'*The Atlantic Experience* has the pot   for
both teachers and students of the A   eri
Jones, Lecturer in History, Aberystwyth University, UK

Providing a succinct yet comprehensive introduction to the history of the Atlantic world in its entirety, *The Atlantic Experience* traces the first Portuguese journeys to the West coast of Africa in the mid-fifteenth century through to the abolition of slavery in America in the late-nineteenth century.

Bringing together the histories of Europe, Africa and the Americas, this book supersedes a history of nations, foregrounds previously neglected parts of these continents, and explores the region as a holistic entity that encompassed people from many different areas, ethnic groups and national backgrounds. Distilling this huge topic into key themes such as conquest, trade, race and migration, Catherine Armstrong and Laura Chmielewski's chronological survey illuminates the crucial aspects of this cutting edge field.

Catherine Armstrong is Senior Lecturer in American History at Manchester Metropolitan University, UK. She is the author of Writing North America in the Seventeenth Century.

Laura M. Chmielewski is Associate Professor of History at Purchase College, State University of New York, USA. She is the author of *The Spice of Popery: Converging Christianities on the Maine Frontier, 1688-1727.*

The Atlantic Experience

Peoples, Places, Ideas

Catherine Armstrong and Laura M. Chmielewski

First published 2013 by
PALGRAVE MACMILLAN

Palgrave Macmillan in the UK is an imprint of Macmillan Publishers Limited,
registered in England, company number 785998, of Houndmills, Basingstoke,
Hampshire RG21 6XS.

Palgrave Macmillan in the US is a division of St Martin's Press LLC,
175 Fifth Avenue, New York, NY 10010.

Palgrave Macmillan is the global academic imprint of the above companies
and has companies and representatives throughout the world.

Palgrave® and Macmillan® are registered trademarks in the United States,
the United Kingdom, Europe and other countries

ISBN: 978–0–230–27273–6   hardback
ISBN: 978–0–230–27274–3   paperback

This book is printed on paper suitable for recycling and made from fully
managed and sustained forest sources. Logging, pulping and manufacturing
processes are expected to conform to the environmental regulations of the
country of origin.

A catalogue record for this book is available from the British Library.

A catalog record for this book is available from the Library of Congress.

Printed in China

Thanks to Maureen and Michael Armstrong, and to Michael Batchelor,
all of whom offered encouragement and love and helped bring this
book to fruition ~ CMA

To Mary and Stanley Chmielewski, who planted the seeds of my love of history;
to Carol Berkin, who taught me how to harvest what grew out of them;
and to Herman and Maria, whose love nourished them all along
the way ~ LMC

Contents

List of Illustrations

Acknowledgements

We thank our employers, Manchester Metropolitan University and the State University of New York at Purchase, and the editors at Palgrave Macmillan, for their support of and faith in this project.

The authors and publishers wish to thank the following for permission to use copyright material:

The John Carter Brown Library for the images of 'Tobacco Production, French West Indies' on p. 109, and 'Die Stadt Havana' on p. 166.

The Granger Collection for the Images of 'Manhattan Purchase, 1626' on p. 58, 'Slave Trading Compounds on the African Coast, 1746' on p. 80, 'Sinners in Hell' on p. 137, Haiti: Slave Revolt, 1791' on p. 195, and 'Hemsley's Engraving of a Slave Ship' on p. 220.

Every effort has been made to trace the copyright holders, but if any have been inadvertently overlooked, the authors and publishers will be pleased to make the necessary arrngements at the first opportunity.

A Note to Instructors

The Atlantic Experience: Peoples, Places, Ideas consists of eight thematic chapters. It was designed this way to encourage instructors to allocate time to analysing and contextualizing the Atlantic world's rich array of documentary and visual evidence. It was also created to conform neatly to the demands of both 12- and 16-week semesters. Courses taught in 16-week semesters can use the thematically organized chapters to frame two weeks of class meetings (with allowances made for the Introduction and Conclusion). Those on a more compressed semester can reduce this coverage to a chapter every one and a half weeks, again with allowances for the Introduction and Conclusion.

Introduction: Studying Atlantic History

'Atlantic History' is both the study of a specific region and an historiographical approach. The origins and significance of each must be understood in order to properly comprehend the lives of the people in the Atlantic past. Atlantic history has been a popular topic among historians in the last 30 years, as shown by the word 'Atlantic' appearing in the title of many academic monographs. However, the topic is only now making a significant impact in undergraduate and postgraduate courses, hence the need for a textbook on the subject firmly aimed at students. Atlantic history concerns the Atlantic-facing coasts of the continents of North and South America, Europe and Africa and the Caribbean Islands from the fifteenth to the nineteenth centuries. These regional definitions and their proximity to the Atlantic are not intended to be limiting. For example, the Scandinavian and Nordic countries and Italy played important parts in the story of the Atlantic world empires without bounding the ocean itself. Broadening the definition further, we might include a Pacific-facing nation like Peru that played a key story in the development of Spain's New World empire, or Indian Ocean-facing regions of Africa such as Ethiopia and Mozambique that, during the sixteenth century, were involved in the Portuguese slave trading system. While coastal areas come to the fore in the stories of contact, trade and transmission of people and ideas, Atlantic historians do not neglect the interior regions of each part of the Atlantic world. Atlantic history examines both the macro structures such as the imperial systems or the slave trade that enabled the Atlantic world to function as an holistic entity, and the individuals of the region, exploring how their experiences and ideas changed their world. This is not a 'top down' history examining the story of the elite; rather, it prioritizes every actor in the Atlantic world story whatever their race, ethnicity or status. Chronologically, this story covers the period from the mid-fifteenth century, when the Portuguese began journeying to the west coast of Africa, to the late nineteenth century, when slavery was finally abolished in the Americas. It includes what scholars studying Europe term 'the early modern period' (roughly 1500–1750), during which colonies were built and trade routes developed. Later, during the eighteenth and nineteenth centuries, the colonial system began to fall apart and the slave trade, and slavery itself, were challenged by abolitionists.

Atlantic history is also a new historiographical approach or 'conceptual leap forward', as Trevor Burnard has called it – a new way of looking at the past. Its fashionable nature during the late twentieth and early twenty-first centuries should give the student pause for thought and encourage them to acknowledge that this is only one of many ways of telling the story of this region. It aims to supersede the history of nations, in which the story of one nation (such as the English, Dutch or Spanish) is taken in isolation and prioritized as important. It also aims to challenge the dominance of the United States in the histories of the region. Hitherto neglected parts of the Atlantic are foregrounded and agency returned to the subalterns (those outside the traditional power structures) of the region.

This is a huge field of study that potentially requires one to be proficient in a number of languages and national stories; and indeed, to write and think in a truly Atlantic way as a scholar is very difficult. In the introduction to his edited collection, *The British Atlantic World 1500–1800*, David Armitage has clarified the study of the Atlantic by suggesting three possible categories: circum-Atlantic, trans-Atlantic and cis-Atlantic studies. Circum-Atlantic history is the history of the entire region, the Atlantic Ocean as a zone of exchange and transmission. Trans-Atlantic history draws comparisons between the national or regional stories within the Atlantic region. Cis-Atlantic history examines the case study of a particular locality in the context of the region as a whole. Consequently, building on Armitage's ideas, very few scholars comprehensively work on every part of the Atlantic region. Despite the field's intention to move away from national stories, some Atlantic historians are specialists in only part of the Atlantic (such as the United States). Many books on Atlantic history are edited collections that comprise the work of a number of scholars, each presenting a small case study, which, taken together, paint a picture of the Atlantic. However, some scholars, such as John Elliott in his book *Empires of the Atlantic World*, emphasizing connections and similarities, compare the regions of the Atlantic governed by Britain and Spain.

One criticism of the field is that it reprises the material covered by the study of the old, 'whiggish' history of seaborne empires, but without the focus on Asia and Africa. This criticism is mitigated somewhat by attempts to give equal footing to the stories of non-Europeans such as Native Americans. Another complaint, as Peter Coclanis put it, is that Atlantic history has become the 'establishment position' but that it has a misleading slant on the history of the early modern (or colonial) period. Coclanis believes that other empires were expanding at this time, including Russia, the Ottomans, Safavid Iran, Mughal India and China. The focus on the Atlantic world, he argues, is another way of artificially prioritizing the story of America. Since its increased popularity as a field of study in the latter years of the twentieth century, scholars have struggled to interpret how they might 'do' Atlantic history and have wondered whether it is valid at all. Is there really one single Atlantic story or a number of smaller ones? Are we justified in looking at the Atlantic in isolation from global history? The following chapters will help you to answer those questions.

Chapter Themes

This textbook distils this huge topic into eight key themes and offers these to students as a way into what would otherwise be a challenging and amorphous topic. Until now, students have had to rely on academic monographs and edited collections in order to learn about the Atlantic world; they have been left floundering with little guidance as to how to be selective and without the tools with which to decide for themselves whether this approach is a useful one.

The first chapter, 'Navigation and Empire', looks at the origins and development of the impulses to explore and conquer that have emerged from the three different regions from about 1450 to 1650. Native American and African empires are mentioned alongside the more commonly discussed Portuguese, Spanish, French, Dutch and English attempts at empire building in Africa and the Americas. The economic and intellectual developments of the Renaissance are explored alongside stories from the lives of key actors such as the Portuguese explorer, Henry the Navigator.

Covering a similar chronological period, Chapter 2, 'Contact and Encounter', takes a social and cultural approach to the question of what Africans, Europeans and Americans thought of each other. The venue for these meetings was not only the New World but also Africa and Europe, as, unusually, Native and African understandings of Europe are also explored. Questions of racism, fear, hatred and cultural confusion are contrasted with sympathetic meetings and understandings between the groups. The difficulties in accessing Native and African voices are assessed here.

Building from the last chapter, Chapter 3, 'Bondage and Freedom', looks at how the impulse to enslave developed across the Atlantic world. Theories offered by Europeans to justify enslavement, from biblical to classical sources, are examined alongside concerns over the shortage of labour and other economic imperatives. This chapter contrasts the experiences of slaves in different sorts of Atlantic slavery, ranging from the plantation slavery of South America, the Caribbean and the southern United States to slavery in New England, Africa and Europe. The story of Atlantic slavery begins when Europeans and Africans first come into contact but the transatlantic slave trade peaks in the eighteenth century.

Chapter 4, 'Exploiting the Atlantic: Trade and Economy', explores the development of an Atlantic system of trade. This system developed slowly over centuries but, like the slave trade, reached its peak during the eighteenth century. The chapter asks whether the triangular trade is a valid way of understanding this system and whether this model of relations between countries mirrors what was happening on the ground. It examines the transfer of goods and people and the impact on each different region of this economic relationship.

Spiritual lives and religious cultures are examined in Chapter 5, 'Atlantic Religion: Beliefs and Behaviours'. Religion was integral to the development of the Atlantic world throughout the period covered by this book, a driving force behind the conquering of and migration to the New World, a justification of the enslavement of Africans, and a comfort to those enslaved. The developments of religious orthodoxy, tolerance and revivalism are traced.

In Chapter 6, 'Lived Lives and the Built Environment', we move on to explore the social stratifications of the Atlantic world and the relationship of class and status to public behaviours and access. The chapter will also examine how geography and climate affected forms of material expression – including architecture, clothing, food-stuffs and decorative arts – in the New World. Materially, these trends can be seen most clearly in the homes and communities built by Atlantic world peoples. In the earliest stages of the Atlantic encounter, these built environments often reflected the architectural and material influences of the places of origin of the colonial founders. Over the course of the sixteenth to the eighteenth centuries, they evolved, however, to adapt to new climatic challenges, the influences of indigenous peoples, and the need to rely on local materials for construction, decoration and manufacture.

In Chapter 7, 'Dependence and Independence', the following questions are asked: When and how did a series of scattered colonial outposts coalesce into international empires? Should historians think of these empires as discrete entities or as an 'entangled world' (i.e., part of the same political and economic system)? This chapter compares the economic and intellectual drivers behind the creation of the different empires of the Atlantic world and looks at some of the key thinkers behind these developments. It explores the borderland spaces where these empires clashed and looks at why various movements for independence occurred in the late eighteenth and early nineteenth centuries in response to efforts to increase control from Europe.

Finally, in Chapter 8, 'The Quest for Abolition', two distinct but related aspects of the abolition movement are discussed: firstly, the move in Britain to abolish the slave trade (and slavery in its own borders), eventually successful in 1807, which preceded the British attempt to enforce this abolition in the waters of the Atlantic; and secondly, the campaigns to abolish slavery in the New World. The actions of Africans, African Americans and Europeans, the role of religious groups as well as politicians, and public opinion are explored.

Thinking Atlantically

One of the advantages of exploring the history of an entire region over several centuries is that it encourages students to think thematically rather than in a narrative way. While the chapters of this textbook do reflect a broadly chronological approach, they are also structured to reveal some of the key themes that reoccur in the history of the Atlantic world. However, there are other themes that students need to be aware of that pervade every section of this book. The most important of these is migration. The movement of people, ideas and goods around the Atlantic is a driver of change and innovation. Demographic reasons for migration are also significant as perceived overpopulation in Britain encouraged many of her migrants, while West African communities which suffered chronic underpopulation did not seek to send out their people to colonize elsewhere. Alison Games has highlighted the importance of migration in her book *Migration and the Origins of the English Atlantic World*. The movement of ideas is obviously partly contingent on the movement of people, but as the opening of the Atlantic to white migrants coincided with the printing revolution, this new medium must also be held responsible for the development of ideas. For example, the shared religious awakenings and the development of the abolition movements operated alongside the development of scientific ways of interpreting the world in which practitioners around the Atlantic world shared ideas. The movement of goods took place as a conscious economic movement, while alongside it occurred the carrying of seeds and weeds, animals and diseases that had a huge impact on the lives of those around the Atlantic world.

Although it should now be obvious that the Atlantic approach to history has been very influential, we do not wish to present this as a fait accompli in the historiography. This book is designed to help you question and challenge what you read. We do not suggest that the Atlantic way of viewing history is the only appropriate way. There are other options available to you, such as using the concepts of local, national or global history. We leave it to you to draw your own conclusions about the usefulness of Atlantic history. Presented here are the tools which you can use to make that analysis. However, the authors of this volume argue that the significance of the Atlantic approach is not that it works as a way of understanding the past, but that, crucially, it would have made sense to people in the past. During this period historical actors did not behave as though they were part of one nation or one race but rather participated in a system that encompassed people from different continents, ethnic groups and national backgrounds.

General Chronology of Atlantic History

Medieval period

1000 Vikings under Leif Erikson explore the coast of Eastern Canada.

1324 Ruler of Mali, Mansa Musa, goes on pilgrimage to Mecca, spending so much on luxuries and slaves that he upsets local economies.

Fifteenth century

1421–3 Date of the highly contested Chinese voyage reaching the Americas.

1430 Portuguese reach Madeira and the Azores under Prince Henry the Navigator.

1440s Portuguese reach the coast of West Africa.

1441 First recorded incidence of Europeans kidnapping an African into slavery (Portuguese seize 12 from Guinea coast and send them to Portugal as a gift to Henry the Navigator).

1452 Sugar production begins on Madeira; experience learned here is beneficial in Brazil later.

1458 Portuguese sign treaties promising to buy African slaves and not kidnap them.

1481 'El Mina' founded on Gold Coast of Africa as a Portuguese trading post.

1482 Portuguese crown establishes the *Casa de Índia* (also known by other names, including the Guinea Mina House), to regulate spice trade with Africa.

1492	Genoan Christopher Columbus, on behalf of the Spanish monarchy, reaches the Americas, landing on Hispaniola. Also the *Reconquista*: Spanish Christian defeat of Moors.
1494	Catholic papacy issues the Treaty of Tordesillas, splitting Spanish and Portuguese claims in the East and West Atlantic.
1497	John Cabot voyage claims Newfoundland for the English while looking for the North-West Passage.
1498	Vasco da Gama reaches India.

Sixteenth century

1500	Portuguese reach Brazil.
1500	The first African slaves are imported into Hispaniola.
1501	Amerigo Vespucci (after whom America was probably named) sails round South America.
1513	Juan Ponce de Leon becomes the first European to reach Florida.
1514	Pope Leo X issues a bull condemning slavery and the slave trade.
1517	Martin Luther produces his Ninety-Five Theses against the Roman Catholic Church, sparking the Protestant Reformation.
1517	Bartolomé de Las Casas protests to Spanish King Charles V about the use of Native slaves on Hispaniola and asks that Africans be used instead.
1518	First smallpox epidemic wipes out the Taino people of Hispaniola.
1519	Hernan Cortés kidnaps Moctezuma II from Tenochtitlan (Mexico City) and loots his gold.
1519	Horses and 'dogs of war' are brought with Cortés and his forces in the conquest of Mexico. Other domesticated animals from across the Atlantic will soon follow.
1521	Earliest recorded slave revolt in the New World, on Columbus's son's plantation in Hispaniola.
1524	Charles V of Spain establishes the Council of the Indies.
1526	Francisco Pizarro reaches Peru.
1531	Indian convert Juan Diego describes his vision of the Virgin Mary, who comes to be known in Mexico as the Virgin of Guadalupe.
1532	Pizarro kidnaps Atahualpa from Cusco and, after collecting a ransom, murders him.
1534	Henry VIII of England breaks from the Catholic Church in Rome, establishing the Church of England in its place with himself as its head.
1535	Jacques Cartier sails up the Hudson River to site of modern-day Quebec.
1538	Slaves are imported into Brazil for the first time; sugar production begins there.
1539	Hernando de Soto reaches south-eastern North America.

1540   Francisco Vasquez de Coronado explores south-western North America.

1542   Bartolomé de Las Casas defends the Indians in *A Short Account of the Destruction of the Indies* (not published until 1552).

1545   Spanish start mining for silver at Potosí (present-day Bolivia).

1547   Las Casas returns to Spain to debate with Sepúlveda on treatment of Indians.

1549   Portuguese establish the city of Salvator on the coast of Bahia, Brazil.

1550s   Hans Staden spends time in Brazil and records the Tupi people there.

1562   John Hawkins sails to Africa in the first English slave trading voyage.

1575   Miguel de Cervantes (author of *Don Quixote*) is kidnapped into slavery in Algiers.

1576   Martin Frobisher sails to the region that became New England looking for North-West Passage and devastates Native population of Baffin Island.

1577   Sir Francis Drake circumnavigates the world.

1584   Manteo and Wanchese (Natives from Roanoke) arrive in England.

1585   Roanoke colony is established and probably destroyed by Algonquian Natives, although its precise fate is unknown.

1595   Walter Raleigh undertakes voyage to Guiana looking for El Dorado and 'monstrous races'.

Seventeenth century

1602   Dutch East India Company founded.

1605   Escaped slaves found the colony of Palmares in Brazil (lasts till 1697).

1607   Founding of Jamestown, Virginia.

1610   Tobacco is cultivated in Virginia for the first time.

1611   First of the Jesuit *Relations* written: these documents have become one of the most important primary sources on Native American and Canadian Amerindian life and culture.

1613   Dutch trading post established on Manhattan Island.

1614   Marriage of Pocahontas and John Rolfe in Virginia.

1616   Pocahontas goes to London.

1619   First African slaves arrive to settle in North America (others had stayed for a short while with Spanish visitors in late sixteenth century).

1620   Puritan separatists arrive in New England and sign the Mayflower Compact with non-separatist shipmates.

1621   Wampanoag Indians teach English immigrants to cultivate native crops at Plymouth.

1622   Virginia Massacre: over 300 English settlers are killed in surprise and coordinated attacks led by Opecancanough.

1624   New Amsterdam established by the Dutch; it becomes a major trade entrepôt on the Hudson River.

1626   Dutch buy Manhattan Island from Natives after getting them drunk.

1627   The French establish the One Hundred Associates to encourage trade and settlement in New France.

1630   Puritans led by John Winthrop reach Massachusetts.

1631   English Puritans found Providence Island in the Bahamas.

1634   North American colony of Maryland founded as refuge for English Catholics.

1636   Governor of Barbados declares all Indians and Africans on the island should be treated as slaves.

1637   Pequot massacre where village of Mystic is burned, trapping women and children inside.

1648   Massachusetts criminalizes striking one's parents with a punishment of death.

1649   The Iroquois Indians destroy rival Hurons to achieve dominance in the fur trade with Europeans.

1650   Final destruction of the Jesuit mission to the Hurons by the Iroquois.

1654   The Jewish congregation Mikveh Israel established in Curaçao, Dutch Antilles.

1660   Catholic-sympathizing Stuart kings return to English throne.

1660   Charles II of England's First Navigation Act applies trade parameters to certain New World commodities.

1661   Earliest Virginian slave codes enacted.

1663   First *filles du Roi* ('King's daughters') arrive in New France to marry settlers and build the colonial population; they will later arrive in New Orleans as well.

1663   England's Second Navigation Act closes off most direct trade between English colonies and Continental Europe.

1671   Connecticut's 'An Act for regulating and orderly celebrating of Marriages; and for preventing and punishing incestuous and other unlawful Marriages Connecticut Law for Orderly Marriage meant to regulate marriage and define suitability' becomes law.

1673   Third Navigation Act closes loopholes that had allowed North American colonists to trade duty-free.

1673   First major slave revolt in Jamaica.

1675   England establishes the Lords of Trade to regulate and oversee, among other things, colonial trade.

1676   King Philip's war results in the destruction of the Wampanoag tribe who welcomed the English at the 'first thanksgiving' in 1620.

1680s	Slave labour is used to build William Penn's experiment in religious toleration, the Quaker colony of Pennsylvania.
1682	French under Sieur de La Salle canoe the length of the Mississippi River.
1684	Massachusetts Bay Company's charter is revoked by Charles II.
1686	James II establishes the Dominion of New England.
1689	England's 'Glorious' Revolution replaces Catholic Stuart king James II with his Protestant daughter and nephew, William of Orange and Mary.
1689	Outbreak of King William's War (War of the League of Augsburg).

Eighteenth century

1700	Comanche begin to use horses, which will completely revolutionize their society.
1700	Asante empire in West Africa (southern Ghana) begins its involvement in the slave trade. Other African tribes and empires involved include Dahomey, Bonny and Kongo.
1701	The Society for the Propagation of the Gospel is founded in England.
1702	Outbreak of Queen Anne's War (War of Spanish Succession).
1704	First colonial English-language newspaper, *The Boston News-Letter*, is printed and distributed.
1712	Slave riots in New York kill nine whites.
1717	By reducing taxes on sugar, the French attempt to corner the market on the commodity.
1723	A new Connecticut law allows women to own property under certain circumstances.
1724	Founding of convent for Indian women in Mexico.
1728	*The Book of Architecture*, by James Gibbs, is published.
1732	Benjamin Franklin begins publishing *Poor Richard's Almanac*.
1733	The Molasses Act aims at curbing smuggling between New England and the Caribbean.
1735	Founders of Colony of Georgia in North America try to ban slavery, but allow it after 1749.
1739	Anglican evangelical George Whitefield begins his tour of North America.
1739	Stono slave rebellion takes place in South Carolina, where 25 whites are killed.
1743	Outbreak of King George's War (War of Austrian Succession).
1750	A spate of economic and cultural reforms under the Marquis de Pombal begin; these will eventually spread to include Portugal's Atlantic world sphere of influence.
1750	Paper money issued in Virginia.

1750	Secret treaty between Spain and Portugal redraws South American geopolitical boundaries, causing a general uprising by the Guaraní Indians and their Jesuit missionaries.
1751	Slave uprising in Saint Domingue, in which 6000 people die.
1756	Outbreak of the Seven Years' War (French and Indian War).
1758	A congregation of African Baptists is founded in Virginia.
1763–74	A series of policies aimed at taxing Britain's North American colonies propels the region towards revolution.
1763	Treaty of Paris: France relinquishes North American holdings to Spain and England.
1773	Society of Jesus dissolved by papal decree; its members are dispersed.
1783	In the wake of the American Revolution, Jewish congregants of the Philadelphia Synagogue petition for full civil rights.
1789	Alexander Hamilton becomes Secretary of the Treasury of the new United States.
1789	British whaling vessel *Amelia* pursues its prey into the Pacific Ocean, reorienting that trade away from the Atlantic; whale oil lamps and candles create cleaner, brighter, longer-burning light sources that enhance domestic life in the Americas and Europe.
1770	British troops open fire on a group of Bostonians, killing five; the event becomes known as the Boston Massacre.
1772	Somerset case rules that slavery has no basis in English law.
1773	Colonists in America attack shipments of British tea that carry a tax to Parliament.
1774	The Quebec Act passed in Britain offers limited toleration to Catholics in Canada, outraging American colonists.
1776	The British North American colonies officially declare separation from the British empire, the first step in becoming the United States of America.
1777	Constitution of the state of Vermont abolishes slavery.
1780–4	Massachusetts, Pennsylvania, Rhode Island and Connecticut gradually abolish slavery.
1783	Quakers begin campaign in England against slave trade; the Zong case catches the public's attention.
1787	Britain establishes African colony of Sierra Leone for former slaves, impoverished free people of colour, and black Loyalists from America.
1787	Society for Effecting the Abolition of the Slave Trade founded in England.
1788	*Société des Amis Noirs* founded in France.
1789	Slavery is preserved under the new United States Constitution.
1791	Toussaint L'Ouverture takes command of slave forces in Saint Domingue.

| 1791 | Haitian slaves and *gens to couleur* lead fight for independence. |
| 1799 | New York gradually abolishes slavery. |

Nineteenth century and beyond

1803	The Louisiana Purchase, made under Thomas Jefferson, promises to reorient American trade and settlement towards the Mississippi River valley and beyond.
1804	Slavery abolished in Haiti; New Jersey gradually abolishes slavery.
1807	Britain and US prohibit the slave trade.
1808	Fleeing an invasion by Napoleon, the Portuguese King João VI and his family establish a new Portuguese capital at Rio de Janeiro.
1812	War breaks out between United States and Great Britain, known by some as the second War of Independence.
1814	African American Methodist minister Richard Allen and his associates found the African Methodist Episcopal Church.
1815	The Treaty of Ghent is ratified, ending the War of 1812.
1816	American Colonization Society founded.
1819	Bernardo O'Higgins leads Chilean independence movement.
1820	Restored Society of Jesus welcomed back to Argentina and other parts of central and South America.
1821	Mexico declares its independence from the Spanish and uses the constitution of the United States as a model.
1824	Mexico establishes Roman Catholicism as a state religion under its constitution.
1829	Slavery is abolished in Mexico.
1830	The founding of the Baltimore and Ohio Railroad hastens the movement of North America's people away from the Atlantic and towards the western interior.
1831	The popularly titled 'Baptist War' slave rebellion breaks out in Jamaica.
1831	The Nat Turner slave revolt in Virginia hardens attitudes towards slavery in the northern and southern states of the United States.
1833	Congregationalism disestablished in Massachusetts.
1833	American Anti-Slavery Society founded.
1834	Slavery abolished throughout the British empire, replaced by system of apprenticeship.
1837	Republican revolt in Bahia, Brazil.
1837	American Theodore Weld publishes *The Bible Against Slavery*.
1838	Apprenticeship abolished in British Caribbean.
1843	Black abolitionist Henry Highland Garnet calls for a slave rebellion.

1847	Liberia declares independence from the United States.
1851	First Argentine novel, *Amalia* by José Marmol, begins to appear in serial form.
1854	Slavery is abolished in Peru.
1860	South Carolina secedes from the United States, triggering the Civil War.
1863	President Lincoln issues the Emancipation Proclamation.
1865	Slavery is abolished in United States.
1884	Congress of Berlin: European powers agree to end slave trade in Africa as part of the justification for carving up territory.
1886	Slavery is abolished in Cuba.
1888	Slavery is abolished in Brazil.
1900	Britain abolishes slavery in Nigeria in areas under its control.
1980	Mauritania abolishes slavery.

1   Navigation and Empire

Origins of Empire

The desire to explore the wider world and to establish settlements and empires in newly discovered territories was not new in 1500. There is a long and important pre-history to this desire. Although Europeans considered themselves at the centre of the known universe, Africans and Americans were also early exponents of using conquest to dominate their neighbours and develop new systems of governance, albeit with significant local variations. The language we use to discuss these new journeys and imaginings is significant. In talking about the European 'discovery' of America we are telling a particularly Eurocentric story, assuming that all innovation and progress was driven from and by Europe. The next chapter explores in more depth what happened when the peoples of the Atlantic world encountered each other for the first time. However, while it is important to acknowledge that Atlantic development represents a departure from previous cultural patterns, this development can also be seen as a continuation and this chapter will explore how ancient and medieval models of empire and earlier technological advances and modes of exploration drove this innovation. Historian Charles Verlinden argues that this continuity can be traced from the fifth century onwards.

While, prior to 1500, most Africans had not encountered a European in person, the 'discovery' of Europe by Africans had certainly begun before that date. Africans soon became aware of the benefits of contact with Europeans and in doing so had redefined themselves and their own identity. Ambassadors and delegations were sent to Europe from 1300 onwards as the European interest in African gold and slaves developed. The Barbary ports on the North African coasts were cosmopolitan places where Europeans of all nations mixed with Africans.

The organization of West African society was hugely varied and constantly changing. Some tribes had grouped themselves together in kingdoms ruled by a king. Others lived in a hierarchical group of tribes, while still others were village-based with only a few hundred people being governed by an elder. Across West Africa disease and famine were obstacles to population growth and these factors led to labour shortages, which defined the models of expansion and conquest employed by the dominant tribes and kingdoms of the region. The kingdom of Kongo used slavery to solve its labour shortages before Europeans even visited the region. The African gold rush gave a new power to Malinke speakers around the headwaters of the Niger

River. They created the Kingdom of Mali in the early thirteenth century. Its suzerainty extended over a thousand miles and it became an Islamic state in the early fourteenth century, Islam having been brought to the region by Berber tribesmen moving south from the North African coast. Mali's court was so wealthy and magnificent that it received praise and admiration even from European writers. As the Malian kingdom declined in power, the Songhai empire took its place and, based on a complex taxation system, it became the most powerful African empire of the period. It flourished from the mid-fifteenth century onwards and is named after its principal tribe. The kings and elites of the empire were Muslims but pagan elements were also blended into the culture. This blend allowed Timbuktu to become an important seat of education. The empire declined after an internal civil war made it vulnerable to attack from Morocco. Other empires such as those of the Asante and Dahomey defined the later history of West Africa, but they rose to power after European contact had changed the region and their power was partly due to the economic advantage given to them by the transatlantic slave trade.

The American model of empire was well developed before the arrival of the Europeans. The Cahokia settlement near modern-day St. Louis existed from the ninth century to the mid-thirteenth century and was an urban settlement that had a number of 'offspring' settlements as far away as Aztalan in Wisconsin. These settlements were influenced by Mesoamerican culture and there may have been trade contact between the two. The Spaniards were successful in establishing the first European empire in the New World because their system simply merged with the existing, but crumbling, imperial systems of the Aztecs and the Incas. The conquistadors joined the failing empires and took part in tribute and labour systems that already existed. The divided nature of Indian society fatally weakened the Native empires, as the Spanish were able to turn Indian against Indian and prevent a pan-Indian feeling developing. Because some Natives were disgruntled with the Aztec and Inca empires they were willing to side with the Spanish. A similar pattern emerged during European encounters across America, especially in Portuguese and Dutch contact with Brazilian Indians. The Aztecs and the Incas were only the final empires in a long line of complex and densely populated societies in Central and South America. The Mayans had lived in a vibrant and complex culture; Incas were more austere.

Europeans were unique among the Atlantic residents because they pursued imperial aims at a great distance from their homeland. Americans and Africans tried to conquer neighbouring territories whereas the Europeans, modelled on the example of the Ancient Greeks and Romans, travelled great distances to undertake their conquests. Greeks were exponents of maritime exploration and pursued the expansion of their empire, which under Alexander the Great stretched east to India, while also philosophizing over the meaning of empire and conquest. The Roman empire operated partly through military conquest and partly through bringing agricultural technology to an area seen as backward. It encompassed Africa, Asia and Christian Europe. It was the model for much of the imperial development in the Atlantic world. For example, the Spanish conquistador, Hernan Cortés, used the term 'empire' in the

Roman sense to mean territory conquered by military force. The Roman idea of *res nullius*, which argued that unoccupied land remained common property until it was put to use, was also important in the Atlantic context. This became a justification for European territorial expansion that lingered in the white mindset for centuries. European understanding of ideas such as 'wilderness', 'savagery' and 'civilization' also emerged from the struggles of Near Eastern peoples as told in the Bible, and was another important intellectual precursor to the fifteenth-century expansion.

The medieval model of empire introduced the theory of economic exploitation: that the colony should provide an income for the mother country. The rise of the feudal state and development of an urban bourgeoisie went hand in hand with an increased interest in empire. This model is seen in the crusading conquests in the Holy Land, and the Crusades also mirror the combination of religious zeal and military display found in the early explorers of the Atlantic world. From the twelfth century onwards European colonies established in the eastern Mediterranean and the Levant allowed Europeans to hone the practical methods and theories that they would later use in their contact with Africa and North and South America. Interest in Mediterranean colonies overlapped with the interest in the Atlantic world so that the two coexisted. There are three models of European imperial development that cross boundaries in the medieval and early modern period: feudal (Crusader and Atlantic colonizers); charter (Genoese in the Mediterranean, and Virginia and Massachusetts); agreement (Genoese in the Bosporus and the Mayflower Compact of Plymouth Rock in North America). Italian innovation, commercial expertise and financial clout drove much of the medieval imperial expansion and triggered the journeys that took Europeans around the Atlantic archipelago and eventually across the ocean. Genoa's trading empire faced both east and west and was created because of a rivalry with Venice and a desire for seaborne expansion, since the geographical barrier of the Alps made expansion across land impossible. During much of the medieval period the Atlantic itself remained a barrier, being perceived as a space to cross rather than an arena of potential trade. As we shall see later in this chapter, Europeans struggled to understand this space. Rivalry between European nations, such as the way that Portugal and Castile competed for influence, also triggered exploration and settlement around the Atlantic.

The internal struggle between the centralizing needs of the state and monarch and the desire of powerful individuals seeking to boost their own power is a recurring theme throughout the exploration of the medieval and early modern worlds. The thirteenth-century conquest of Majorca by the Aragonese under King Jaime is important as an early example of European seaborne conquest. Majorca became part of the Aragon dominions, but was not referred to as an empire. Crusaders working under a system of private enterprise conquered Ibiza and Formentera; the crown legitimized but did not lead the missions. In England under the Tudors, empire denoted England's independence from European powers and Elizabeth I used imperial iconography to reinforce the idea that she was a strong, independent ruler. Ulster provided the model for English adaptation of the Roman idea of empire as overseas conquest, and also provided an example of English and Scots working alongside one another.

UP FOR DEBATE   Atlantic interlopers: Vikings and Chinese?

Two groups do not usually form part of the Atlantic narrative but their claims to be part of it are interesting. Did the Vikings and the Chinese reach the New World before the southern Europeans?

In the Viking case the answer is yes. We have no contemporary written evidence to corroborate the archaeological evidence found at L'Anse aux Meadows in Newfoundland, but sometime between the tenth and fifteenth centuries Viking explorers such as Leif Ericson, based in Greenland, sailed west and reached the coast of what is now Canada, which was only 16 miles away. These stories are told in later sagas.

In the Chinese case, historians hotly debate the evidence. The existence of some archaeological evidence and detailed Chinese maps of the Americas seems to suggest that the Chinese visited the west coast of North America during the middle of the fifteenth century. But others claim this is fictional and spurious.

What Drove Exploration?

New technology played an important part in the exploration of the Atlantic empire. Renaissance thinkers rejected the traditional learning of the medieval church and looked back to the ancients and their models of knowledge of the world and its people. However, looking back could only provide so much impetus. The physical capability for crossing the Atlantic or navigating the coast of West Africa had to be developed. As important was the will of the individuals, rulers and states undertaking and supporting these expeditions. Without the desire to push further into the unknown, the voyages would never have taken place. In terms of ship design, the replacement of old-style galleys with new broadside 'ships of the line' was important but did not cause an overnight revolution. The ships' weaponry was also changing in the sixteenth century, as cheaper iron guns became available. But the real problems were the small size of the ships, which were not designed for long voyages, and the issue of supplying those ships. The techniques for preserving food were woefully inadequate for voyages of several months. English ships increased in size under James I with the largest being the East Indiaman. At the same time the distinction between warships and merchant ships was defined, with the former required to protect the latter on the long trading voyages to the east and west. Naval innovation took place in response to opportunities not only in the Atlantic world but also globally.

Myth and exploration were closely tied together throughout the medieval period. One of the most popular books was Sir John Mandeville's *Travels*, a fictional account, written towards the end of the fourteenth century, of a journey in which Mandeville encountered unusual races of people in far-flung corners of the earth. The writings of Mandeville influenced Columbus and this is why he expected to find so-called 'monstrous races' at his destination. More detail about the origins of these ideas is found at the start of Chapter 2. The settlement of the Canary Islands in the early fourteenth century also shows how myth influenced the process of conquest. The Islands were given names such as Hesperides and the Elysian Fields. Part of the motivation for the Portuguese exploration of the West African coast was a desire to find the legendary land of Prester John, a Christian ruler initially supposed to live in the Far East but by the fifteenth century sited in Ethiopia. In the 1480s an early attempt at crossing the Atlantic, undertaken from Bristol, intended to search for the mythical 'Isle of Brasil'.

The role of classical myth in triggering exploration did not cease once the Europeans had reached America. Amerigo Vespucci's 1503 work *Novus Mundus* was a Renaissance fable that expressed and created excitement about the New World by portraying the Natives as natural and pure. Peter Martyr went further, saying that the peaceful Caribbean Natives were like the people of the golden age of classical antiquity. Significantly, Martyr had never been to America so his understanding was based not on visiting America but solely on reading about it. But by 1526, eyewitness Gonzalo Fernandez de Oviedo y Valde, who spent most of his life in the New World, expressed how his observations in America showed classical authorities could no longer be reliable. But his pleas were ignored and thus the disconnect began between the eyewitness reports and the more fanciful humanist accounts written in Europe, which looked back to the models of the ancient world and were written by those with no experience of the Americas. By 1590 Acosta's *Natural and Moral History* categorically challenged the errors of Aristotle and Saint Augustine and proved that America was not Atlantis or Ophir and the Natives were not part of the twelve tribes of Israel. But this did not prevent Peruvian creoles from using European myths to proudly describe their home. Peru was associated with Ophir throughout the seventeenth century and in the eighteenth century creole patriots reiterated this connection. The term 'creole' can be confusing. Here, it means Peruvians of either Spanish or mixed Spanish and Native heritage born in Peru who saw themselves as different from '*peninsulares*' or Spaniards born in Spain. However, the term 'creole' can also refer to a person of any mixed racial or cultural heritage especially in the Caribbean but also throughout the New World, or more specifically in Louisiana to the people, language and culture of French and Spanish origin.

The Spaniards' seizure of Inca gold from Atahualpa in 1532–3 and the discovery of the vast silver mines at Potosí in 1545 caused the quest for El Dorado, the fabled city of gold mentioned by ancient authors, to reach its peak. The Spanish pushed into the interior of South America searching for mines in the Amazon jungle. The search for El Dorado inspired other European nations, especially the British led by Sir Walter Raleigh. In 1542 the Portuguese expedition, led by Orellana, had supposedly encountered members of a tribe of warlike female Amazons after whom the region was named, and this had whetted the appetite of Raleigh. He had heard about the mythical city and its supposed location in South America and in 1595 these rumours persuaded him to sail to Guiana in order to find it. Raleigh believed that he would find the creatures described by the Roman writer Pliny in his *Natural History*, such as the Amazons and the *Ewaipanoma* who were men with mouths in their chests. This belief in the existence of strange, alien races influenced the way that Europeans treated Africans and Native Americans on their travels, as shown in later chapters.

Gold was present in the interior of the Amazon region but Europeans did not discover it until the eighteenth century, and Raleigh's voyage to El Dorado was a failure. He fell out of favour with James I and spent much of the remainder of his life imprisoned in the Tower of London. The English quest for a South American El Dorado was abandoned early in the seventeenth century when South America ceased to be a model for English expansion in the New World, but Englishmen did not stop fruitlessly seeking gold in North America.

ATLANTIC HISTORY IN FOCUS

Why did exploration of the Atlantic world increase in the late fifteenth century?

▸ Improved naval and military technology
▸ A desire for fame, wealth and salvation that was no longer fulfilled in Crusades
▸ Rivalry between European nations
▸ Being shut off from Eastern trade routes after the fall of Constantinople in 1453
▸ Visionary individuals such as Henry the Navigator, Christopher Columbus
▸ State willingness to sponsor exploration in order to boost national fame
▸ Religious imperative: the desire to take Christianity abroad

---

Exploration and the Economy

The Atlantic trade system did not emerge fully formed following Columbus's voyages. Many aspects needed for its success were in place before Columbus even received permission for his first journey.

C. R. Boxer has called the Portuguese the 'pathfinders' of the Atlantic world. They were keen to expand their horizons because of their geographical position on the edge of Europe and also because of a lack of good soil in Portugal itself. Portugal and Castile, the regions that drove Atlantic interest, were also on the periphery of Europe in terms of their influence and power and this gave them something to prove. The Portuguese captured the Moroccan city of Ceuta in 1415. This was the first permanent European presence outside Europe in modern times. From Arabs they encountered there, the Portuguese learned about the gold mines in the African interior and this sparked their interest in that continent. The European desire for gold was promoted as a religious mission: this wealth would help Christians liberate Jerusalem from the Muslims. However, by 1550 the Portuguese had lost their foothold in North Africa and this opened up the region for the other European countries to trade.

A Portuguese prince, known as Henry the Navigator or Dom Henrique, inspired much of the early exploration of the West African coast. He wanted to be remembered by posterity as a chivalrous Crusader knight and this meant that he was prepared to invest in voyages of exploration. The European naval involvement in the African slave trade began when Captain Goncalvez kidnapped a black man and woman to take to court to please Dom Henrique. This occurred after Goncalvez's attempts at trading were rebuffed by the Africans. By the 1450s regular trading voyages searching for gold were taking place and by 1482 the Portuguese had established a permanent trading post on the West African coast at El Mina (or Elmina). They exchanged European goods for gold and, to a lesser extent, slaves. This wealth allowed Dom João II to send out more voyages of exploration and trade to the East.

Sugar production using slave labour is, surprisingly, not an Atlantic world innovation. The Venetians ran sugar colonies in Palestine following the First Crusade. The Venetians, Genoese and French also cultivated sugar in the fourteenth century on the island of Cyprus using Arab slave labour and local serfs. Occasionally a black African was enslaved but the slave communities were cosmopolitan; slavery was not associated with only one race. Sugar production was already an industrial process, with huge boilers set up to process the raw sugar. From the mid-fifteenth century onwards, in the Atlantic archipelago, Portugal copied the Mediterranean model of island hopping to conquer territory and thus expanded the slave-produced sugar industry into Madeira, the Azores, the Cape Verde Islands and finally São Tomé and Príncipe, off the coast of Africa. These places became important trading centres. Once again Dom Henrique was the inspiration for establishing settlements on these islands. The Portuguese possession was not unchallenged since merchants of other nations, especially the Italian states, also invested in these islands. In 1452 the first sugar mill on Madeira was established, in which Dom Henrique was a partner. The islands attracted immigrants from Portugal who began using African slave labour in these mills, associating slavery solely with the black African. On São Tomé and Príncipe, African slave labour was used, but the population was a cosmopolitan one with criminals, orphans, Gypsies and Jews also settling there. On those islands and the Cape Verde Islands few white women settled and so a creole, mestizo population emerged very quickly. ('Mestizo' is a term that was used in colonial Spanish America to describe someone of mixed race with both European and Native American ancestry.) A similar trend occurred in the areas of Portuguese control on the African mainland, once factories had been established. Columbus took sugar to the Caribbean on his second voyage, so the experiments with the crop began early in the New World.

During the late fifteenth and early sixteenth centuries the lure of the Far East was arguably more important to the European powers. There had been a demand for Eastern goods in Europe since Roman times and the historically small trade developed in the sixteenth and seventeenth centuries when the bullion from Africa and later America triggered more interest in the East. The East held the key to the spice and silk trades, and when Constantinople fell to the Ottomans in 1453, Europeans were worried that their trade routes would be blocked. The aim of Columbus in setting out towards the West was partly to find a new route to the East, a search continued by successive navigators until the opening of the Panama Canal in the nineteenth century. Accidents also took fleets bound for India westwards. The Portuguese sighted Brazil in April 1500 because 13 of its ships were blown westwards off course from their trip to India. On arrival they discovered the potential of Brazilwood, after which the country is named, and later sugar growing became important, but many merchants and explorers were not deterred from their Eastern focus. By the 1530s, the Portuguese interest in the

African coast was beginning to wane as their attention was captured by India and China, although a sufficient presence was maintained to sustain the slave trade.

In 1495–6 the Italian John Cabot arrived in Bristol and began preparing for his voyage in search of the North-West Passage, a sea route that supposedly connected the Atlantic and Pacific oceans. He hoped to make direct connections with the markets of the East so that Europeans would not be reliant on traditional trade routes. His journey also triggered an interest in the Newfoundland cod fishery, and, in 1501, Bristol merchants worked with Azorean Islanders for the first time to undertake explorations of the northern Atlantic between Greenland and Newfoundland with the purpose of recording commodities there but with no intention of going on to the East. However, America did not interest merchants until the later sixteenth century. Cabot, like Columbus, misunderstood where he had reached. He thought he had reached Cathay (China). The North-West Passage was not seen as the sole option for reaching the trade rich lands of the East. From the mid-sixteenth century onwards courtiers such as Sir Hugh Willoughby with the Muscovy Company and explorers such as Sebastian Cabot tried to open up a North-East Passage to the East via Russia. The North-West Passage was still driving exploration well after the Atlantic trading system itself had been established and fascination with it touched the lives of many varied individuals. During the eighteenth century Olaudah Equiano, the former slave and abolitionist, and British naval officer Horatio Nelson were both involved in voyages to find the North-West Passage. This quest, along with the search for gold, obsessed many of the explorers in the Atlantic world during the early period of contact.

Once the existence of Africa and the Americas had become a reality for Europeans, they began to prepare to exploit the resources that they found there. For example, slaves were not the only commodity that the Europeans desired from Africa; they also traded for dyes, wood, gold and spices. Africans and Native Americans were not merely passive recipients in this trade: they took an active part in the negotiations and often drove a hard bargain, refusing to allow Europeans to get away with offering a low price. In America, in the early years, many of the commodities purchased from the Natives were designed to sustain the young colonies themselves. It was not until staples were established that Europeans managed the production and distribution of the crops. In Brazil, the Portuguese and Dutch sometimes worked with the Native producers who harvested their trade crop for them and took it to the coast for sale. But in most parts of America, Europeans did not simply stay on the coast and wait until traders came to their factories, as they did in the East and Africa.

The trading companies not only controlled trade but also encouraged exploration. These companies were focused on a particular area of the globe, but the policy behind them was globally conceived. An example of this is the Dutch West India Company, modelled on the Dutch East India Company, which in turn imitated the 'fort and factory' model used by the Portuguese in Africa and the East, which in turn was an imitation of the Italian factories in Byzantium. The Europeans came to Africa not as conquerors but as customers. The fortunes made by the Portuguese in Africa and America caused the Dutch and British to follow their example, although England's historic alliance with Portugal and resultant pressure from the Portuguese restricted

England's interest in Africa. Economic rivalry developed but this was a global story rather than an Atlantic one. However, it was jealousy of the Spanish that made the English seek their fortunes in North America. Portugal may have prepared the way by offering a model for colonial development, but the Spanish discovered the gold and silver riches of Mexico and Peru and their experience provided the inspiration for many Europeans.

Exploration and National Identity

Historians used to remember the voyages of Columbus as epics of 'discovery' and described the man himself as a heroic innovator who single-handedly changed the course of human history. More recently it has been recognized that it is important to put Columbus into the context of his time and also to judge his achievements from a less Eurocentric point of view. His journeys were a disaster for the Native Americans, for instance, because many other Europeans were encouraged to follow him, carrying their diseases with them. Also, other factors apart from his undoubted bravery and self-belief allowed Columbus to leave Europe in the first place. Spiritual regeneration and the expansion of the Catholic faith drove the Iberian interest in the Americas. The Spanish found a new confidence because of the *Reconquista*, the reclamation of their land from the invading Moors. The symbolic unification of the crowns of Aragon and Castile also changed the way Spaniards viewed their place in the world, and Ferdinand and Isabella tried to cement their position as the true heirs of Visigothic Spain. The Visigoths were a Germanic tribe of late antiquity who dominated the Iberian Peninsula before the Moorish (Muslim) invasion of the early eighth century. This religious fervour and national pride influenced Ferdinand and Isabella in their decision to award permission to Columbus for his voyage, but even then there were many protesters among the examiners at Salamanca who assessed his project and thought Columbus a charlatan who would be unable to fulfil his goal.

Castilians had been interested in territorial expansion since the early fifteenth century when they conquered the Canary Islands. Italians were also involved in the developing of the sugar trade there; they had easier access to ready currency than the Spaniards. Ferdinand and Isabella were also interested in using the Islands as a trade route for supplying African gold to Castile. The treatment of the Islands' natives presaged the Spanish treatment of the Native Americans. Slave trading and disease had depleted Canarians' numbers and, once they were pacified, Spanish representations of them in literature depicted them living in pastoral idylls in idealized simplicity. The experience in the Canary Islands offered a precursor to the way that the Spanish empire would be run. The conquistadors in both places were only nominally tied to Ferdinand and Isabella; they wanted to be feudal lords. The monarchs resisted this urge by using land and labour as a means of securing loyalty to the crown.

Around the ports of the southern Mediterranean, the spread of knowledge about the Atlantic, by word of mouth, was an important method of cultural exchange. Sailors who had had experience of visiting the European Atlantic seaboard, Africa and the Atlantic archipelagos shared stories and expertise in informal ways and literate members of the crews transmitted maps and journals to those collecting such information in the universities of Italy and Iberia. For example, Columbus learned about the Atlantic both from books and from speaking to sailors, but the knowledge he gathered still did not prevent him from grossly miscalculating the distance across the Atlantic.

The reconquest of Spain was political as well as religious. Influenced by the ideas of early Christian theologian Saint Augustine, it was seen as a just war to reclaim stolen territory. The victory boosted Spain's morale but also engendered a climate of paranoia and intolerance. It allowed the country to turn its attentions elsewhere. Hostility towards the Moors was in evidence throughout the period as Spain's activities were designed to challenge the power of the Islamic eastern Mediterranean by circumventing their trade routes. They also hoped to spread Christianity to any peoples they encountered. Rituals of claiming possession show how important the Europeans' religious identity was to them. They claimed territory in the New World by planting a large cross and giving the region a European name. Using his religious authority the Pope divided up the Americas on Columbus's return. In 1493 a papal bull from Alexander VI gave the Portuguese the eastern portion of the Atlantic and the Spanish the western. The Portuguese challenged this and under the agreement that followed, known as the Treaty of Tordesillas, the line was moved 600 miles to the west. Later, sixteenth-century writers used the papal donation to justify their territorial ambitions in the New World. Religious authority initially undertook land division, although those in temporal authority also played their part. The European nations now had to move to settle and use this land that they had acquired, both by making use of its natural resources but also – a more important duty – by taking Christianity to the Natives.

ATLANTIC HISTORY IN FOCUS

The significance of Columbus

1451	Born in Genoa.
	Spent time in Portugal learning from sailors; visited Iceland and Ireland.
1480	Visited Madeira to buy sugar for Portuguese.
early 1480s	Visited Gold Coast of Africa, but Portuguese would not support a trans-atlantic mission so went to Castile.
1492	Permission finally given for voyage.
But:	He didn't do it alone; Portuguese precursors; also used advice of others.
	Was confused about where he was/misunderstood span of ocean.
	Thought he'd arrived in the East Indies; no concept of America.
	Fell out with monarchs over use of Indians as slaves.
	Never found the huge gold mines he sought.
	Died in relative obscurity.

Exploration and International Rivalry

The motivation to explore the far-flung corners of the earth emerged from the rivalry between the European powers. Nations who had not yet reached the Americas wished to emulate the success, fame and religious honour gained by the Iberians. This dynamic was especially important for the English and the Dutch who had their own reasons – chiefly enmity with Spain – for pursuing interests across the Atlantic. A distinction is often drawn between the formalized systems of conquest used by the Iberian world and the commercial system of northern Europe's empires, but there were important similarities; the two sorts of empire were bound closely together and did not operate in isolation. The Spanish provided an example of how to exploit the natural resources but also how not to behave towards the Natives. The emergence of the Black Legend, the idea that the Spanish Catholics were behaving in a particularly cruel and inhumane way in Central and South America, flourished in northern Europe from the late sixteenth century onwards. In 1542, the work of Bartolomé de Las Casas defended the Indians and criticized the behaviour of his fellow Spaniards, inspiring the Black Legend, as will be seen in Chapter 2. It was cemented in the minds of Englishmen and the connection was made between global expansion and the Protestant faith by the collector of travel narratives, Richard Hakluyt, and the observer of Natives, Thomas Harriot. Despite seeing the Spanish treatment of Natives as a terrible example, the English settlers did not behave any better and pursued a policy of exclusion, removal and annihilation where necessary. From 1585 to 1603 when England and Spain were at war, the Spanish empire in the New World was a reality and many Englishmen attacked Spain via her Atlantic empire. Elizabeth's official policy was defensive but many of her sailors led a more offensive policy.

The first English forays into the Americas were by privateers lying in wait for the Spanish treasure ships returning from Mexico and Peru. Raiding continued, tacitly supported by Robert Cecil, Elizabeth's chief minister, even after peace was concluded by the two nations in James I's reign. After the defeat of the Spanish Armada in 1588, the Dutch and English challenged the naval power of the Spaniards in the Atlantic. Not only was the Armada's defeat a morale boost for the English and devastating for the Spanish, but in practical terms it reduced the size of Spain's navy to such an extent that it was unable to prevent challenges from other nations. Sir Francis Drake's circumnavigation voyage of 1577, during which he attacked Spanish ports along the Pacific coast, and his successful action at Cadiz prior to the Armada also increased anti-Spanish feeling and Protestant nationalism in England. Drake worked with anyone who saw themselves as enemies of the Spanish, such as the *cimarrones* (free blacks) who, in 1573, helped him to seize silver shipments from an overland mule convoy at Nombre de Dios, in present-day Panama. In 1585 he also held the city of Cartagena to ransom in a lucrative raiding voyage. Through the work of privateers such as Drake, the English became successful interlopers in the Iberian trade.

Once settlements had been established, the rivalry between European powers triggered further expansion into wilderness areas, such as the Spanish and Portuguese competition in the Brazilian interior. The English were more concerned about the

Spanish and the French than about any threat from the Native Americans. The Caribbean was another important site where international rivalries played out. For example, the Spanish were forced to give up Jamaica by the English Puritan government of the mid-seventeenth century following a mission driven by religious and patriotic zeal.

A similar pattern emerged in West Africa where initial Portuguese dominance was challenged by the Dutch and the English, creating a situation in which Africans had to choose sides and could be disadvantaged by picking the wrong one. In the 1560s commercial rivalry between the English and the Portuguese over the Guinea trade in Africa developed into war. In the 1550s and 1560s the English, who desired a foothold in the gold trade, privately financed voyages to Guinea. In 1558 Mary paid for a royal voyage and in 1564 Elizabeth partnered John Hawkins in a slaving voyage, loaning him one of her ships. These were successful plundering voyages and they marked the start of the English involvement in the triangular trade, but they were also characterized by brutality towards Africans and very high mortality rates among the sailors. The Portuguese sank English ships that they encountered off the coast of Africa, forcing the English out of the trade until the seventeenth century. Even the attempt in 1618 to form a Guinea trading company came to nothing in terms of participation in the slave trade, although some gold and timber were acquired.

The Portuguese war with the Dutch in the early seventeenth century could be described as the first world war, as the Dutch challenged the Portuguese in Brazil, gaining Pernambuco and Bahia, and on the African coast, gaining São Tomé and Príncipe and some Gold Coast forts; they even pushed the Portuguese temporarily out of the Malabar coast of India. The Dutch had been encouraged by Linschoten's account published in 1598, which revealed the vulnerability of the Portuguese empire. The Dutch rise to power was rapid and global. However, the Portuguese proved difficult to dislodge because they had already created a settled community and established a number of Native alliances. Some Dutch at Pernambuco actually converted to Catholicism, such was the force of the Iberian cultural tradition there. There is also one recorded case of a Jesuit working for the Portuguese turning renegade and joining the Dutch Calvinists. The Dutch defined themselves as enemies of Hapsburg Spain who, they felt, had colonized them in Europe, and so their enmity of the Spanish was a reaction against tyranny. The unity of the Spanish and Portuguese crowns in the late sixteenth century brought the Dutch and Portuguese into conflict. The Dutch saw the New World as a site of Iberian cruelty and hoped to rescue the Natives. They were surprised to discover that the relationship between the Europeans and the Native Americans was not as simple as the colonizer taking advantage of the colonized. The French were also a significant Atlantic power during this early period, and their challenges to Portuguese dominance of Brazil and to Spanish dominance of Florida forced both Iberian nations to further fortify and solidify their holdings.

A desire to emulate the trading and colonizing success of the Italians, especially Genoa and Venice, was an important factor in the emergence of the Iberians into the Atlantic world. The growth in the economic wealth and power of Venice was based on its success in the Levant trade that other Europeans wanted to emulate. The

Barbary ports along the North African coast were cosmopolitan places where traders of many European and African nations lived and worked alongside one another. But it is important to remember that many individuals who played a part in the Atlantic story operated across national boundaries. For example, Columbus was a Genoese who had worked for the Portuguese before sailing across the Atlantic for Castile, but he always remained nostalgic for his home city. Although national rivalry drove much of the expansion, the story of the individuals involved reveals a more cosmopolitan aspect and there was a significant sharing of knowledge both orally by sailors of different nations and on paper through Latin works or the translation into the vernacular of books about the newly discovered parts of the world. Internal competition within one country could also trigger interest in the Atlantic, as shown by the development of the merchant class in Bristol and their sponsorship of trips to find a North-West Passage and to open up fisheries and settlements in North America. They defined themselves in opposition to and in competition with the merchants of London. During this period London's merchants were wary of exploiting the Atlantic trade, preferring instead to focus on opportunities in Continental Europe. This lack of support was a serious weakness in England's approach to overseas trade during the sixteenth century. It must be remembered that local pride and patriotism was as important in the early modern period as national identity.

Extra-national Conquest

So far, we have examined the role played by the crown, the state and individuals in the exploration of the Atlantic world. But the Catholic Church along with other denominations also played their part. In Catholic countries the secular church and the religious orders defined European expansion, but Protestantism was also an important motivator, both in its relationship with nationalism and in driving the migration of particular groups. Missionary zeal was central to the expansion. The desire on the part of Christians to convert 'the heathen' drove exploration and migration to all parts of the Atlantic world and caused a religious revival in southern Europe. The Catholic Church was successful in converting millions of Natives, slaves and freemen and gave the Iberian colonies an important coherence. The Continental Catholic Church was in a state of uncertainty in the late medieval period. The burning of heretic enemies was seen as redemptive and this provided the backdrop to the behaviour of the church in the New World. As shown in Chapter 2, Christian beliefs about the pagan Indians and Africans and the way they should be treated influenced the developing racial ideology of America.

The Catholic Church responded quickly to the explorations of the Atlantic with the papal bull of 1493, which divided the region between the Portuguese and the Spanish. The territory was given to them with the proviso that the conquerors and settlers take with them missionaries to evangelize any Native populations they encountered. This division of territory was respected by the nations as they pushed into the Americas and Africa. Papal bulls that had been used in the conquest of the

Mediterranean islands became the model for the bull dividing the Atlantic. For example, in 1478 a Bull of Indulgence was given by Sixtus IV to encourage the conversion of the Canary Islanders. This in turn was modelled on the papal declarations encouraging crusades.

Representatives of the Catholic Church duly followed migrants and conquistadors into the New World and the religious orders followed. In New Spain, Franciscans arrived in 1524, Dominicans in 1526 and Augustinians in 1533. However, the relationship between the secular parish-based Catholic priests and the members of the religious orders was sometimes a challenging one and the orders often operated outside the remit of the national, imperial structures. Initially, in New Spain, the mendicant orders had a leading role in evangelizing and in debating the role to be played in society by the Native Americans, but then the crown established parishes and appointed secular clergy who took over from the orders. They used a system of mass baptism coupled with attempts to instruct individuals (especially the young) about Catholicism. They learned local languages such as Nahuatl in Mexico and Quechua in Peru in order to instruct the Indians in their own language. They also instituted a policy of resettlement for the Indians, forcing them to move from their tribal homes and to live in settlements controlled by the religious orders.

The Jesuits were not a uniquely Atlantic organization; they operated in a global context. The Jesuits were managed by a complex administrative system of procurators based on the geographical unit of the province. Their independence upset the diocesan churches, especially in frontier areas where Jesuits took over roles usually undertaken by the secular church. The Jesuits were most influential in Brazil, having failed to get a foothold in Kongo. However, there was some success in the conversion of Africans. As early as 1488 King Jeleen of the Wolof people (in modern-day Senegal) and six of his chief followers were baptized, with members of the Portuguese royal family as godparents. C. R. Boxer has argued that Jesuit activity was all that kept some regions Portuguese, for example in East Africa and Timor. Although they owned thousands of slaves in Brazil, Jesuits also sent missions to enslaved Africans both in Africa and in the Americas. The Jesuits were keen founders of libraries and distributors of medicines, although they struggled to help the Natives overcome the horrors of the European plagues such as smallpox and measles, using them to teach the lesson that God was punishing the Natives for their sinful ways. Some Indians saw the Jesuits as loyal allies who defended them against the aggressive settlers. While the Jesuits tried to prevent illegal slavery, the settlers needed labour and the Jesuits were powerless to stop the raiding by *bandierantes*, although by the seventeenth century they had begun arming the Indians at their missions.

However, by the mid-eighteenth century the Jesuit Atlantic was being dismantled by the national governments of Spain, France and Portugal who wished to reduce the power of the Jesuits in the Americas. They were accused of being greedy and corrupt, and it was true that the Jesuits were very wealthy. The religious houses also became a battleground for the struggles for power and influence between American-born creoles and Iberian-born *peninsulares*. The Inquisition was employed in the Americas and globally to stamp out superstition and sorcery but it was more tolerant than it first appeared.

Magic borne of ignorance was not seen as an evil heresy and was tolerated until it was possible to 're-educate' the Natives. However, in some cases the heavy-handed tactics of the Inquisition may have hindered conversion by intimidating the Natives.

The idea of a colony in America as a refuge from religious persecution began in the 1560s with the French Huguenot migration to Florida. They were the first to see America as a haven, but were soon followed by the religiously pluralist colonies of England in North America: the Catholic exile colony planned by George Peckham, the Catholics in Maryland and, perhaps most famously, the Pilgrim Fathers at Plymouth and the Puritans in Massachusetts. These groups established transatlantic communities of dissention designed to help anyone who was a victim of religious persecution. Quakers were especially good at maintaining these networks and this explains the cosmopolitan nature of the Pennsylvania colony, which attracted dissenting migrants from all over Europe.

Who Held These Nascent Empires in Place?

The founding of the overseas empires was undertaken by various groups of people. Critics of Columbus say that he was a decent navigator but a poor administrator and without the help of others the Spanish empire in the New World would have been a complete failure. Who were these groups that bound the new European empires together?

Soldiers and sailors were an important force, especially in the early years of exploration. These military men were often a motley transnational and even interracial collection who worked both for the state they represented and for their own financial gain. In New Spain, Hernan Cortés and the four Pizarro brothers saw themselves as representatives of Spain and the Catholic monarchs, but much of their activity was undertaken to secure plunder and honour for themselves and their men. The relationship between the soldiers and the crown was strained at times. Gonzalo Pizarro was a rare example of a conquistador who turned completely against his own crown because he disagreed with the New Laws and their more sympathetic treatment of the Natives. He was executed in 1548.

The settlements at Roanoke in present-day North Carolina (founded 1585) and Jamestown, Virginia (1607) also contained a number of military men alongside civilian settlers and, although the soldiers were very good at exploring and mapping the local area, they were poor at growing crops and establishing friendly relationships with the Indians. Although without sailors the voyages would never have taken place, they did not hold a position of respect in the societies of Europe. They often worked against the settlers if their interests clashed, leading to tensions between the two groups. The Puritans in Massachusetts were upset by the behaviour of the soldiers and sailors whom they considered to be ungodly and coarse. Public opinion in Europe was also critical of the worst excesses of the military representatives of empire. After the Spanish conquistadors murdered Atahualpa in Peru and divided into factions, Spanish public opinion turned against them.

Alison Games believes that to understand the story of the Atlantic world it is important to study the patterns of migration. There were two sorts of migration to and around the Americas: free and forced. Free migrants were either economic or religious settlers seeking exile and security in the New World. Often these two motivations were combined. Free migrants were encouraged by a series of push and pull factors: push factors such as poverty or debt in their own country that encouraged them to leave, and pull factors such as the possibility of making a fortune that attracted them to their new home. In New Spain and New France, only Spanish or French Catholic settlers were welcomed, and they travelled in small numbers. However, in Brazil, Portuguese, Dutch and French settlers appeared, while English North America was more cosmopolitan still, with a wide variety of different nationalities settling in that region. Migrants were especially important in the establishment of the English colonies, in which the main focus was the creation of white settlements rather than the management of Natives. The nationality of the settlers did not threaten the imperial government of the colonies and all were welcomed. In São Paulo, Brazil, the white settlers encouraged the use of Indian slave labour and gained dominance over the gold mines of the interior. They formed groups of *bandierantes*, who set out on harsh, long journeys to kidnap slaves or explore for gold mines. These *bandierantes* were mixed-race groups formed initially because the soil of the São Paulo region was poor for growing sugar. They were hostile not only to local Indians but also to other white settlers who moved into the region following the gold rush.

In Africa few European settlers stayed permanently. The European presence consisted of merchants who stayed on the coast of West Africa for a few years. Some took African wives but many also had families in Europe and their move was not intended to be permanent. From the 1580s onwards merchants were an especially important part of the English exploration, with their ships and money allowing the voyages to North America to take place. Merchants also worked against the trend towards centralized empire by indulging in illicit trade. Africans also sent out emissaries and negotiators to European courts, realizing the importance of engaging with the crown of Portugal in order to improve trade. Their traders and merchants played a key role in the development of the Atlantic system. Arguably, without them the transatlantic slave trade would not have been a success.

Forced migration also ensured the success of the New World empires. The most obvious and numerous cause of this was the transatlantic slave trade, without which the sugar industry in the Caribbean and Brazil would not have developed. However, initially Indian slave labour provided the workforce for settlements in New Spain and Brazil. Settlers and missionaries combined to 'reduce' the Natives to civilization by moving them to Spanish- and Portuguese-controlled villages from where they could hire out their labour. Although imperial authorities forbade Indian slavery, demands for labour meant that the kidnapping of Indians into slavery continued. Despite their denials and opposition, Jesuits colluded in this system. White labourers were also part of the forced migration, such as criminals who were exiled and labourers who were kidnapped from the streets of London to work in the plantations of Barbados and Jamaica.

Missionaries held many of the European empires in the New World together, especially in frontier regions. Although religious orders operated outside the imperial structure, their activities allowed the Europeans to gain control of the Americas using Indian labour. They were also important in New France, Brazil and New Spain in defending the rights of the Natives and ensuring that they were considered full imperial subjects. In British North America missionaries were not a significant factor. Although individuals – such as John Eliot of seventeenth-century Massachusetts, who was known as 'the apostle to the Indians' – concerned themselves with converting the Natives, there was never a concerted effort on behalf of the Protestant denominations or the crown to make the Indians Christian, but missionaries transmitted information about the geographical realities of the Americas and its people to interested audiences in Europe. In Africa missionaries attempted to ply their trade, but were mostly unsuccessful due to the reluctance of Africans to replace their own religions with Christianity. The Portuguese Jesuits in Angola and Kongo had some success and missionaries there worked with the African elites and with captives on board the slave ships about to cross the Atlantic. However, the missionary effort did not have a significant impact on Africa until the nineteenth century, when the imperial relationships morphed into a new form.

All empires needed administrators and a system of government in order to survive. In Central and South America, governing the large Indian populations was the main concern for administrators. They used the *encomienda* system, offering Natives protection in return for their taxes and forced labour. The Spanish were the most efficient at putting an imperial organization into place because they had the incentive of wanting to gain access to the mineral wealth of Mexico and Peru. Their portion of the Americas was divided into the viceroyalties of New Spain and Peru, and a Board of Trade and a Council of the Indies was set up to control the area from Spain. However, some of the Spanish governors ruled almost as absolute monarchs, for example, Francisco de Toledo in Peru in the 1570s. He conducted a survey of the Natives within his region and forced them to move into small towns, although he did not actually take their land from them. He also mobilized a slave labour force to mine less accessible ores at Potosí. This meant that the financial benefit of his methods prevented criticism from Spain. Other European nations were slower to create a structure and were more haphazard in their methods of managing their new colonies. The Portuguese began distributing land to a group of donatories who were in charge of pacifying the Indian threat in their area. The most active of these was Duarte Coelho, who was in charge of Pernambuco in the 1540s and 1550s; he made use of Indian slave labour in his sugar mill and managed to enforce Portuguese control of the region by playing the local Indian tribes off against one another. Royal governors oversaw the donatory system. In British North America a system of local assemblies began in Virginia in 1619, and settlers had representative rule during the reign of Charles I – whilst the residents of England did not because the King had dissolved Parliament. From 1660 onwards, royal governors, who received a mixed reception among the settlers, oversaw the local assemblies, but overall the royal control imposed on the Americas was much more tolerant than that imposed by Spain.

A final group who held these nascent empires together were the authors who wrote about the Americas and Africa and triggered European interest in the regions, their people and their commodities. Some of these authors were religious or economic migrants who had travelled to the New World, but many were 'armchair travellers' who stayed at home but saw it as their religious and national duty to encourage interest and investment in the colonies. John Dee, who coined the idea of a seaborne British empire, and Richard Hakluyt were the leading English exponents of this. As John Donne, poet and supporter of the Virginia Company, wrote, 'he who prints, adventures'. Despite the way that Europeans portrayed their own successes during this period, without the connivance of Native Americans and Africans they would not have been able to gain a foothold in the Americas, so while Europeans were masters of their own destiny, they had to work with the other races of the Atlantic world in order to truly dominate the region.

Conclusion

As this chapter has shown, the European impulse to cross the Atlantic and establish settlements had important precedents. An interest in trade, plantation slavery and conquest had flourished in the Mediterranean for centuries. European rivalry in this region encouraged some states to push further in their attempts to seek economic gain and religious salvation. As the Crusades ended, the desire to take Christianity to other parts of the world motivated those crossing the Atlantic or travelling down the coast of West Africa. The desire for personal gain and power also cannot be ignored. Every explorer, conquistador and settler from Columbus onwards saw the New World as a place where he or she could gain a heroic reputation and undreamed of wealth or influence. So, national pride, religion and personal gain united to drive the development of the Atlantic world. It is important to look at the explorers in the context of the time. Although we might be tempted to see them as heroes, they did not act alone. Similarly, white Europeans could not have achieved what they did without the assistance of other participants in the Atlantic story.

CHAPTER CHRONOLOGY

1440s	Portuguese explorers reach the coast of West Africa.
1492	Genoan Christopher Columbus on behalf of the Spanish monarchy reaches the Americas, landing on Hispaniola.
1519	Conquest of Mexico by Hernan Cortés.
1526	Francisco Pizarro reaches Peru.
1535	Jacques Cartier sails up the Hudson River to site of modern-day Quebec.
1576	Martin Frobisher sails to region that became New England looking for North-West Passage.
1585	Roanoke colony (present-day North Carolina) established.
1607	Founding of Jamestown, Virginia.

■ PRIMARY SOURCES AND STUDY IMAGE

Popol Vuh – Chapter 1: A Mayan Creation Story

This is the account of how all was in suspense, all calm, in silence; all motionless, still, and the expanse of the sky was empty. This is the first account, the first narrative. There was neither man, nor animal, birds, fishes, crabs, trees, stones, caves, ravines, grasses, nor forests; there was only the sky. The surface of the earth had not appeared. There was only the calm sea and the great expanse of the sky. There was nothing brought together, nothing which could make a noise, nor anything which might move, or tremble, or could make noise in the sky. There was nothing standing; only the calm water, the placid sea, alone and tranquil. Nothing existed.

There was nothing standing; only the calm water, the placid sea, alone and tranquil. Nothing existed. There was only immobility and silence in the darkness, in the night. Only the Creator, the Maker, Tepeu, Gucumatz, the Forefathers, were in the water surrounded with light. They were hidden under green and blue feathers, and were therefore called Gucumatz. By nature they were great sages and great thinkers. In this manner the sky existed and also the heart of Heaven, which is the name of God and thus He is called. Then came the word. Tepeu and Gucumatz came together in the darkness, in the night, and Tepeu and Gucumatz talked together. They talked then, discussing and deliberating; they agreed, they united their words and their thoughts.

Then while they meditated, it became clear to them that when dawn would break, man must appear. Then they planned the creation, and the growth of the trees and the thickets and the birth of life and the creation of man. Thus it was arranged in the darkness and in the night by the Heart of Heaven who is called Huracán.

Traveller Leo Africanus describes Timbuktu (1600)

The name of this kingdom is a modern one, after a city which was built by a king named Mansa Suleyman in the year 610 of the hegira [1232 CE] around twelve miles from a branch of the Niger River. The houses of Timbuktu are huts made of clay-covered wattles with thatched roofs. In the centre of the city is a temple built of stone and mortar, built by an architect named Granata, and in addition there is a large palace, constructed by the same architect, where the king lives. The shops of the artisans, the merchants, and especially weavers of cotton cloth are very numerous. Fabrics are also imported from Europe to Timbuktu, borne by Berber merchants. The women of the city maintain the custom of veiling their faces, except for the slaves who sell all the foodstuffs. The inhabitants are very rich, especially the strangers who have settled in the country; so much so that the current king has given two of his daughters in marriage to two brothers, both businessmen, on account of their wealth. There are many wells containing sweet water in Timbuktu; and in addition, when the Niger is in flood canals deliver the water to the city. Grain and animals are abundant, so that the consumption of milk and butter is considerable. But salt is in very short supply because it is carried here from Tegaza, some 500 miles from Timbuktu. I happened to be in this city at a time when a load of salt sold for eighty ducats. The king has a rich treasure of coins and gold ingots. One of these ingots weighs 970 pounds. The royal court is magnificent and very well organized. When the king goes from one city to another with the people of his court, he rides a camel and the horses are led by hand by servants. If fighting becomes necessary, the servants mount the camels and all the soldiers mount on horseback. When someone wishes to speak to the king, he must kneel before him and bow down; but this is only required of those who have never before spoken to the king, or of ambassadors. The king has about 3,000 horsemen and infinity of foot-soldiers armed with bows made of wild fennel which they use to shoot poisoned arrows. This king makes war only upon neighbouring enemies and upon those who do not want to pay him tribute. When he has gained a victory, he has all of them – even the children – sold in the market at Timbuktu. Only small, poor horses are born in this country. The merchants use them for their voyages and the courtiers to move about the city. But the good horses come from Barbary. They arrive in a caravan and, ten or twelve days later, they are led to the ruler, who takes as many as he likes and pays appropriately for them. The king is a declared enemy of the Jews. He will not allow any to live in the city. If he hears it said that a Berber merchant frequents them or does business with them, he confiscates his goods. There are in Timbuktu numerous judges, teachers and priests, all properly appointed by the king. He greatly honours learning. Many hand-written books imported from Barbary are also sold. There is more profit made from this commerce than from all other merchandise. Instead of coined money, pure gold nuggets are used; and for small purchases, cowrie shells which have been carried from Persia, and of which 400 equal a ducat. Six and two-thirds of their ducats equal one Roman gold ounce.

The people of Timbuktu are of a peaceful nature. They have a custom of almost continuously walking about the city in the evening (except for those that sell gold), between 10 p.m. and 1 a.m., playing musical instruments and dancing. The citizens have at their service many slaves, both men and women. The city is very much endangered by fire. At the time when I was there on my second voyage; half the city burned in the space of five hours. But the wind was violent and the inhabitants of the other half of the city began to move their belongings for fear that the other half would burn. There are no gardens or orchards in the area surrounding Timbuktu.

Richard Hakluyt's *Discourse on Western Planting* (1584) encouraging English involvement in the Americas

And where England now for certain hundreth years last passed, by the peculiar commodity of wools, and of later years by clothing of the same, hath raised itself from meaner state to great wealth and much highr honour, mighty and power than before, to the equaling of the princes of the same to the greatst potentates of this part of the world it cometh now so to passe, that by the great endeavour of the increase of the trade of wools in Spain and in the West Indies, now daily more and more multiplying that the wools of England, and the clothe made of the same, will become base, and every day more base then other; which, prudently weighed yet behoveth this realm if it mean not to return to former olde means and baseness but to stand in present and late former honour, glory, and force, and not negligently and sleepingly to slide into beggery, to foresee and to plant at Norumbega [New England] or some like place, were it not for any thing else but for the hope of the vent of our wool endraped, the principal and in effect the only enriching continuing natural commodity of this realm.

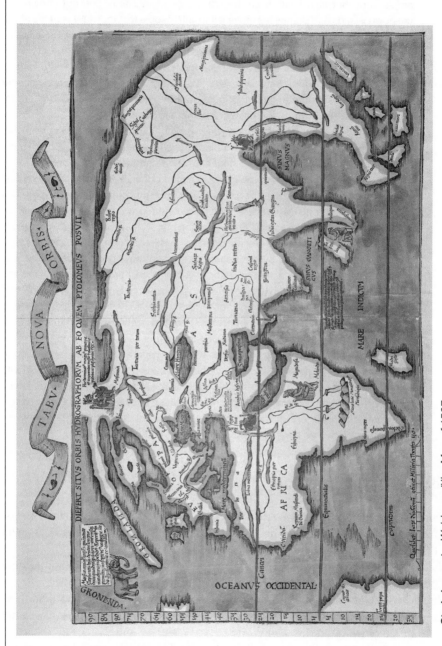

Study image 1 *Waldseemüller Map of 1507.*

And effectually pursuing that course, we shall not only find on that tract of land, and especially in that firm northward (to whom warm clothe shall be right welcome), an ample vent, but also shall, from the north side of that firm, find out known and unknown islands and dominions replenished with people that may fully vent the abundance of that our commodity, that else will in few years wax of none or of small value by foreign abundance &c.; so as by this enterprise we shall shun the imminent mischief hanging over our heads that else must needs fall upon the realm without breach of peace or sword drawn against this realm by any foreign state; and not offer our ancient riches to scornful neighbours at home, nor sell the same in effect for nothing, as we shall shortly, if presently it be not provided for ...

This enterprise may stay the Spanish King from flowing over all the face of that waste firm of America, if we seat and plant there in time, in time I say, and we by planting shall [prevent] him from making more short and more safe returns out of the noble ports of the purposed places of our planting, then by any possibility he can from the part of the firm that now his navys by ordinary courses come from, in this that there is no comparison between the ports of the coasts that the King of Spain doth now possess and use and the ports of the coasts that our nation is to possess by planting at Norumbega, ... And England possessing the purposed place of planting, her Majesty may, by the benefit of the seat having won good and royall havens, have plenty of excellent trees for masts of goodly timber to build ships and to make great navys, of pitch, tar, hemp, and all things incident for a navy royall, and that for no price, and without money or request. How easy a matter may yet be to this realm, swarming at this day with valiant youths, rusting and hurtful by lack of employment, and having good makers of cable and of all sorts of cordage, and the best and most cunning shipwrights of the world, to be lords of all those seas, and to spoil Phillip's Indian navy, and to deprive him of yearly passage of his treasure into Europe, and consequently to abate the pride of Spain and of the supporter of the great Anti-Christ of Rome and to pull him down in equality to his neighbour princes, and consequently to cut of the common mischiefs that come to all Europe by the peculiar abundance of his Indian treasure, and this without difficulty.

Recommended Reading

Kenneth Andrews, *Trade, Plunder and Settlement* (Cambridge, 1984). Provides assessment of reasons for English expansion into the Atlantic and a balanced assessment of why it lagged behind the Iberians.

Charles Boxer, *The Portuguese Seaborne Empire* (New York, 1975). The classic account of Portuguese expansion from the fifteenth century onwards.

Alfred Crosby, *The Columbian Exchange* (Westport, 1972). A seminal work describing the exchange of foods, drinks, medicines, ideas, and diseases that took place after the arrival of whites in the New World.

Felipe Fernandez-Armesto, *Before Columbus* (Philadelphia, 1987). Examines the Mediterranean and African precursors to the building of Atlantic colonies, discussing themes such as religious missions, staple crops and plantation culture.

Alison Games, *Migration and the Origins of the English Atlantic World* (Cambridge, MA, 1999). Shows the importance of the movement of people to the story of the English Atlantic, surveying the experiences and motivations of over a thousand English migrants.

John Hemming, *Red Gold* (London, 1978). Provides a detailed account of the conquest of the Brazilian Indians between the sixteenth and eighteenth centuries.

Peter Hulme, *Colonial Encounters* (London, 1986). Shows how Native Americans were incorporated into the European mentality by analysing literary and theatrical representations.

Sidney Mintz, *Sweetness and Power: The Place of Sugar in Modern History* (New York, 1985). Takes one staple crop as a case study and shows how it has affected human history.

Benjamin Schmidt, *Innocence Abroad: The Dutch Imagination and the New World* (New York, 2001). A rare examination of the origins of the Dutch interest in the Atlantic world, exploring how Dutch rivalry with the Hapsburg Spanish drove their understanding of the Americas.

Charles Verlinden, *The Beginnings of Modern Colonization* (Ithaca, NY, 1970). Shows how classical, biblical and medieval forerunners of empire building influenced Renaissance Europeans.

TEST YOUR KNOWLEDGE

1 Prior to 1492, what were 'colonies' like?
2 What drove European exploration of and settlement of the Americas?
3 What role did rivalry between the European nations play?
4 Apart from states and monarchs, how did other organizations become involved in this process of expansion?

2 Contact and Encounter

Models of Racial Understanding

This chapter will explore what happened when Africans, Native Americans and Europeans encountered each other for the first time. It discusses physical responses such as trade and warfare as well as psychological and intellectual developments. Racial misconceptions rooted in the colonial period are still rampant today. Even modern historians often portray Native Americans as unchanging and simple. But we need to ask whether these attitudes were present before first contact took place, or whether it was contact between the races that caused prejudice to develop. Because immigrants wanted to create a 'new world' modelled on the places they had left behind, and not simply to observe and assimilate themselves into whatever they found, this meant that contact between the races was naturally strained. We must go back to the period before Columbus reached the New World to examine when and how these racial ideas emerged. Renaissance Europeans derived their understanding of the racial 'other' from several sources. In northern Europe, few whites had met someone from another race, so their ideas came from the culture around them. In southern Europe, such as the courts of Madrid, Lisbon and the Italian city states, contact with Africans was much more common. Isabella d'Este, Marchesa of Mantua from 1490 to 1539, instructed her agents to find her some black African servants, whom she treated well and saw as symbols of her status and wealth. Africans even reached as far as Peter the Great's court in Russia where he proudly displayed his black servants, but the Russian Africans, including novelist Alexander Pushkin's great-grandfather, came from East Africa. By the mid-sixteenth century Africans made up nearly 10 per cent of the population of Lisbon. Delegations were sent from African rulers to Mediterranean ones. But most people still relied on classical and biblical models to help them interpret what people of other races were like. Ordinary people based their understanding on rumour, myth and word of mouth, while the more educated people relied on information from their reading of ancient sources.

The classical model of race is drawn from the work of natural history of the first-century Roman author Pliny the Elder. In his monumental *Naturalis Historia* (Natural History) he depicted monstrous races from far-flung corners of the world such as the Blemmye and the Cynocephalus (the dog-headed man). For centuries Pliny's work was the authority on the natural world and many of the early travellers along the coast of Africa and across the Atlantic truly believed that they would encounter these monstrous races. They were not only hideous in appearance but were also alienated from God, so therefore were not truly men. Columbus believed he would encounter these sorts of monstrous races, as did Walter Raleigh on his 1595 voyage to Guiana; and the Orellana expedition in the Amazon basin in 1542 found the mythical tribe of Amazons who were large warrior women, mentioned by Homer in his *Iliad* and by Herodotus.

The Bible was another source of knowledge during this period and was taken as an historically accurate representation of the origins of man. The story of Noah's sons is crucial to the understanding of how hatred of the racial 'other' developed. Noah's son Ham was seen as the ancestor of all black Africans, and Ham had transgressed, offending his father, so his descendants were destined to be forever slaves. Early Christian authors reinforced the meaning of this biblical text with their own interpretations. An influential thinker was Origen, who lived in the first half of the third century CE. He wrote about the Ham story in his *Homilies on Genesis 16:1*:

> For the Egyptians are prone to a degenerate life and quickly sink to every slavery of the vices. Look at the origin of the race and you will discover that their father Cham, who had laughed at his father's nakedness, deserved a judgment of this kind, that his son Chanaan should be a servant to his brothers, in which case the condition of bondage would prove the wickedness of his conduct. Not without merit, therefore, does the discoloured posterity imitate the ignobility of the race [*Non ergo immerito ignobilitatem decolour posteritas imitatur*].

Europeans did not live in cultural and geographical vacuums and had practical experiences of other races. Long before the so-called dark ages isolated much of the western European peninsula, traders from the West were making their way along the Silk Road, amassing and passing on goods, ideas and stories. Traders were the importers of stories about the lands that lay beyond European Christendom. Even when trade routes were disrupted, the tales of fabulous wealth, mythical rulers and strange people and animals left their cultural mark and became a part of Europe's cultural legacy. By the late thirteenth century, Spanish and Italian merchants were trading throughout the Mediterranean rim and confirming, at very least, that places far away did indeed contain the goods that wealthy Europeans wanted. Still, few if any Europeans travelled far from home, and the remoteness of other lands, and lack of the means or motive to visit them, reinforced ideas of their inherent difference.

The stories of a mythical English traveller named Sir John Mandeville contributed to the perception among Europeans that the remainder of the globe was comprised of strange, vaguely human creatures. Period woodcuts used to illustrate Mandeville's stories depict an array of perplexing figures. Some had human bodies and the long necks and heads of storks; for some it was dogs. Others were creatures with no heads but with facial features on their torsos. Still others had the same number of arms as an octopus, or possessed a single gigantic foot or the head of a stork, or the single eye of the Cyclops. These mythical creatures had some basis in fact: they were reflections of sustained contact through trade and travel, in which Europeans observed (though did not necessarily pursue an understanding of) various cultures around the Mediterranean rim and along the old Silk Road. The dog-headed people, for example, were likely variants of Anubis, the Egyptian god of embalming. An image of sheep protruding from the blossom of a plant likely depicted a cotton plant. The origins of others remain mysteries.

Other mythologies were more general, reflecting the missing pieces of a perceived global Christian past. As William Phillips and Carla Rahn Phillips point out, a common belief among educated Europeans was that the peoples of the Far East – modern China and India, most specifically – held beliefs that were intrinsically sympathetic to and philosophically compatible with European Christianity. Seaborne travel to create a smooth line of access to these mythical pre-Christians was one reason to pursue maritime innovations. From the middle of the twelfth century onward, there were rumours of a king of Central Asia, known in English as Prester John, who reigned in a Christian kingdom far to the east. Genghis Khan, the Mongolian leader whose armies expanded aggressively in the thirteenth century, was thought by returning Crusaders to be 'King David', a nephew of Prester John. Legends such as these persisted until the Atlantic discoveries and even beyond: Vasco da Gama, who rounded the Cape of Good Hope on his way to India, carried letters of introduction to the legendary Prester John. When he and his men successfully made landfall in India, they conflated Hindu temples and objects with Christian ones.

The natural world was also the subject of much myth making and speculation by Europeans. The myth of the travels of Saint Brendan, a sixth-century Irish monk, fed imaginations about what lay to the west of Europe. What waited, according to Brendan's legend, was a wonderful island called Paradise (or Saint Brendan's Isle), rich with edible foliage and natural beauty. Rumours of Paradise's location in the middle of the ocean near the equator persisted for many centuries. It even appeared as fact on German cartographer Martin Behaim's 1492 map of the western hemisphere.

The Europeans who explored the Atlantic littoral (the coast) carried knowledge of these tales and rumours with them. These in turn acted as a catalyst for some New World explorations. Both Gonzalo Pizzaro (brother of Francisco) and Francisco de Coronado spent years, fortunes and Spanish lives attempting to track down mythical societies of fabulous wealth. The failure to find the cities of El Dorado or Cibola heightened their suspicion of Native peoples, who often told the conquistadors what they wanted to hear in order to move them out of the area. Europeans who saw the stories fail to pan out used them as evidence of Indian deceit, and yet another reason to subdue them harshly.

Legend also tells of Juan Ponce de Léon's search for Bimini, a magical land that was home to a fabled fountain of youth. Though modern historians debate whether or not such a factor actually motivated Ponce de Léon, the persistence of the myth well into the modern era itself underscores the common perception that Europeans were looking for their Atlantic world adventures to validate durable legends – and in the process, they created new ones.

By examining where people thought racial difference came from we can under-stand more about how racial ideas developed. Most early modern scholars believed that differences in skin colour were caused by climatic variation. So, the hotter countries near the Equator in Africa produced very dark-skinned Africans, tropical regions produced brown-skinned Native Americans and the cooler climate of Europe produced white people. Northern Europeans differentiated between themselves and more 'swarthy' Mediterranean dwellers such as the Spanish and Italians. It was only later in the nineteenth century that ideas emerged claiming that those with black skin were subhuman and even perhaps a different species.

The harsh treatment of the 'other' was a reality of life in the early modern world, not just the stuff of literature. Witches, Jews and the Irish were among the groups demonized, and the rhetorical techniques used to describe these groups were imitated by travellers encountering Africans and Americans for the first time. Both witches and Jews were represented in European accounts as being outside the normal realms of society in both appearance and character. Both were suspected of horrendous cruelty and also were tainted with rumours of cannibalism and sexual deviance. Witches and Jews made others feel vulnerable and this produced the aggression and rage that led to persecution. This model was transferred onto Native Americans when it became convenient for Europeans to tarnish them as the enemy savages. The Spanish especially had developed ideas of racial and religious purity in relation to their own national identity, culminating in the *Reconquista*, the final defeat of the Muslims in the Iberian Peninsula and their removal from Al-Andalus. That this happened in the same year as Columbus's voyage to the New World is culturally no coincidence. The new confidence felt by the Spanish, who had made their geographical area a truly Christian country, was part of the reason why in 1492 Ferdinand and Isabella countenanced Columbus's voyages.

The way that the English treated and understood the native Irish also acted as a training ground for the development of later racial ideas. Native Irish, although not visibly of a different race, were religiously and culturally different and were seen as inferior savages, incapable of looking after themselves and needing order to be imposed on them by the English. The English created a safe area for themselves near Dublin, surrounded by a protective fence or 'Pale'. This led to the expression 'beyond the pale', meaning something outside the realms of normal behaviour. Although this was not a racially driven decision, it shows the ways in which Europeans treated those that they considered unlike them.

Class and status were other important reasons for prejudice in early modern Europe, and explorers and settlers took these attitudes with them to America and Africa. Authors of travel narratives constantly distinguished between elite and ordinary Indians and Africans that they encountered. The cultural practices of the elite were treated with interest and respect. The hierarchical structure and the power and jurisdictions of Native leaders fascinated Europeans, whereas the mass of the population were often dismissed as cruel, ignorant or savage. In Europe, members of the elites also criticized the behaviour of the poor of their own race in similar ways. The poor were seen as a group who could be manipulated and used, ripe for exploitation. As Karen Kupperman argued, low-born Englishmen and Natives were both seen as 'treacherous, lazy or disgusting in some way'. Commentators described what was different about the Natives: clothes, hair, tattoos, jewellery and posture. These aspects, not morality or character, determined one's status in society, thus showing that Europeans viewed Natives through the prism of a hierarchical society rather than one defined by racial difference.

• **UP FOR DEBATE**   Can we use the concept of racism to talk about this period?

For:
• Europeans understood black-skinned people as different and associated them with evil.
• People who looked different were seen as inferior and 'other'.

Against:
• Prejudice was based on cultural and religious differences (i.e., people behaved differently, were not Christian) rather than the fact they had different skin colour.
• Racism as we know it today emerged in the nineteenth century based on pseudo-scientific ideas of racial determinism. It meant nothing to people in earlier centuries.

Fitting New Races into Existing Models

Once Europeans actually began encountering Africans on a regular basis, their skin colour was often the first thing to strike authors. Within the first few decades of exploration of the West African coasts, Africans had become 'black' even to sympathetic Europeans, who showed little distinction between Africans of different ethnic or racial heritage, although later commentators categorized 'moors' (African Muslims of Arab descent) who would not be enslaved and 'black moors' (black Africans) who would.

It was not only whites who developed a pejorative view of Africans. Early on, members of the Native elite in New Spain began to write about the black slaves they encountered and the position they should hold within society. In the early seventeenth century Guamán Poma de Ayala, a member of the Inca elite in Peru, wrote a manuscript letter to the King of Spain demanding that Native voices be heard and situating them in the history of Christendom. Poma obviously had some respect for the 'modest and decent-living' African slaves that he met, but also saw that Christianity could be used to subdue them and make them more obedient. He thought their affectionate natures made them excellent slaves. He believed that slaves ought to be able to elect their own mayor, magistrate and clerk who dealt with serious transgressions; however, he believed that physical punishment – the use of 'good hard iron' – would correct a slave who had gone bad. So, Poma advocated kindly treatment and even some measure of slave autonomy, but fundamentally believed that black Africans ought to be enslaved.

The relationship between Indians and blacks in North America was also very complex. In Florida between the late seventeenth and early nineteenth centuries, the Seminole Indians helped former slaves to stay hidden from their masters and welcomed them into the tribe, creating a mixed-race group. However, in the Tennessee/Georgia border area, the Cherokee, imitating white patterns of land ownership, had plantations and held slaves in much the same manner as whites did.

Once whites had had a chance to examine Native Americans they attempted to fit them into the racial hierarchy that they had brought from the Old World. In the early seventeenth century, it was thought that all men were descended from the same creation in Genesis. Only later would pseudo-scientific ideas emerge excluding certain races from full humanity. But this begged the question of how the Natives got to America. Authors answered this question by trying to find their ancestors from among the tribes of the ancient world. An intimate knowledge of Native language was required in order to make this comparison. Men such as Roger Williams, first of Massachusetts and then Rhode Island, learnt the Narragansett language and became an important cultural ambassador between the English settlers and their Indian neighbours. This is in stark contrast to Columbus, who refused to acknowledge the validity of Native language and believed it to be simply erroneous; he believed that his own language was a sign of his authority. Ironically, Columbus struggled to communicate not only with the Natives but also with many of his own men, who themselves were not a homogeneous group.

Until he died, Christopher Columbus claimed that the people he encountered in the Americas were the inhabitants of islands near India. As it became obvious that the Americas were a distinct set of land masses, learned Europeans strove to fit Native Americans into some continuum of human history. To that end, they scoured ancient texts for guidance and points of cultural similarity. Consistent with the precepts of the Scientific Revolution (an outgrowth of the European Renaissance that helped give rise to the Enlightenment), Europeans attempted to classify the peoples they encountered. Part of their interest was born of the belief that the world, and all human relationships therein, was naturally hierarchical, and that one's origins, family and class were part of a God-ordained natural hierarchy and dictated one's treatment by others.

From their earliest encounters with new peoples, European philosophers and theologians grappled with the implications of so vast a number of new, non-Christian people. In his seminal book, *The Columbian Exchange: Biological and Cultural Consequences of 1492*, Alfred Crosby describes how at least one European thinker, Isaac de Peyrère, imagined a human creation that pre-dated Adam and included 'the ancestors of all non-Jews'. Crosby also notes that while the Roman Catholic papacy had little problem with Genesis's description of human origins, other religious thinkers such as Joseph de Acosta grappled with ways of explaining the Indians' origins that the church found troubling, as they suggested a 'polygenesis', or multiple creations. Others took a different tack, with Spanish historian Gonzalo Fernández de Oviedo y Valdés equating the Indies with the mythical Hesperides, supposedly ruled by an equally mythical, pre-Christian Iberian king who pre-dated Christ.

Some Europeans became convinced that the Indians were indeed related to common European ancestors: in this case, the Greeks, Romans and other Mediterranean people. In 1724 a Jesuit priest named Pierre-Joseph Lafitau produced his *Moeurs des sauvages américquains* (Customs of the American Natives), in which he argued that the Mohawk Indians were the descendants of the ancient peoples, including the Romans and Egyptians. Lafitau worked from the assumption that events and ceremonies described in ancient sources were too similar to those he observed for there *not* to be a connection. Lafitau's approach to his subjects, however, is notable for its detachment, objectivity and dispassion, leading some scholars to credit him with the founding of the discipline of sociology.

The *Leyenda Negra* or 'Black Legend' was the focus of European Protestant writers, who hoped to use tales of Spanish cruelty as ammunition to challenge their religious enemy's New World claims. Yet the variation they devised contained far more than a kernel of truth. Works such as Bernal Díaz del Castillo's *True History of the Conquest of New Spain*, Las Casas's *Devastation of the Indies* and even Columbus's own *Diario* seemed to demonstrate conclusively that the Spanish were inherently bloodthirsty, ruthless and vicious both at home and abroad. Still, after the first phases of bloody conquest and forced conversion, the Spanish- and Portuguese-American cultures showed themselves to be somewhat flexible in terms of race and ethnicity. Cultural and ethnic blending was more common among Iberian Americans than among the English, who in general frowned upon and discouraged official and unofficial unions between English settlers and Native peoples or Africans. Racial mixing, and mixed-race children, were far more common in Iberian Atlantic world societies – spanning the Caribbean, the Atlantic Islands and the Americas – than they were in most English societies. Still, human sexual interactions, ranging from coercive to consensual to based on mutual love and respect, resulted in racial mixing in every Atlantic world society.

Nevertheless, the *Leyenda Negra* became an important propagandistic tool for Protestant Europe. It justified resistance to Spanish continental power in Europe, as well as discrete attacks on the Spanish New World empire (chiefly through privateering). The same Theodor de Bry who copied John White's drawings adapted those that showed the cruellest abuses of the Spanish. Images of Indian men, women and children being burned at the stake, torn to pieces by dogs, and slaughtered with impunity were frequently reproduced for European audiences. Certainly the Spanish stories and accompanying images resonated with the Dutch, who in the early seventeenth century were in the process of challenging Spanish control of their homeland. Such stories emanating from the New World provided powerful justifications against the enemies of the Old and rallied the support of fellow Protestants.

Though it should be noted that this was the result of trial and error, of all the New World Europeans, the French and the Dutch were most flexible in terms of cultural mixing and integration, especially in regard to Native Americans. The French in particular practised an informal policy of *le même sang* ('the same blood'), which proposed that French peasants should intermarry with Native Americans to create a new, mixed people who were part Old World, part New, and all Catholic. This already happened frequently, yet as a matter of policy that was encouraged by both colonial administrators and clergy, it stood to create a new francophone class who saw themselves as French yet also Native, who could help control the flow of resources into the French empire. New ethnicities were created, however, and persisted long after the seventeenth century. In the nineteenth century, the mixed Native/French/Scottish Catholic *Métis*, who had migrated far into the Canadian interior, mounted challenges to the government in a drive to control their own destinies as a sovereign people.

ATLANTIC HISTORY IN FOCUS

John White's illustrations

Many European artists who depicted New World encounters did so without the benefit of ever seeing the lands or people they portrayed. This was not the case with John White, whose talents as an artist were richly enhanced by his ability to live among and observe the Algonquians who lived near the first English North American settlement, Roanoke. His sympathetic yet almost anthropological depictions of New World people had an electrifying effect in Europe, where other artists copied and appropriated his work for (literally) centuries. White's exquisite 'documents' of encounter continue to inspire new lines of enquiry for historians.

His parentage and the circumstances of his birth are unclear, but John White was likely born in Cornwall some time between 1540 and 1550. While in his twenties, he joined Martin Frobisher's expedition to Baffin Island (between Greenland and Hudson's Bay). Later, he was chosen as a leader and chronicler of Humphrey Gilbert's Roanoke colony, of which he eventually became governor. He returned to England to secure supplies. It was during his absence that the colony was 'lost', including White's daughter and granddaughter.

White worked with writer Thomas Harriot to describe for his fellow Europeans what he saw while living among North Carolina's Indians. The result was Harriot's *A Briefe and True Report of the New Found Land of Virginia*, which, by 1590, was already widely read throughout western Europe. Rich in ethnographic detail, White's compelling images were a source of curiosity to Europeans. In a period before copyright laws, they served as a guide for others to copy. Dutch engraver Theodor de Bry made a name for himself that persists to this day as an artist of encounter and conquest, copying and embellishing the work of others who had seen new lands first-hand. Other artists who appropriated White's work changed the meaning altogether. As Karen Kupperman points out, White's depiction of an eastern Algonquian village was even transformed into an Apache community by French artist Guillaume de l'Isle. In an age before copyright and fact checking, White's images were turned to multiple purposes.

Source Materials: How Do We Know What Natives and Africans Thought?

Native Americans, Africans and Europeans have all left their own records of the Atlantic world's periods of contact and encounter. The forms these records take, however, vary dramatically. The variety of types of communication and record creation leads to difficulty in assessing what these peoples thought as they encountered one another. For many historians, the accounts of Europeans, despite problems of bias, the evolution of language and cultural chauvinism, remain the only option. In addition, historians are limited by the state of research in other fields, including anthropology, archaeology and linguistics, that contribute to our knowledge of Indian and African languages and forms of communication. The problem for many remains how to reconstruct that past with, at best, a one-sided record.

The fact that Europeans in most Atlantic world enterprises were determined to make some sort of record of their encounters or conquests is nevertheless a blessing for historians. It is beholden upon the individual historian, however, to discern the background of the document's production and its author's reasons for creating it. The literary forms these records take are numerous. Some wrote tales of triumph, casting explorers and conquerors in the roles of either crusaders, heroes from antiquity, minions of a modern king, or saints. In his book *Marvelous Possessions*, scholar Stephen Greenblatt describes how these explorers (most notably Christopher Columbus) deliberately distorted encounter experiences to dehumanize Indians and justify conquest. The writings of others, such as the Spanish Dominican priest Bartolomé de Las Casas, were more polemic in nature, and therefore meant to demonstrate a point and persuade an audience (in Las Casas's case, that the Americas were rife with abuse of Native peoples). Las Casas was ahead of his time in support of the Native peoples of the Atlantic world. His opinions of Africans and slavery in general are quite another issue. Las Casas himself was inspired by the fiery Dominican preacher Antonio de Montesinos, who challenged Hispaniola planters on their abuses of the local Indians. The Jesuits were writing for yet another set of reasons: to stimulate financial support for their missions and create a record of their achievements to inspire and instruct newcomers to the mission field. The business records of Dutch and Portuguese traders in slaves, as well as those of colonial administrators, were intended to be straightforward analytical and bureaucratic documents, meant to keep their enterprises functional.

Scholars who explore African or Native American societies therefore need to become ethnohistorians. Ethnohistorians are skilled at 'reading between the lines' of European records. They are capable of scraping away layers of Eurocentric bias and period interpretation to attempt to reconstruct plausible scenarios of what the lives of those who were observed were really like. Ethnohistorians also rely on the intellectual tools of social scientists, including anthropology, sociology, psychology and economics, to create plausible models of non-European cultures. But the talent of reading between the lines can rely quite simply on insightful, detailed readings of the sources themselves. For example, the Jesuits of New France perhaps thought that the Huron Indians sought baptism because they were moved by the Christian concept of the Holy Spirit to do so, but ethnohistorians who have explored other details the priests recorded see in the Indians' actions a willingness to 'hedge their bets' by incorporating as many belief systems as possible into their religious systems.

First Contact: Misunderstandings and Confusion

For some early travellers the fear and wonder engendered when they encountered the racial other was as severe as it would have been had they come across a member of a monstrous race. The cultural shock caused by encountering unexpected people and environments meant that it was difficult to assimilate them into existing patterns of understanding. This was as true for Natives and Africans as it was for whites. They too misunderstood the nature and intentions of their unusual white visitors.

Africans were instantly frightened of the European visitors they encountered, believing them to be spirits or creatures from another world, because in their culture whiteness was associated with death. They had not considered that it was possible for humans to have white skin, and so when they met white people, they assumed that they were not people at all. Until they were sure their visitors were human sometimes Africans were unwelcoming, but their overall response to visits from Europeans was hospitable. Interestingly, the fears that Europeans have about those they perceive as 'the other' are mirrored in Africans. Many enslaved Africans on encountering whites on the African coast for the first time assumed that these strangers were capturing them in order to eat them. Thus it was not only white Europeans who linked cannibalism with savagery and otherness. The gunpowder that Europeans bought with them was also a source of fear for Africans. Although Europeans mostly received a favourable welcome, their ignorance of African customs and religious practices led them into difficulties that temporarily soured the trading relationship. In 1482, the Portuguese trampled on a sacred site and later, in 1598, the Dutch cut down branches in a sacred grove for their May Day celebrations. Because the Europeans were dependent on the Africans for trade, they had to apologize and rebuild the relationship.

Native Americans too found it difficult to assimilate the arrival of whites in the New World into their belief systems about people and the world. It was not skin colour that surprised them but rather cultural and technological differences such as clothes, beards, method of transport and religious practices. Because they could not imagine how the whites had arrived in America and across so long a distance, some Indians believed that they had come from the sky. According to Spanish accounts, others believed that they were gods. Aztec society was heavily focused on the past and dominated by tradition. They found it very difficult to accept that something completely new was happening in their world and relied on soothsayers to offer prophesies as to future events rather than organizing a military response to the arrival of the Spaniards. The idea that Hernan Cortés was the reincarnated Aztec god Quetzalcoatl (or at least his emissary) arose among the Indians very quickly after the Spaniards arrived in Mexico. It had been prophesied that Quetzalcoatl would return around 1519 and would have a beard and white skin, and Cortés seemed to fit this description. Of course, he did nothing to dispel these ideas but rather used them to his advantage and even mentioned this deception in a letter to Spanish king Charles V. Cortés also had his horses' corpses buried after dark to perpetuate the impression that the animals were immortal creatures.

Some historians dismiss the importance of this misunderstanding and argue that the more significant mistake made by Moctezuma was to welcome Cortés and his soldiers into the heart of Tenochtitlan (modern-day Mexico City) in order to better get to know them and judge whether they were friend or foe. The Aztecs also had little understanding of an enemy who declared himself a friend initially, and the use of siege warfare was also alien to them because of its deliberate, dishonourable weakening of an opponent and the use of civilians. Peace was very important to Moctezuma and so he allowed himself to be taken captive in order to preserve peace. In contrast, the Mayans were more wary of the Spaniards because they had previously been victims of foreign invaders, the Toltecs. David Stannard argues that the settlers appropriated Native knowledge and technology, used up their stores of food and took advantage of their hospitality to crush their culture. Had Moctezuma immediately acted to remove Cortés, there would have been little response the Spaniard could make. First-contact history is littered with instances where Natives offered assistance or friendship to Europeans, only to find their culture overrun by them, such as the 1536 rescue near the modern city of Montreal of icebound explorer Jacques Cartier by the Hochelaga Natives.

These misunderstandings are all the more surprising as, with hindsight, it is possible to see that, in some areas, Natives and Europeans were culturally similar. For example, there was a reliance on magic and spirituality, on religious explanations for environmental crisis among members of both groups. Some Spanish writers such as Diego Duran and Bernadino de Sahagun learned the Nahuatl language and explained how similar the Aztecs were to the Spanish, not to reinforce their humanity and equality but to show how they were ripe for conversion by missionaries, although Sahagun appeared to have respected Aztec culture and history and wanted to record it for posterity. Not all authors were hostile towards their Native neighbours but they often had an ulterior motive for writing admiringly about them. They were implicitly criticizing their own society rather than genuinely representing 'the other' favourably. Thomas Morton, who did allow Natives into his community, wrote that in Indian society respect was given to those who deserve it: their king was a good leader and parents were good to their children; society's hierarchies were respected. He was implicitly attacking contemporary English society where these values no longer prevailed.

In his book *Guns, Germs and Steel*, Jared Diamond illustrates how these powerful elements changed the course of human history. This was the case with European technology, as illustrated by the 'guns' and 'steel' of the book's title. Early guns were loud, unreliable and inaccurate: the primitive harquebuses that Europeans brought with them frequently misfired. They were, however, good for a terrifying show and, when they actually hit their targets, to injure and kill humans as well. As these weapons improved both in target accuracy and reliability throughout the sixteenth, seventeenth and eighteenth centuries, they became ever more useful, indeed critical, to Africans, Indians and Europeans alike. Europeans tended to control the supply of these weapons and the accessories they needed, contributing to what historians have dubbed the 'gun–slave cycle'. This entailed a close relationship between the number of guns sold to Africans and the number of slaves procured for them. In essence, the availability of guns encouraged an African state to go to war with a rival. War brought captives for slavery and, for the victors, more guns and greater regional power. A version of the cycle also operated in colonial Carolina, where the stakes were to separate, often through death, Indians from their land and thus pave the way for Europeans to move in.

Perhaps more terrifying were the 'dogs of war' – large and powerful canines which Europeans had learned to weaponize. America's indigenous peoples had small, domesticated dogs that they used for hunting, companionship, transportation and food. The dogs that Europeans used in conquest, however, were large, incredibly strong and trained to attack. The ancestors of modern-day bull mastiffs, presa-canarios and greyhounds, these enormous animals had jaws that exerted hundreds of pounds of pressure on the flesh of their prey. For the Spanish conquerors, human opponents were prey, and their dogs, as directed, literally tore their victims apart. In a particularly cruel twist, conquistadors were also reported to use the dogs to 'hunt' Native Americans as they would deer or other large game animals back in Spain, or to improvise gladiator games that pitted captured warriors against particularly vicious dogs.

Horses were likewise brought by the Spanish and likewise served the purposes of warfare. But Native peoples throughout the Americas were very quick to grasp their usefulness. Some mastered their use and added their own innovations, and thus revolutionized their societies. A prime example of this situation is the Comanches of what is now north-western Texas. Historian Pekka Hämäläinen's work describes how the Comanches built on the relationship between grasslands and horses to dominate the region's other, horseless Native people.

Indians and Africans used and appreciated European knowledge, innovation and resources. But that does not mean they rejected and forgot their own. One of the chief weapons that Indians throughout the Americas had to defend themselves was knowledge of their particular landscape's topographical features. Such knowledge at least allowed for the possibility of escaping and hiding, ambushing one's enemies, and hiding stockpiled resources to save them from aggressive settlers. The English in Virginia suspected as much of the Powhatans when the latter refused to trade their stores by pleading shortage. Europeans knew that Indian knowledge was superior to their own and often hoped to use it to their own advantage. When Europeans clashed, they frequently cultivated local Indians of relevance in the service of defeating their enemies. At the same time, however, the European victors were acquiring more of their own knowledge of the local area. For many groups, this willingness to share eventually led to their displacement once hostilities had ended. Though long in coming, this was the ultimate fallout of the Seven Years' War and American Revolution.

Africans brought skills to the New World that were likewise compatible with harnessing the power of the Americas' new landscapes. Some of the most valuable enslaved Africans were those who could act as 'surfmen', that is, navigators of tricky, shallow coastal waters. Known as *grumetes*, these were highly skilled African mariners. Other African mariners were river pilots, possessing the talent to move vessels along the continent's many interior rivers. In the New World, African mariners and seafarers could be seen working at their trade in almost every culture, piloting vessels, crewing merchant ships, traversing the Atlantic, Caribbean and all their affiliated waterways, and practising their maritime crafts.

Perhaps the greatest sources of wonder for early American Indian people were the technological feats, including the written word, which Europeans brought across the Atlantic with them. The European capacity to read, make use of timepieces, and predict natural phenomena such as eclipses was also impressive to Indians, who at times came to view the newcomers as particularly powerful shamans – that is, prophets and healers who worked with Indian leaders on tribal business, warfare and local resource management. The shaman also acted as a bridge with the supernatural, leading religious ceremonies and interpreting signs. It was this latter function that most closely resonated with Europeans, who deployed technology to support the idea that they possessed great power.

Nevertheless, the newcomers were ignorant of numerous other things of which the Indians had well-developed knowledge. Though communication problems were rife, Indians, Africans and Europeans were often able to demonstrate their ideas through signs and gestures. An imperfect form of communication, it had the potential to lead to cultural collision. But the sharing of knowledge was also common. Native Americans taught newcomers how to grow new foodstuffs. Fishing and hunting techniques were also shared, with Europeans using American-style weirs and blinds. Europeans, especially those on frontiers, made use of snowshoes, moccasins and buckskins. Indians, in turn, integrated European textiles, clothing styles and jewellery into their fashion repertoires.

Much of this type of encounter came through trade, the observations of which often led to cultural misinterpretations. Europeans marvelled at the piles of 'greasy' (used, and therefore more valuable), beaver pelts that were sometimes worth small fortunes, received in exchange for items they simply dismissed as trinkets. An Iroquois trader, on the other hand, could not understand why a trader would give him a fine assortment of useful and beautiful objects that his fellow Indians found culturally useful.

The Columbian Exchange

The Europeans who crossed the Atlantic in the wake of Columbus encountered an array of new botanical products, animals and microbes. Alfred Crosby has termed this collective encounter 'the Columbian Exchange'. The by-products of the Columbian Exchange had the power to kill or heal, enrich or deprive, feed or starve. In short, this exchange revolutionized life on both sides of the Atlantic. European explorers encountered numerous new foodstuffs, including potatoes, tomatoes, squashes, beans of various kinds, maize, batata (sweet potato), manioc and chocolate, to name a few. Domesticated animals were few among Indian peoples throughout the Americas. Europeans brought with them cattle, horses, goats, and fowl of various kinds. Native peoples who had access to these animals innovated with raising them, making them their own. In other places, the unchecked animals thrived and permanently changed the landscape. Tensions over these animals could disrupt relationships between Indians and Europeans. Marauding pigs and cows, for example, had the power to inflict severe damage on the crops on which New England's Indians depended. When these animals destroyed Native hillocks and the Indians killed and ate the animals, they were hauled into court to pay damages to the livestock's owner and faced possible additional penalties. Needless to say, the intrinsic unfairness of this situation was not lost on the local Wampanoag Indians, who added the severely lopsided sense of justice to a list of grievances against the English. Such grievances exploded into King Philip's War in 1675.

European animals often thrived in the New World. Cattle ranged freely on the *pampas*, or grasslands, of South America. The size of the herds swelled, creating new markets in tallow and hides, as well as meat. As Alfred Crosby notes, these trades even influenced seemingly unrelated areas such as Iberian architecture. With cheaper tallow came greater reliance on tallow candles, which in turn created changes in domestic structure and home-based activities for both colonists and Europeans. They also made another form of exploitation of the natural world – mining – possible. Without cheap sources of illumination, Alfred Crosby notes, 'mining could never have been carried on as extensively as it was'. Mining carried with it its own social evils: those unlucky enough to be enslaved in its service were treated with tremendous brutality, and the ships that carried the treasure from America to Europe fuelled European rivalries and piracy.

Africa and Africans made tremendous contributions to colonial cuisines. Numerous African crops grew well in the New World. Their means of crossing the Atlantic was yet another dimension of the Middle Passage: slave ships needed large stores of starchy and preservable foodstuffs to feed their captive cargo. ('Middle Passage' is the name given to the transatlantic sea voyage that took African slaves to their new home in North or South America or the Caribbean.) Curious Europeans and Africans who travelled the Atlantic as free people also likely experimented with new crops in an exchange that was already common between Europe and America. Rice, black-eyed peas, okra, sorghum, millet, yams, cassava, lima beans and semolina were all staples of regional African cuisines. Africans who had the means to cultivate these familiar plants did so in the New World, and Europeans and Native Americans used them in their cuisines as well. Crops from the Americas could also grow well in Africa and revolutionized landscapes and cuisines there. Maize, peanuts, sweet potatoes and pumpkins all grew well and were easily integrated into African diets that relied heavily on stews, breads and grain-based dishes.

African cooking techniques were another transforming element. Some African women held in bondage were forced to cook for their masters, and integrated their own ethnic cooking traditions into food preparation. As Frederick Douglass Opie demonstrates, African foodways were culturally predominant in the Caribbean. The traditional stews integrated new ingredients into traditional forms of soup and stew cookery. Fish were local staples and were dried, fried, boiled or eaten fresh. Mixing cooked rice, vegetables and fish produced gumbo and other creolized dishes. Potatoes roasted in ashes, corn breads of various kinds, and meats prepared using various African techniques were staples on the tables of white slaveholders.

As a result of converging food cultures, more people had more varied and balanced diets than they had enjoyed at other times. Meat and fish provided protein; vegetables and fruit were varied and added critical vitamins; milk products provided calcium. For Native Americans who survived the encounter with Europeans and Africans, these dietary inclusions stood to dramatically improve personal health. Varied diets made possible by the Columbian Exchange contrasted sharply with the health problems created by over-reliance on a few select foods. Yet these problems continued to happen. One of the most severe cases of over-reliance on a foodstuff was the Irish potato famine of the 1840s. The New World potato grew well in Ireland. Cheap, easy to grow, filling and nutritious, it was the preferred comestible for Irish farmers, who were forced to sell the foods they grew and raised to their English overlords. When a blight known as *Phytophthora infestans* attacked the crop, it caused widespread famine and death. One million Irish died, and another million emigrated to England, Scotland, North America, Canada or Australia, causing a significant demographic shift of people native to Ireland. News of the famine was, of course, widespread. In an ironic twist with an Atlantic world dimension, a group of Choctaw Indians, who had been forced from their own homes less than two decades before, responded to the tragedy by collecting $710 for relief efforts for the starving Irish.

The most useful, but accidental, weapon the Europeans bought to help them subdue Native peoples in the Americas was disease such as smallpox, measles, dysentery, typhus, cholera and the bubonic plague. Because the Natives had no immunity against these pathogens, huge numbers were killed. In some places 90 per cent of Natives died within a decade of first contact. Although the Europeans carried these diseases – and, weakened by their Atlantic crossing, some died – many had built up some natural immunity and so survived their bouts. Scholars estimate that as many as 100 million people inhabited the Americas in 1491, but imported diseases, and strains of old ones that morphed in a new environment, killed as many as 95 per cent of the pre-contact population in some places.

As Alfred Crosby says, the effects of disease on the Native community were awesome and bewildering. This meant that the Natives thought they were being saved by the white man's gods or that their medicine men were particularly powerful. The whites did not challenge this misunderstanding and in fact themselves thought that the diseases were a sign from God that he approved of their actions. Thus, a misunderstanding on both sides about the nature of disease meant that Europeans were able to get the upper hand and appear superior to the Natives. Hans Staden was treated as an oracle by the Tupi people of Brazil in the 1540s, and later, in the 1580s, the Englishmen who prayed for the recovery of Wingina, the Algonquian chief at Roanoke, were thought to be medicine men when he recovered afterwards. According to Harriot, the death of many other Indians was attributed by Wingina to the gods being displeased with them. Disease was most rife among the populations of California, Florida, and Central and South America who had been herded into missionary towns and forced to live in close proximity with Europeans.

Interestingly, the relationship between Europeans and Africans was also coloured by disease. Africans were the most disease-resistant of the three groups and this encouraged whites to believe that this made them most suitable for slave work in the New World. Also, D. W. Meinig has argued that white susceptibility to African diseases like yellow fever prevented them from establishing more substantial enclaves on the African coast.

The diseases themselves were particularly cruel, often disfiguring their victims and taking their lives amid much pain and suffering. Smallpox was one of the most virulent, and could wipe out large populations quickly. Diseases that did not kill everyone often at least killed the most vulnerable – the old and the young – thus robbing Native communities of the keepers of cultural traditions and the sources of hope. This was also happening at a time when Indian culture was under siege by Europeans, who sought either to transform or destroy it.

Whole communities could be destroyed by disease. This was likely the case with the Indian village of Patuxet, the home of Tisquantum ('Squanto'), who was kidnapped by English fishermen and taken across the Atlantic for a period of three years. Upon his return to New England in 1619, Tisquantum discovered that all his fellow Patuxets, as well as a majority of other coastal Indians, had died of a raging epidemic. In some places in New England, the bones of the dead lay above ground where the dead and dying had fallen.

In the initial phases of contact, and even long after, few Europeans wrote of their concern about the high mortality rate the 'Old World' disease wrought on their Indian neighbours. Some interpreted the mass deaths as part of God's plan for the New World. One of these was Massachusetts minister Cotton Mather, who mused that the disease that killed the Patuxets was part of a divine plot to rid New England 'of those pernicious creatures, and make room for better growth'. The 'better growth' was, of course, the Puritans.

The fact that Indians succumbed so quickly to European diseases for the most part destroyed any hope that they could be forced to labour for the conquerors. The combination of Old World diseases and New World epidemics had tragic consequences for Africans too, who then became the coerced labourers of choice. For centuries, Indians were considered to have given one deadly scourge – syphilis – to Europeans, for whom this would have been a virgin soil epidemic. Certainly, outbreaks of syphilis in European port cities after Columbus's voyage seemed to confirm the hunch. Recent scholarly work, however, suggests that further research is needed into the disease's origins in order to conclude beyond doubt that all forms of the disease were American in origin.

Europeans brought more than microbes back to Europe. The New World was full of wondrous products to exploit, and some Europeans did so with gusto. The French Jesuits were quick to recognize the properties of certain New World botanical products. A trade in ginseng from Canada developed quickly. In Brazil, guaiacum, also known as 'Jesuit's Bark', was reputed to help ease the effects of syphilis. Pernambuco wood, as well as products from other exotic trees, possessed resonant qualities that led to the success of the violin as an instrument of choice for European chamber musicians. The wood also supplied a highly valued red dye that had previously only been available from Asia. The climate of the Americas allowed for other valuable exotic crops to be cultivated for growing markets. The long list of these items eventually expanded to include – aside from the obvious, sugar – cotton, indigo, lemons and oranges, coffee and rice.

Natives' Responses

Some conventional views of encounter have depicted powerful Europeans menacing cowering, powerless Indians. Yet the primary documents of encounter suggest a different reality. Yes, Europeans more often than not were convinced of their own cultural and military superiority. But Indians, too, could harbour long-standing hostilities against their neighbours. To that end, the groups that survived the initial wave of contact with Europeans sought to incorporate the latter's resources and allegiance into their own struggles.

Africans did this as well. From the first period of contact with the Portuguese, powerful local African families sought to garner the newcomers' support to enhance their own power. Their children intermarried with the Portuguese, which cemented alliances among merchant families and helped some gain primacy over local rivals. The Spanish followed similar patterns when they married the daughters of local Indian *caciques*. Though some of these marriages were bigamous, with the wives of the Spaniards back at home or elsewhere, they succeeded in creating bonds between the conquerors and were a means for powerful Incan families to retain some of their prestige. Additionally, there was the issue of long-standing Indian hostilities that strategic unions addressed. When Hernan Cortés united with the México slave Malintzen (or La Malinche, as she's also known), he united with a Native woman who had her own scores to settle. Her own people held in involuntary tribute by the Aztecs, she allied with the invaders whom she saw as her best hope for freedom from her people's overlords. Similarly, the Huron Indians west of the Saint Lawrence Valley were eager to build strategic alliances against their long-standing enemies, the people of the Iroquois League. This strategy had been encountered by the French before: when Samuel de Champlain encountered the Hurons and Montagnais, he and his troops were enlisted to fight against the Iroquois near what is now Crown Point, New York. Wahunsonacock, also known as Powhatan, was the leader of many tributary tribes in tidewater Virginia. As head of the Powhatan Confederacy, he hoped to use the English at Jamestown as vassals within his own empire of Native peoples. His daughter Pocahontas, who was long credited with saving the life of Jamestown administrator John Smith, was actually likely playing a role in an arrangement aimed at bringing the Englishman into his power structure.

Natives did not passively accept the arrival of the white Europeans. There are many examples of violent resistance but this response failed either because of the numbers of European settlers or their technological superiority. It is important to give Native peoples the agency they deserve and not to simply depict them as passive reactors to the white onslaught. However, accessing their thoughts and actions is difficult because the sources we have are almost all left to us by white Europeans. The decision over how to respond to the arrival of the Europeans often divided Native communities, as it did in the nineteenth century in the western United States. In Virginia, on the death of his kinsman, Wahunsonacock, Opecancanough of the Pamunkey tribe decided to mount resistance against the English settlers. Opecancanough's war against the English lasted two decades, beginning with the Virginia Massacre of

1622. One-third of the white settlers were killed as bands of Indians attacked settlers in their homes over breakfast. An Indian loyal to the whites tipped them off, meaning that Jamestown itself was spared, but many outlying settlements were destroyed completely. Although this attack created great shock among the English in Virginia and in England, it did not deter the settlers and in fact probably strengthened their resolve to defeat and subdue the Natives and the landscape. No longer was there any attempt to convert or educate the Natives; they were now seen as an obstacle and an annoyance, cruel savages who, if necessary, could be killed en masse. Indians were routinely hunted with dogs and plans for mass poisonings were hatched. Opecancanough did not forget his vendetta against the English and, eluding their attempts to capture him, attacked again in 1644. But by this time the numbers of English settlers were so great that he was unable to significantly threaten the settlement and instead, despite being an old man, suffered a humiliating death, being shot in the back by his enemies.

The greatest act of Indian resistance in North America in this period was that of King Philip (or Metacom) in the New England region. Philip's father was Massasoit, the leader whose treaty and friendship with the English at Plymouth is still commemorated in the Thanksgiving celebrations today. Again, as in Virginia, it took the death in 1661 of one leader who had advocated peace for his warmongering son to take control and turn on the English. He united a number of tribes in the Massachusetts and Connecticut area, although some Natives did remain loyal to the English in order to protect themselves from attack. Also some Natives had learned to write English, and others had converted to Christianity and grew crops by the European method. They lived in what were called 'praying towns'. The majority of other Natives disliked the literate, Christian Indians, and they existed on the edges of society.

The most significant of Philip's allies were the Narragansetts who had been friends with the English but were pushed into hostility after the Great Swamp massacre of 600 of their number at the start of the war. Cotton Mather said that the Natives had been 'terribly barbecued'. When war came it was very sudden and took the English by surprise. Many English women and children were kidnapped and taken north to Canada where they were ransomed to the French. In 1675 Philip's combined Native forces initially did well, but by 1676 the English began to gain the upper hand, especially after a harsh winter left the Native armies weak and short of food. As Philip's forces split into smaller and smaller groups, the English sent out raiding parties to massacre the Natives. Scalp bounties were offered by the colonies of Massachusetts and Connecticut. In August 1676 Philip's wife and child were captured and shortly afterwards he was taken. He was murdered and his head displayed at Plymouth, the site of his father's friendly encounter with the English, so his defeat gave the English a great symbolic victory.

A French Protestant visitor to Brazil recorded seeing the Tupi people engaged in war with another Native tribe. Their bellicose nature fascinated him, but another observer, Hans Staden, recorded that the Tupi only indulged in warfare to satisfy their desire to cannibalize their enemies. The Tupi tried to drive the invading Europeans out, but were divided among themselves, which the French and Portuguese used to their advantage. But during the 1540s the Tupi were temporarily able to hold the whites out of the Bahia region. Some other Brazilian Natives such as the Potiguar allied themselves with the French and later the Dutch in the hope of preventing the expansion of the Portuguese. One Potiguar leader, Anthonio Paraupaba, spent time in Europe learning Dutch, which he then used to his tribe's advantage when he returned to Brazil. This tactic worked for much of the sixteenth century. Other Native tribes used the European skills in warfare against their Native enemies. Because Europeans tended to see the Natives' life as unchanging and static, many commentators did not understand the complex rivalries between Native groups, often caused by struggles over land. For example, in Connecticut, one part of the Mahican tribe had split off before the English came to the region. This tribe was much feared by their neighbours and was named the Pequot ('the destroyer'). This explains why so many Natives from other tribal groups were willing to ally themselves with the English against the Pequot in the mid-1630s (for more on the Pequot War, see Chapter 3). In the case of the Potiguar and the Pequot, Europeans defined particular Native groups as 'our Indians' and distinguished them from the Natives of other regions who were often described as monstrous or cannibalistic. This was a natural reaction based on the allegiances of the Europeans, but also was a response triggered by information received from the friendly Native tribes who realized that they might ally themselves to the Europeans by creating the image of a common enemy somewhere out there in the wilderness.

Some Native groups initially trusted whites but, after years of annoyances, finally turned to violence. In the sixteenth century the Maya in the Yucatan peninsula and the Taki Onquy revolt in Peru are examples of this sort of relationship breakdown. Other tribes, such as the Tainos on the island of Hispaniola, initially worked for the Spanish *encomenderos* in their mines, but as disease and overwork ruined the Native society, in desperation the Tainos began committing suicide and aborting their offspring in large numbers: a last act of resistance by a desperate people. The population was almost eradicated even before Columbus's death in 1506.

Conclusion

Europeans, Africans and Native Americans had religious and cultural preconceptions that determined their responses to encounters with other races. These views were often subtly changed but not fundamentally challenged at first contact. Cultural misunderstanding, economic exchange and gradual development of hostilities characterized this period.

CHAPTER CHRONOLOGY

1492   Columbus arrives in the Americas.

1519   Cortés kidnaps Moctezuma II from Tenochtitlan (Mexico City) and loots his gold.

1542   Bartolomé de Las Casas writes The *Destruction of the Indies*.

1585   Roanoke colony probably destroyed by Algonquian Natives, although its precise fate is unknown.

1614   Marriage of Pocahontas and John Rolfe in Virginia.

1622   Virginia Massacre when over 300 English settlers are killed in surprise and coordinated attacks led by Opecancanough.

1676   King Philip's war results in the destruction of the Wampanoag tribe who welcomed the English at the 'first thanksgiving' in 1620.

1700   Comanche begin to use horses, which will completely revolutionize their society.

■ PRIMARY SOURCES AND STUDY IMAGE

John Smith describes Jamestown (1609)

It might well be thought, a country so faire (as Virginia is) and a people so tractable, would long ere this have been quietly possessed, to the satisfaction of the adventurers, and the eternizing of the memory of those that effected it. But because all the world do see a failure; this following treatise shall give satisfaction to all indifferent readers, how the business has been carried: where no doubt they will easily understand and answer to their question, how it came to passe there was no better speed and success in those proceedings …

On the 19 of December, 1606, we set sail from Blackwall, but by unprosperous winds, were kept six weeks in the sight of England; all which time, Master Hunt our preacher, was so weak and sick, that few expected his recovery. Yet although he were but twenty miles from his habitation (the time we were in the Downes) and notwithstanding the stormy weather, nor the scandalous imputations (of some few, little better than atheists, of the greatest rank among us) suggested against him, all this could never force from him so much as a seeming desire to leave the business, but preferred the service of God, in so good a voyage, before any affection to contest with his godless foes whose disastrous designs (could they have prevailed) had even then overthrown the business, so many discontents did then arise, had he not with the water of patience, and his godly exhortations (but chiefly by his true devoted examples) quenched those flames of envy, and dissension …

The first land they made they called Cape Henry; where thirty of them recreating themselves on shore, were assaulted by five savages, who hurt two of the English very dangerously …

Newport, Smith, and twenty others, were sent to discover the head of the river: by divers small habitations they passed, in six days they arrived at a town called Powhatan, consisting of some twelve houses, pleasantly seated on a hill; before it three fertile isles, about it many of their cornfields, the place is very pleasant, and strong by nature, of this place the Prince is called Powhatan, and his people Powhatans. To this place the river is navigable: but higher within a mile, by reason of the rocks and isles, there is not passage for a small boat, this they call the falls. The people in all parts kindly entreated them, till being returned within twenty miles of Jamestown, they gave just cause of jealousy: but had God not blessed the discoverers otherwise than those at the fort, there had then been an end of that plantation; for at the fort, where they arrived the next day, they found 17 men hurt, and a boy slain by the savages, and had it not chanced a cross bar shot from the ships struck down a bough from a tree among them, that caused them to retire, our men had all been slain, being securely all at work, and their arms in dry fats.

Hereupon the president was contented the fort should be pallisaded, the ordnance mounted, his men armed and exercised: for many were the assaults, and ambuscades of the savages, and our men by their disorderly straggling were often hurt, when the savages by the nimbleness of their heels well escaped.

What toil we had, with so small a power to guard our workmen by day, watch all night, resist our enemies, and effect our business, to relade the ships, cut down trees, and prepare the ground to plant our corn, etc., I refer to the reader's consideration.

The Mayflower Compact (1620) Agreement Between the Settlers at New Plymouth

IN THE NAME OF GOD, AMEN. We, whose names are underwritten, the Loyal Subjects of our dread Sovereign Lord King *James*, by the Grace of God, of *Great Britain*, *France*, and *Ireland*, King, *Defender of the Faith*, &c. Having undertaken for the Glory of God, and Advancement of the Christian Faith, and the Honour of our King and Country, a Voyage to plant the first Colony in the northern Parts of *Virginia*; Do by these Presents, solemnly and mutually, in the Presence of God and one another, covenant and combine ourselves together into a civil Body Politick, for our better Ordering and Preservation, and Furtherance of the Ends aforesaid: And by Virtue hereof do enact, constitute, and frame, such just and equal Laws, Ordinances, Acts, Constitutions, and Officers, from time to time, as shall be thought most meet and convenient for the general Good of the Colony; unto which we promise all due Submission and Obedience. IN WITNESS whereof we have hereunto subscribed our names at *Cape-Cod* the eleventh of November, in the Reign of our Sovereign Lord King *James*, of *England*, *France*, and *Ireland*, the eighteenth, and of *Scotland* the fifty-fourth, *Anno Domini*; 1620.

Bernal Diaz's account of Cortés and Moctezuma (1632)

When Montezuma knew of our coming he advanced to the middle of the hall to receive us, accompanied by many of his nephews, for no other chiefs were permitted to enter or hold communication with Montezuma where he then was, unless it were on important business. Cortés and he paid the greatest reverence to each other and then they took one another by the hand and Montezuma made him sit down on his couch on his right hand, and he also bade all of us to be seated on seats which he ordered to be brought.

Then Cortés began to make an explanation through our interpreters Doña Marina and Aguilar, and said that he and all of us were rested, and that in coming to see and converse with such a great Prince as he was, we had completed the journey and fulfilled the command which our great King and prince had laid on us. But what he chiefly came to say on behalf of our Lord God had already been brought to his [Montezuma's] knowledge through his ambassadors, Tendile, Pitalpitoque and Quintalbor, at the time when he did us the favour to send the golden sun and moon to the sand dunes; for we told them then that we were Christians and worshipped one true and only God, named Jesus Christ, who suffered death and passion to save us, and we told them that a cross (when they asked us why we worshipped it) was a sign of the other Cross on which our Lord God was crucified for our salvation, and that the death and passion which He suffered was for the salvation of the whole human race, which was lost, and that this our God rose on the third day and is now in heaven, and it is He who made the heavens and the earth, the sea and the sands, and created all the things there are in the world, and He sends the rain and the dew, and nothing happens in the world without His holy will. That we believe in Him and worship Him, but that those whom they look upon as gods are not so, but are devils, which are evil things, and if their looks are bad their deeds are worse, and they could see that they were evil and of little worth, for where we had set up crosses such as those his ambassadors had seen, they dared not appear before them, through fear of them, and that as time went on they would notice this.

The favour he now begged of him was his attention to the words that he now wished to tell him; then he explained to him very clearly about the creation of the world, and how we are all brothers, sons of one father and one mother who were called Adam and Eve, and how such a brother as our great Emperor, grieving for the perdition of so many souls, such as those which their idols were leading to Hell, where they burn in living flames, had sent us, so that after what he [Montezuma] had now heard he would put a stop to it and they would no longer adore these Idols or sacrifice Indian men and women to them, for we were all brethren, nor should they commit sodomy or thefts. He also told them that, in course of time, our Lord and King would send some men who among us lead very holy lives, much better than we do, who will explain to them all about it, for at present we merely came to give them due warning, and so he prayed him to do what he was asked and carry it into effect.

As Montezuma appeared to wish to reply, Cortés broke off his argument, and to all of us who were with him he said: 'with this we have done our duty considering it is the first attempt'.

Montezuma replied – 'Senor Malinche, I have understood your words and arguments very well before now, from what you said to my servants at the sand dunes, this about three Gods and the Cross, and all those things that you have preached in the towns through which you have come. We have not made any answer to it because here throughout all time we have worshipped our own gods, and thought they were good, as no doubt yours are, so do not trouble to speak to us any more about them at present. Regarding the creation of the world, we have held the same belief for ages past, and for this reason we take it for certain that you are those whom our ancestors predicted would come from the direction of the sunrise. As for your great King, I feel that I am indebted to him, and I will give him of what I possess, for as I have already said, two years ago I heard of the Captains who came in ships from the direction in which you came, and they said that they were the servants of this your great King, and I wish to know if you are all one and the same.'

Miantonomo's (Narragansett) plea for unity among the Natives (1630s–40s)

Brothers, we must be as one as the English are, or we shall all be destroyed. You know our fathers had plenty of deer and skins and our plains were full of game and turkeys, and our coves and rivers were full of fish.

But, brothers, since these Englishmen have seized our country, they have cut down the grass with scythes, and the trees with axes. Their cows and horses eat up the grass, and their hogs spoil our bed of clams; and finally we shall all starve to death; therefore, stand not in your own light, I ask you, but resolve to act like men. All the sachems both to the east and the west have joined with us, and we are resolved to fall upon them at a day appointed, and therefore I come secretly to you, cause you can persuade your Indians to do what you will.

Study image 2   *Manhattan Purchase, 1626. Painting by William T. Ranney, 1855.*

Recommended Reading

Alfred Crosby, *The Colombian Exchange: Biological and Cultural Consequences of 1492* (Westport, 1972). Seminal work describing the exchange of foods, drinks, medicines, ideas and diseases that took place after the arrival of whites in the New World.

Jared Diamond, *Guns, Germs and Steel* (New York, 1997). An ambitious global history investigating the question of seeming European superiority since the fifteenth century, combining biology, science and history.

Stephen Greenblatt, *Marvelous Possessions* (Chicago, 1992). Uses a postmodern literary approach to explore the way that Europeans represented the Native Americans during the first contact period and tried to assimilate them into their world view.

Pekka Hämäläinen, *The Comanche Empire* (New Haven, 2008). Shows that successful empire building was not restricted to the Europeans by examining the Comanche empire in south-western North America that survived until 1875.

Karen Kupperman, *Indians and English: Facing off in Early America* (Ithaca, NY, 2000). Explores how the Indians and English reacted to one another by looking at the seventeenth-century intellectual context and integrating colonial American history with early modern English history.

D. W. Meinig, *The Shaping of America*, vol. 1 (New Haven, 1986). Offers a geographical perspective on the history of North America, showing the importance of 'place' in influencing human history.

Frederick Douglass Opie, *Hog and Hominy: Soul Food from Africa to America* (New York, 2010). Shows how African cultural influences on food in the Americas have endured and evolved between the fifteenth and twentieth centuries.

William Phillips and Carla Rahn Phillips, *The Worlds of Christopher Columbus* (Cambridge, 1993). Places the story of one man's life in its historical and intellectual context, thus moving away from the idea of a single hero 'discovering' the New World.

David Beers Quinn, *Set Fair for Roanoke* (Chapel Hill, 1985). Gives a standard account of the background of the Roanoke expeditions of 1584 onwards with some thought-provoking speculations about the fate of the settlers.

David Stannard, *American Holocaust* (Oxford, 1992). Controversially depicts the European treatment of Native Americans in North and South America and in the Caribbean as genocide.

TEST YOUR KNOWLEDGE

1 What were the origins of racial thought that existed before Europeans encountered 'the other' in African and the Americas?

2 How did Europeans fit Native Americans into their world view?

3 To what extent did 'the shock of the new' cause cultural misunderstanding when two races met each other?

4 How were skills and technology shared in the New World?

5 What role did disease play in the period of early contact between whites and Natives?

6 How did the Native Americans respond to the arrival of Europeans?

3 Bondage and Freedom

Identifications of racial difference were based on two independent facets: physical, observable differences such as an African's black skin, and cultural differences such as alien clothing, religious practices or language. As we saw in Chapter 2, in Renaissance Europe black skin was associated with negativity and pollution; but as well as inferiority, bodily difference was also used to reinforce suitability for work. Africans were perceived to have sturdy bodies, and, unlike Native Americans, to be disposed to hard work in fierce climates, but to be incapable of intelligence and creativity (witness Thomas Jefferson's comments on the lack of African American poets and playwrights in the 1780s). Native Americans were initially thought by the Spanish and the English to be suitable labourers; however, by the early sixteenth century, the African had become the labourer of choice for the Spanish. This was partly due to the impassioned plea by Bartolomé de Las Casas that Natives should not be enslaved but rather converted to Christianity, whereas Africans were natural slaves whose only destiny was as labourers for the white population. We will look at this belief in more detail later in this chapter. The biological susceptibility of Native Americans to the diseases brought over by Europeans rendered them less useful as slave labourers. Estimates vary, but in some areas over 90 per cent of the Native population succumbed to European diseases such as smallpox and measles within a few decades. The pattern was repeated as white settlements spread westward and southward.

Slavery in Africa

The clichéd view of slavery is that white Europeans came to peaceful African nations and seized slaves, victimizing the black Africans for racial reasons and later because labour was needed for the developing sugar plantations around the Atlantic world. There is some truth to that, but we must also acknowledge that Islamic traders and Africans themselves played a pivotal part in creating the system of slave seizing and trading that stretched down much of the West African coast, but centred on the Gold Coast area to the north and Angola to the south. Once it became obvious that trading people rather than land was the way to make money, ruthless, money-hungry local leaders became eagerly involved in the slave trade, exploiting the fragmented nature of West African society. The rulers of Dahomey (modern-day Benin, known to historians of slavery as Lower Guinea, and to contemporaries as 'the Slave Coast') were able to found their powerful state on profits gleaned from the Atlantic slave trade in the eighteenth century. From 1721 local tribes traded slaves with the Portuguese at the fort of Ouidah (now a museum documenting the slave trade) and the Dahomey seized control of the trade by subduing their neighbours in war. War also provided the opportunity for acquiring the slaves to sell to the Europeans; most of those shipped across the Atlantic from Ouidah were prisoners of war. This helps us to understand how Africans were able to sell fellow Africans into slavery: to them the concept of 'an African' would have been meaningless. Those who were being sold into slavery were from another – therefore alien – tribe, making it easier to disassociate oneself from their fate. This view is reinforced by Olaudah Equiano's description in his 1789 book of his kidnap into slavery and his six-month journey from the interior of the continent to the coast. He describes the cultural and linguistic differences of the tribes whose lands he passed through on the journey, saying of one, 'I was amazed to see no sacrifices or offerings among them.' The shocks and surprises he faced on this leg of his journey were nothing compared to the horrors of the Middle Passage: the sea voyage across the Atlantic that held so many terrors for the enslaved people.

In West Africa some prisoners of war were ritually slaughtered, so probably viewed becoming a slave as a preferable option. Wars that would have taken place with or without the presence of the Europeans resulted in the seizure of slaves: the Europeans were simply profiting from a pre-existing practice. Europeans also took an active part in the wars themselves, rarely pushing into the interior but providing weapons and offering advice to their African allies, and also using alliances with African tribes to gain an upper hand against their European rivals. An example of this is in Portuguese Angola when European involvement in Angolan wars of the 1580s created a surge in the numbers of slaves arriving in Luanda to be shipped across the Atlantic.

Another prominent slave 'factory' or trading post in Lower Guinea was Elmina ('the mine'), at various times owned by the Portuguese, the Dutch and the British. It was the first slave factory on the African coast, being built by the Portuguese in 1482 to tap into the local gold mining. At its peak in the eighteenth century it had a population of 12,000, larger than the most important North American slave port of Charleston. One of Elmina's major slave suppliers was the powerful Asante empire whose leaders conquered much of the surrounding territory with arms bought from Europeans. They gained such power that they resisted incursions from the British in the early nineteenth century. The slave trade was so beneficial to some African leaders that they were disturbed by the change of heart of the British in 1807 when they ended the transatlantic trade. The King of Bonny (now Nigeria) said: 'We think this trade must go on. That is the verdict of our oracle and the priests. They say that your country, however great, can never stop a trade ordained by God himself.'

As historian John Thornton explains, Africans were not coerced into participating in the slave trade; it was rather that Europeans were tapping in to existing trading relations and practices for disposing of prisoners of war. But Walter Rodney challenges this view. His work centres on the Upper Guinea coast, north of Dahomey and Asante, less significant in the trade in terms of statistical numbers, but still an important region for slave trading. It was one of the earliest regions to be exploited by the

Portuguese. Slaves were taken from here to work in the sugar plantations of Madeira and the Canary Islands, but in the early sixteenth century the slave trade changed direction to meet the needs of the Spanish Caribbean market. Early European slavers kidnapped their cargo, but later Europeans realized it was far more profitable to buy slaves than risk penetrating inland to kidnap them. As in other areas of Africa, most were sold on by other Africans; some Africans even volunteered themselves in times of crop failure or food shortages. Rodney argues that wars and local disputes were triggered by the need for slaves, rather than slaves being an unintended by-product. Slave raiding became a profession amongst Africans as the prices paid by Europeans rose, and the trade was sanctioned, protected and driven by the African ruling classes, liaising with Europeans.

As shown in Chapter 1, the Portuguese were the first Europeans to explore the African coast and it was a natural progression for them to become the first slave traders there. Their dominance lasted over a century, with only the occasional voyage to the region by other powers during the sixteenth century. The Dutch took an interest in the region in the 1590s and by the 1640s had successfully taken over the Portuguese factories on the coast, including the original one at Elmina. Simultaneously the English were trying to establish a trading presence to rival the Dutch, but had little interest in slaves at first. But once the English realized how profitable sugar produc-tion was in Barbados, the English slave trade developed, cemented in 1660 with the founding of the Royal African Company. This governmental attempt to secure trading rights represents one of the earliest actions of the British empire, both in economic terms and in its establishment of forts on the coast that became centres of British rule once the slave trade had ended. But until the eighteenth century, this control was only an 'informal empire'. The Royal African Company's monopoly lasted until the end of the seventeenth century, when the slave trade was opened to commercial traders and developed into the economic system that will be explored in Chapter 4. The British slaving empire was established from Cape Coast Castle, only a few miles along the coast from Elmina. A motley gang of British soldiers staffed the factories. Often these men were convicted criminals or deserters, who were offered a posting in Africa to avoid execution, a common story around the Atlantic world. But the largest proportion of the population of the castle forts were the castle slaves: male labourers who were responsible for a variety of tasks such as bricklaying (unpaid and working longer hours than their white counterparts but supplied with decent rations of tobacco and rum); and the female concubines who provided sexual services to the British soldiers. Some African women were forced into sexual slavery, but others voluntarily took the soldiers as their husbands following local customs of polygamy, producing children conversant in both cultures but fully accepted by neither. The European Victorian commentators did not distinguish between either practice, both of which they considered to be sexual transgression, so it is difficult to measure the numbers of women who entered into these liaisons voluntarily.

White Europeans were not the only slave traders and slave owners in the Atlantic world; there were others who had their own reasons for taking slaves. Islamic North Africa had been slave trading for centuries before the arrival of the Portuguese. The relationship between Islam and slavery is long and complex and the understanding of scholars in 'the West' is coloured by twenty-first-century relationships with Islam. As in the Bible, there are many passages in the Qur'an which permit the taking of slaves but also recommend their good treatment and manumission for good behaviour. In Islam slavery is not a permanent state determined by race, but rather a temporary situation in which someone of any race or religion (apart from other Muslims) may find themselves. Islamic law regulates the lives of slaves, concubines and their offspring in great detail, as did the law in the New World from the seventeenth to the nineteenth centuries. In practice, this meant that black Africans were transported from West Africa across the Sahara to the Nile and into the Middle East. Europeans from the Mediterranean and even as far north as Cornwall in the west of England were seized and taken into slavery by Islamic pirates from the North African coast. In the late seventeenth century relatives of victims seized by the so-called Barbary pirates appealed to the government to rescue them, citing the dreadful atrocities that they were undergoing. However, the slavery experienced by both black and white captives of the Islamic North African pirates was very different to the systematic plantation slavery suffered by Africans in the New World. The pirates' victims were often much freer during their term of captivity: some were able to continue their business dealings, for example, and their term of slavery almost always had a time limit.

After the United States became a nation, its citizens were also seized by the Barbary pirates, and this became such a problem that John Adams, through the Continental Congress, asked John Lamb to negotiate a treaty, such as that held by European nations, to ensure that American vessels went unmolested. It said:

> we leave it to your discretion to represent to the Dey Government of Algiers or their Ministers if it may be done with Safety, the particular circumstances of the United States, just emerging from a long & distressing war, with one of the most powerful nations of Europe; which we hope may be an apology if our presents should not be so splendid as those of older & abler Nations ....

Historians debate over whether these white captives can truly be classed as 'slaves', for while many were forced to work, including one American sailor whose job it was to look after the Dey of Algiers' lion, others were simply kept as prisoners awaiting ransom. James Walvin has challenged the idea that Islamic 'slavery' was really slavery at all: its scale was a trickle compared to the torrent of transatlantic slavery, and black African slaves taken by Muslim traders were employed in a variety of roles throughout society rather than predominantly as cheap, unskilled and disposable labour. Muslim traders occasionally looked to the West and sold slaves to Europeans – and sometimes found themselves taken as slaves to the New World – but for the most part their trade was focused on the North and East, the Mediterranean rather than the Atlantic.

When writing about New World slavery, Ira Berlin called the first generation of African slaves to go to the Americas 'the charter generation', and said that they inhabited a truly Atlantic world. Their story is often ignored in historians' race to identify an African American culture. Berlin said that 'Black life' was not born in Africa or America but rather somewhere in between: that you cannot distinguish the story of this race from the story of slavery. The castle slaves in European factories are as much 'Atlantic creoles' as the slaves taken from Africa to work on plantations. In fact Berlin's creoles had more room to manoeuvre, creating more of a life for themselves, unlike the slaves born into plantation life who had little flexibility. The early creoles could buy their freedom, were more likely to rebel and also to own slaves themselves – as did Anthony Johnson of the Eastern Shore in Virginia between the 1640s and 1660s, whose grandchildren named his slaveholding plantation 'Angola' in memory of his birthplace. Islamic slavery of black Africans and of white captives (with the exception of a handful of American captives) does not really fit this mould: so not all slavery has a direct Atlantic context.

However, this chapter will go on to show that the story of that entire Atlantic world cannot be separated from the story of slavery. All the Atlantic is tainted by slavery, even if all slavery does not easily fit into the concept of 'the Atlantic'.

New World Slavery: the Native Americans

When we think of New World slavery we automatically think of African slavery, but black Africans were not the only victims of European labour-hunger during the sixteenth and seventeenth centuries. When Columbus arrived in Hispaniola in 1492, his wonder and confusion at encountering a Native population soon subsided as he anticipated to what uses they could be put. Being familiar with plantation slavery on a small scale from living in Madeira, Columbus saw opportunities granted by the Native population in the Caribbean to make a lot of money for himself and his sponsors Ferdinand and Isabella, the Spanish monarchs. He wrote in his journal, rewritten by Las Casas and not published until the nineteenth century:

> your Highnesses may believe that this island (Hispaniola), and all the others, are as much yours as Castile. Here there is only wanting a settlement and the order to the people to do what is required. For I, with the force I have under me, which is not large, could march over all these islands without opposition. I have seen only three sailors land, without wishing to do harm, and a multitude of Indians fled before them. They have no arms, and are without warlike instincts; they all go naked, and are so timid that a thousand would not stand before three of our men. So that they are good to be ordered about, to work and sow, and do all that may be necessary, and to build towns, and they should be taught to go about clothed and to adopt our customs.

Bartolomé de Las Casas, the editor of Columbus's words, was an important figure in the Spanish debates over whether the Natives could or should be enslaved. Unlike Columbus, who had a merchant's blood, the religious man Las Casas felt they should not be enslaved and spent much of his writing career exposing the Spaniards' mistreatment of the Indians and recommending that Africans be used as labour instead. The relationship between Spanish settlers and their Native neighbours were defined by the *encomienda* system: land was to be held by the Spanish crown and Natives were to work for local Spanish settlers in return for protection and Christian instruction. Las Casas felt that this system was open to abuse and he described it in a famous passage: 'It was upon these gentle lambs … that from the very first day they clapped eyes on them the Spanish fell on them like ravening wolves upon the fold.'

Las Casas's writing became famous in England because England and Spain were at war and it contributed to the development of the 'Black Legend' that told horrific tales of Spanish cruelty and encouraged the English to settle in the area to rectify some of these wrongs. Some of Las Casas's descriptions are incredibly graphic and are similar to European accounts of Native butchery and cannibalism: 'The way they [the Spanish] normally dealt with the native leaders and nobles was to tie them up to a kind of griddle … and then grill them over a slow fire.' His descriptions reflect his horror at the treatment of the enslaved Natives:

> A host of cruel, grasping and wicked men …were put in charge of these poor souls. And they discharged this duty by sending the men down the mines, where working conditions were appalling, to dig for gold, and putting the women to labour in the fields … properly only a task for the toughest and strongest of men … in short they were treated as beasts of burden…

Because the Americas were unfamiliar to the Europeans of the late fifteenth century, they were unsure how to fit their inhabitants into already existing schemes of knowledge. Some Spanish thinkers, such as Juan Gines de Sepúlveda, argued that Aristotle's idea of natural slaves fitted the Native Americans perfectly. Sepúlveda illustrated this by arguing that Moctezuma II, the bravest of the Natives, had capitulated to the conquistador Hernan Cortés without a fight. Sepúlveda and Las Casas took part in the Valladolid Controversy, a debate set up by Charles V in 1550 during which the two parties never actually met, to determine whether Native Americans were capable of self-government, of civilization, or whether they were naturally slavish people, as Sepúlveda argued. Although no 'winner' was declared, Las Casas's case was not refuted and he believed for the rest of his life that Natives did deserve freedom. His *Short Account of the Destruction of the Indies* was published in Seville in 1552 (and eagerly translated by Spain's enemies, the English, to form the backbone of the 'Black Legend') to inform a wider audience of the sufferings of Native slaves in the Americas and further refuting Sepúlveda's arguments. But events in America had already advanced further than debate and Natives were being used as slave labour for building work, agriculture and mining.

The Spanish were not the only Europeans who thought the Natives would make good slaves. The English used Native slaves in North America for a time, especially in the early days of the settling of South Carolina. Although the plantations in South Carolina were worked mostly by Africans, following the model of the Barbadian Goose Creek Men who had settled in South Carolina, the demand for slave labour of any race was increasing so rapidly that local Native tribes and confederacies began to provide slaves for the whites, partly in an effort to achieve economic betterment, but also to prevent themselves becoming targets for slave traders. Some of the Native slaves traded remained in North America but most were shipped to the Caribbean. The trade penetrated far into the interior; at a time when the white settlement remained anchored to the eastern seaboard, some of the slaves came from as far west as the Mississippi region.

ATLANTIC HISTORY IN FOCUS

Pequot War, Connecticut, 1636

During the violent Pequot War, New Englanders, wanting to move south into what is now Connecticut, massacred a Native group to force them to leave the territory. Those defeated Natives who did survive were sold into slavery in Bermuda. John Mason, one of the English captains involved in the massacre, did not fully acknowledge this in his account, saying that about 180 Pequots were taken prisoner and divided up for use as 'servants', but that they 'could not endure that yoke' and did not stay long with their masters. The name of the ship that took the Natives to Bermuda is not recorded, but it may have been the *Desire*, which returned to Massachusetts in 1638 with a variety of goods and African slaves, the first recorded arrival of slaves into Boston – less than a decade after the settlement of the English there. The Pequot tribe was almost completely erased from North America but their heritage on St David's Island, Bermuda, is celebrated to this day. In 2002 the remnants of the North American Pequots met with their Bermudan cousins in a ceremony of 'Reconnection' as the tribe was symbolically reunited once more.

The Atlantic 'Other' in Europe

Africa and the Americas were not the only sites of racial clash and confusion; Europe too, had its cultural tensions within its borders between whites, blacks and Native Americans, although for different reasons and with different results to the meetings on the other two continents. It is wrong to think of Europe as a white society with no one there having the opportunity to meet a non-white person. Richard Hakluyt recorded in his *Principall Navigation* the visit of a Brazilian king (that is, a Native leader) to England following the voyage of William Hawkins (father of the famous slave trader John) to South America in the 1530s. Ralph Burton, one of the readers of Hakluyt's book, made copious notes in his copy and was especially interested in the visit by the Native leader. Native Americans were treated partly as visiting dignitaries, afforded a status equal to any other important foreign person, but also as a spectacle of the exotic, proudly shown off by their supposed superiors, the English monarchs. Natives who came to Europe were often treated like the animals from their own countries taken to be exhibited in European menageries, as something strange and fascinating to be observed and wondered at. They were defined by their very difference to Europeans and were never considered to be of equal status because of this psychological alienation.

The most famous visit by a Native American to London was made by the most famous Native American of the colonial period, a young woman by the name of Pocahontas (known to Natives as Matoaka). Immortalized in cartoons and feature films, the Pocahontas of myth is a far cry from the reality. She was a young girl used by powerful men to make alliances and consolidate power, and while it is probably true that her intervention saved the life of Captain John Smith and that she did genuinely love her husband, John Rolfe, she is not the romantic figure of film. Pocahontas agreed to come to England with her husband in 1616, having married him three years earlier. She spent a number of months meeting members of the court in London and becoming an attraction, before falling ill and dying before she had a chance to return to her homeland. Reportedly, Pocahontas and Rolfe stayed in the Belle Sauvage inn at Ludgate Hill while in London, but this is unsubstantiated. Ironically, the inn later gained notoriety for displaying a live rhinoceros during the 1680s, charging large sums for the public to view it. Much hype surrounded this animal that was connected in people's minds with the mythical unicorn, and this interest mirrored that shown in visiting Native leaders. The aim of the visit by Pocahontas was to encourage investment in the Virginia Colony to give the ailing community a lifeline, her husband having earlier successfully cultivated tobacco there. White Europeans also wanted to demonstrate how it was possible to work with and pacify the Natives, with Pocahontas, baptized Rebecca and wearing English clothes, typifying these possibilities.

Although for Pocahontas the visit ended tragically with her early death, some Natives who were brought to Britain used the experience for their own benefit. Squanto became friendly with English explorers in New England but was kidnapped by Captain Thomas Hunt in 1614 and taken to Spain to be sold as a slave. He managed to escape and made his way back to the custody of the English where he spent his time as a translator, interpreter and guide on various expeditions to New England, finally being released to enjoy life as a free man back in his native land. When the Pilgrim Fathers arrived at Plymouth in 1620 they met Squanto, who spoke decent English, and also his compatriot Samoset, and another North American foundational myth of the first thanksgiving was born. Squanto's story shows the complex ways in which Natives were viewed by Europeans and demonstrates how they managed to carve out their own place in their new, multiracial Atlantic world.

Europe must not be treated as a single homogeneous unit. Natives' and Africans' experiences in Iberia were very different from those in London. As well as being hubs of the international slave trade, which will be explored in Chapter 4, Lisbon and Seville were also cities where a number of Africans and Native Americans spent part of their lives. In 1495 Columbus sent to Seville four boatloads of Native Americans seized on Hispaniola during the suppressing of violent resistance to the Spanish. Only a few years later in 1502 Juan de Cordoba, a merchant of Seville, became the first Spaniard allowed to send African slaves to the New World. Seville soon became the largest city in Spain because of the successful transatlantic trade, and the presence of

West Africans, North Africans and Native Americans in the city added to its cosmopolitan reputation. Some members of these groups were enslaved but blacks also visited Mediterranean cities of their own free will, to gain knowledge of European culture. Although the majority of Africans in Europe were in bondage, a significant minority population of free blacks were also present. Lisbon had an active internal slave trade and a large enslaved black population: at any one time up to 10 per cent of the city's population was black. From the late fifteenth century, Africans were taken to Lisbon to be sold on as slaves to the elite of Spain and Italy, thousands passing through the Lisbon slave house, the Casa dos Escravos de Lisboa. Only later did this trade acquire its transatlantic aspect.

Native Americans were not the only non-white group in London society; Africans too, were present in substantial numbers. In London, Africans appear in the earliest extant parish registers, showing that they took a full and varied part of city life. Many black Africans were imported as slaves and spent most of their life in London, but this caused a number of problems for the courts as the 'slaves' challenged and redefined their legal status. Many did remain domestic servants, but a few established themselves as free and independent workers, the black population in England acting as a visible reminder to whites of the means by which the country was becoming very rich through African labour in the colonial sugar or tobacco plantations. In the 1580s, when blacks first appeared in the parish registers of London, their racial status was somewhat confused and mixed-race relationships were openly acknowledged. An entry for St Boltoph's, Bishopsgate, records the baptism of 'Elizabeth a negro child born white, the mother a negro'. In the registers many Africans were recorded as 'servants'; their status was explicitly viewed as no different from white servants. In the parish clerk's memorandum book for 1593 of St Botolph's, Aldgate, the burial of 'Robert' was recorded thus:

> Robert a negar being servant to William Mathew a Jentelman dwelling in a garden being behynd Mr Quarles his howse and neare unto Hogg Lane in the libertie of Eastsmithfield was buried in the owter church yeard being withowt the crosse walle before Mr Soda his tenementes ... Yeares xxvi. He had the second cloth and fower bearers.

In the margin the word 'plague' is written, so despite this being a death of the plague every effort was made to give Robert a decent Christian burial, with a number of bearers and the second-best burial cloth being chosen, probably at considerable expense to his master. However, not all black servants received a Christian burial. An unnamed 'blackamore' belonging to John Davies of St Mary Woolchurch had his burial described in Latin as if to protect the meaning from some readers: '*sine frequentia populi et sine ceremoniis quia utrum christianus esset necne nesciebamus*' which translates as 'without the company of people and without ceremony because we did not know whether he was a Christian or not'. The same John Davies appears again in another register; this time a servant of his was baptized. The register gives details about the origins of this young man, giving his African name, his father's name, his place of origin and the reason for his arrival, which was that his father had deliberately sent him to England. John, the man's Christian name, was said to 'belong' to John Davies. However, the word 'slave' is never used in the records, and white servants and apprentices could also be said to 'belong' to their masters. Poor treatment of Africans in London is hard to find in the records; most masters appear benevolent in having their charges baptized or given a good burial. In the late seventeenth and early eighteenth centuries Africans in the parish registers do not seem to warrant such detailed comment, being listed in a similar format to their white neighbours with only 'black', 'blackamore' or 'negro' included in the entry to differentiate them. Many servants were baptized, taken by their masters who then pledged surety for them. In the eighteenth century blacks born in the Caribbean began to appear in the registers, showing that they were no longer being transported only from Africa, but were coming to England from the Americas. By the early nineteenth century, where a place of origin for the person was mentioned these transatlantic black migrants figured more frequently in the records than Africans arriving direct from Africa, due to the criminalizing of the African slave trade in 1807.

UP FOR DEBATE   Prejudice versus profit

Slavery and race are contentious issues and historians enter into passionate debates about the origins of slavery, the experiences of both whites and blacks, and how and why the institution began to collapse.

It is difficult to get into the mindset of people in the past but many historians, including Oscar and Mary Handlin and Eric Foner, have argued that the concept of 'race' as we understand it in the twenty-first century would have meant little to someone living in the fifteenth or sixteenth centuries. Instead, people were delineated by social status, so the concept of being 'free' or 'unfree' would have made sense. Initially being 'unfree' was unconnected to being black or racially 'other'. This view is supported by the evidence in the 'Atlantic History in Focus' box below on Irish 'slaves' in the Caribbean. The Handlins argue that Virginians, desperate for labour on their tobacco plantations, initially attracted white indentured labourers from England. The life of white indentured servants was harsh: they 'belonged' to a master for a fixed number of years and, like African slaves later, did not have freedom of movement. In 1619 when the economy of Virginia was still in a perilous state, Edwin Sandys of the Virginia Company wrote to the City of London asking for 'superfluous' city children to be sent to Virginia to work on the tobacco plantations. Although the children were promised 'favourable conditions' after their terms of indenture ended and money for their 'apparel', Sandys also suggested, less charitably, that this scheme would be profitable to the City too, as undesirable children such as criminals, paupers or orphans could be sent to America and 'under severe masters they may be brought to goodness'.

In the 1660s Virginia became less attractive to poor white migrants and the planters had to solve their labour problems elsewhere. The first African slaves to work in Virginia, the Handlins argue, were treated the same as white indentured servants and worked alongside them and sometimes married them. However, at the end of the seventeenth century Virginians codified the differences between races in a series of laws. Despite this, the status of blacks remained in flux for a number of years. Thus the use of slave labour in Virginia actually caused racist ideas to develop, not the other way round. Whether Africans coming to Virginia were quickly treated differently to poor whites or whether the idea of racial difference only emerged gradually is the crux of the argument. In 1661 Virginia passed a law that said all children of slave mothers would themselves be slaves, but this provided only the first step towards a racial definition of slavery. By 1705 black and white servants were definitely being treated differently. The Virginia slave code of that year stated that all imported servants who were not Christians in their own country would be slaves. And all black, mixed-race and Native American slaves already there were henceforth classified as 'real estate'. The passing of these laws was mirrored in England's other American possessions, Barbados and Jamaica, which had a far higher number of black slaves than Virginia by this period. Initial racial codes were passed in the 1660s and by 1700 the law assumed that to be a slave meant to be black. It was not the case that all blacks were slaves – to complicate the picture further, the Caribbean plantation system allowed for the establishment of free black communities.

Other historians disagree with this picture. Winthrop Jordan argues that racism and economic necessity combined to cause the establishment of the slave system in North America. As shown in the previous chapter, Europeans held views about racial difference before whites settled in North America. Prejudices based on skin colour and religious differences were rife in medieval and Renaissance literature and art. As well as being seen as tarnished because they were black and inferior due to not being Christian, Africans were also thought to be especially suited to the physical and mental rigours of slavery. Jordan sees the codification of racial difference in the late seventeenth century as merely rubber-stamping the treatment that slaves were already receiving. He shows that as early as the 1640s black African slaves in Virginia had to serve for their lifetime whereas whites always had a fixed period of indenture (usually five or seven years).

When applied to an Atlantic context this model also seems to be complicated. Carl Degler argued that the existence of Roman law about slavery and the European familiarity with the African prevented the development of outright racial prejudice in Iberia, whereas these taming factors did not exist in England. When the Portuguese settled Madeira they initially farmed the archipelago for grain, but the demand for sugar grew and soon African slaves were planting sugar. By the end of the fifteenth century parts of Madeira, especially around Funchal, were operating as slave plantations, albeit with a different industrial model to that adopted later in Brazil. This development was authorized by the Pope in his bull *Dum Diversas* of 1452 which granted Christians the right to enslave any non-Christians. While this was not an explicitly racial instruction, religious prejudice certainly played a part in its use. By this time slaves had also been brought to Portugal itself for several decades, but now due to the labour needs of the sugar crop, the birth of the slave plantation economy occurred – prejudice and economic necessity going hand in hand. A century later the newly discovered colony of Brazil became a sugar colony almost immediately. The Spanish also worked fast. Columbus, who had himself seen sugar production in Madeira, took the idea of planting cane sugar with him to Saint Domingue and within less than a decade African slaves were taken to the region to work the crop. Unlike the English, the Spanish and Portuguese did not make any sustained trials with white indentured labour. As shown above, the Spanish used Natives in the face of protests from men such as Las Casas. This indicates that in the Spanish mind slave labour *was* connected with the concept of the racial 'other'.

ATLANTIC HISTORY IN FOCUS

Irish 'slaves' in the Caribbean

Slaves were not only black. Anyone who fell foul of the English monarch might be transported to the New World as a 'labourer' – but with few rights and the prospect of never-ending labour they were almost 'slaves'. A significant number of these in the seventeenth century were Irish, being banished or transported by Elizabeth I, Charles I, Cromwell and James II. Their exchange of labour was not always an agreement between two parties, as with indentured servitude. Sometimes they were kidnapped and sold for profit just as Africans were. In 1612 the first group of Irish were sent to South America as labourers and later more went to Guiana, Montserrat (forming the majority of the population there) and Antigua. The exodus increased during Cromwell's rule when many thousands of Irish children were sent to the New World, especially Barbados, causing a severe depopulation of Ireland itself. Irish slaves suffered religious prejudice: the Protestant British did not recognize Catholics as Christians. In some parts of the Caribbean the Irish married Africans to create families known colloquially as 'black Irish'.

Plantation Slavery and Other Forms

When we think of Atlantic slavery, plantation slavery comes to mind. Rightly or wrongly, the image of a slave is of an African growing and harvesting a staple crop for distribution in Europe. We will look at this economic trade relationship in more detail in the next chapter, but here it is important to look at other types of slavery in the Atlantic world, and how these other 'slaveries' fit our understanding of race in this period.

Plantation slavery existed in Madeira and the Azores; in the Caribbean islands settled by the Spanish, English and French; in South America, especially Portuguese and Dutch Brazil; and in North America, predominantly in the Chesapeake region (Virginia and Maryland), and in the Carolinas, Georgia and later in the cotton belt of the south-eastern United States. In many of these areas not all slaves were plantation workers: industrial, craft-working and semi-professional slave labourers were also employed. But these regions are predominantly remembered for their plantation systems.

What are the differences between slavery in different parts of the Atlantic world? In attempting to evaluate this, demography is important: where slaves came from, how many lived together, how many children they had, when they died, the gender ratios. Historians assess which slaves had a harder life: those harvesting sugar in the Caribbean or South America, or those working on tobacco or rice and indigo in North America. In Virginia, those slaves working on tobacco lived on smaller plantations of around ten slaves each. They had close contact with their master and soon began to reproduce their population by natural increase. This meant that importations from Africa became less frequent. By contrast, in South Carolina, due to the conditions needed for growing rice there, slaves lived on larger plantations with higher mortality rates and lower reproduction rates, so, well into the eighteenth century, regular importations of new slaves from Africa were needed to maintain numbers. Slaves were less likely to have close contact with their masters, too, because white planters thought it unhealthy to spend a lot of time on their Low Country estates, preferring the society of Charleston. Louisiana, where slaves grew sugar and rice under Spanish, then French, then United States control, also had a very high mortality rate among the slaves due to the humid climate. Charleston and New Orleans were the largest centres of slave trading in North America, so always had a large population of recent arrivals from Africa until the transatlantic trade was made illegal in 1807.

On sugar plantations of the Caribbean the life of slaves was extremely hard with high mortality. Again, slaves were regularly imported from Africa. These factors contributed to frequent revolts and runaways, with slave rebellions commonplace especially in Jamaica. In Brazil slaves were owned by private individuals and by organizations such as the church and state. Again, the mortality rates were very high and Brazil relied on importation of African slaves, mostly from Angola, to keep the workforce numbers high even into the nineteenth century when illegally traded slaves were brought into the country. Slavery was everywhere: many slaves worked in sugar or coffee plantations but some were urban workers, 'negroes de ganho' able to hire themselves out and split the profits with their master. Slaves who were taken to Catholic countries benefited from more regular holidays too, but the slave population was far from passive and happy. The Palmares maroon or free slave community (now known as a 'quilombo' in Portuguese) in Pernambuco, Brazil, survived for most of the seventeenth century, and at times had a population of tens of thousands and was run as an Angolan kingdom with Catholic influences.

It is difficult for us to access information about what slavery was really like because slaves themselves left few written records before literate former slaves began writing their testimonies for the abolitionist movement in the mid-eighteenth century. However, we do know about changing white attitudes to slavery and these differed depending on which part of the Atlantic world we focus on. The Caribbean was in many ways the most racist of the slave societies, with racial theories developing early in the eighteenth century reflecting the long, troubled history of the plantation system. Ideas of racial difference – that different skin colour reflected a more insidious inferiority – started here earlier than in North America due to the sheer numbers of black people within the Caribbean societies. Seemingly contradictory is the white planters' tolerance of mixed-race liaisons and of a large free black population. But perhaps it was because of these quirks that some writers felt it necessary to define racial difference. In North America, where to be black always meant to be a slave, virulent racism was slower to develop.

Although they left few written records, we know that the lives of slaves were dominated by their work culture. Their experience was defined by the seasonal patterns of the crop they were employed to harvest. In some areas slaves were also required to tend livestock and cultivate a secondary staple, but most of their work was focused on one main crop. During the few short breaks from work, some slaves cultivated their own gardens, even selling produce or livestock for profit on rare occasions. In South Carolina this was more common due to the 'task' system where slaves were given an allotted task and, if they worked quickly, they were allowed time to till their own gardens. By contrast, in Virginia slaves worked the 'gang' system where they worked a specific number of hours, giving them no incentive to finish their work quickly.

Slaves developed their own cultural pursuits too, although it is difficult to gain an overall picture, as each plantation was different. On plantations where many slaves were recent migrants from Africa, singing, dancing, craft-making, storytelling and religion had a strongly traditional African flavour, whereas on plantations with a creole (American-born) slave population white American culture influenced the slaves' behaviour and produced an African American identity. Survival of the African language Gullah in the islands off Carolina shows that slaves valued their African heritage and used it to mark themselves out as culturally different from their white masters. The adoption of Christianity by slaves is an equally complex topic. On some plantations masters encouraged their slaves to become Christians and used this as a tool to pacify them and to justify their own paternalistic intentions. Missionaries in both Catholic and Protestant areas were concerned for the spiritual wellbeing of slaves and in Brazil the Jesuits owned slaves. Africans who fell into the hands of Portuguese traders were given a perfunctory baptism before boarding ship for the Middle Passage across the Atlantic. Elsewhere, such as seventeenth-century Barbados, the conversion of slaves was forbidden as it was thought unlawful to keep Christians as slaves. Those slaves who did become active, practising Christians did not do so to assimilate with white culture; rather they adapted the Christian message for their own purposes, giving hope of salvation and freedom in the future.

Plantation slavery – blacks of African origin owned by whites of European origin – though important, is not the only story in the Atlantic world. Earlier in this chapter the stories of black servants in Europe were told. Before the War of Independence Africans had a similar status in northern North America. In colonies such as Rhode Island and Massachusetts Africans were used as domestic servants and as labourers on small family-run farms with one or two slaves each. Africans were given a separate status to white indentured servants in slave codes enacted in the mid-seventeenth century. But although they were treated differently because of the colour of their skin, Africans in the northern colonies had very different experiences because they were living surrounded by whites. They were less likely to develop their own independent slave culture and were more likely to have a one-to-one relationship with their master. New England became a hub of the slave trade, supplying slaves to southern colonies and the Caribbean, as some planters preferred not to buy slaves direct from Africa but to have them 'seasoned' first by spending time in the Americas.

The story of slavery in the Atlantic is literally not only 'black and white'. Native Americans were used as slaves, by the Spanish, and by Carolinians who shipped Natives to the Caribbean for profit. In 1657 Richard Ligon described the differences in Barbados between the Natives from the mainland, 'whom we make slaves', and the Africans who constituted the majority of the slave population. Although Ligon described both racial groups in terms of their physical attributes, he also said that the Natives were better cooks than the Africans, so they were employed in bread-making. The male Natives made good footmen and fishermen, this observation indicating that the two races were placed not in a racial hierarchy but classified according to expertise and usefulness.

Natives were also slave owners and traders themselves. As in Africa, Natives in America had practised a form of slaveholding before the arrival of the Europeans, but it was on a small scale and did not represent a coherent slave system. Early Native slaves were war captives, taken as prizes rather than bought or sold. They were used for some labour, exchanged for ransom or used in ritual sacrifice. The Native practice of kidnapping whites, much feared by Europeans, was an extension of this understanding of slavery. Once the English arrived and built slave plantations, some Native groups in south-eastern North America offered assistance to runaway slaves, perhaps marrying them and integrating them into Native society; others sold them back to their white owners. By the early nineteenth century Natives of the Five Civilized Tribes (Cherokee, Choctaw, Creek, Chickasaw and Seminole) owned their own black slaves, sometimes treating them as separate and inferior, at other times allowing them to play a part in Native society. Since the 1990s the descendants of mixed-race African Natives have been pursuing court cases in the United States to gain recognition and legal rights as full members of the tribes to which they belong.

Conclusion

The story of the Atlantic world is inseparable from the story of the horrible abuses perpetrated in the name of the slave trade. However, this chapter has shown that the story is not as simple as it seems. Slavery need not be Africans living on a plantation in the Americas; there are many other sites and victims of slavery in the region that need to be acknowledged. From the fifteenth to the nineteenth century every nationality and racial group that lived in the Atlantic world was affected by slavery. Its economic significance will be more fully explored in the next chapter, when we look at how the slave trade became tied in to the so-called 'triangular' trade and why it became so lucrative. Slavery, racism and its painful political legacy also figure strongly in the story of Haiti and its independence movement (see Chapter 7), and it is the dangerous 'wolf', as Thomas Jefferson put it, in the story of the American Revolution. Thomas Jefferson said that dealing with slavery was like holding a wolf by the ear – you didn't want to hold on, but you didn't want to let go either – illustrating that he understood slavery to be a hidden threat to the nation.

So yes, slavery does define the Atlantic world. Of course there are early dissenting voices; the Atlantic is certainly not a homogeneous entity. Abolitionism will be explored more fully in Chapter 8, but early anti-slavery voices included the Mennonites of Germantown, Pennsylvania, who, in their resolutions of 1688, argued that just as whites fear being kidnapped into slavery by 'Turks', so African slavery was an abomination because it was being undertaken by Christians. They explicitly stated that they 'stand against' those who 'rob and sell them [Africans] against their will'. Samuel Sewell, a Puritan from Boston, who recorded in his diary his growing discomfort with slavery, published the first explicitly anti-slavery tract *The Selling of Joseph* in 1700. Visitors to the New World, who lived in societies with less visible engagement with slavery, such as Hector St John de Crevecoeur, changed the tide of feeling towards slavery. Africans in America and in Africa also campaigned against the trade. Some African leaders realized that despite the slave trade's economic potential, it was bad for their people, leading to depopulation and dramatic cultural changes.

Sewell's friend Cotton Mather disagreed strongly with him and argued that the system of slavery should be maintained, but that slaves should be afforded the comfort of being baptized into Christianity. So, even those places that we assume to be the bedrock of abolitionist feeling such as New England and Pennsylvania were involved in the slave trade and slave owning. The Quakers, who led the abolition movement and who built Pennsylvania as a tolerant, liberal settlement during the late seventeenth century, did so with the assistance of slave labour. Their leader William Penn himself owned slaves.

Arguments to justify the use of Africans as slave labour emerged alongside the slave trade itself. Many of these were arguments based on racial difference, although true racist doctrines took another few centuries to emerge. Europeans debated about who should be enslaved and whether Native Americans or Africans made the best slaves. Europeans and Africans worked together to develop the transatlantic slave trade, but they were not the only people seizing and selling slaves; Native Americans and North African Muslims also took part in trading and slaveholding and as witnesses to the white involvement in slavery. Plantation slavery differed in its impact on workers and masters and in any case not all African American chattel slavery fits the plantation model. And finally, all the Atlantic is tainted by slavery even if all slavery in the region does not fit the concept of 'the Atlantic'.

CHAPTER CHRONOLOGY

1441 First recorded incidence of European kidnapping an African into slavery (Portuguese seize 12 from Guinea coast and send to Portugal as a gift to Henry the Navigator).

1500 African slaves imported into Hispaniola.

1517 Las Casas protests about the use of Native slaves and asks that Africans be used instead.

1538 Slaves imported into Brazil for the first time; sugar production begins there.

1619 First African slaves arrive in British North America

1636 Governor of Barbados declares all Indians and Africans on the island should be treated as slaves.

1661 Earliest Virginian slave codes enacted.

1700 Asante empire in West Africa begins its involvement in the slave trade (southern Ghana). Other African tribes and empires involved include Dahomey, Bonny and Kongo.

■ **PRIMARY SOURCES AND STUDY IMAGE**

Early slave codes from Virginia (1660s)

December 1662

Whereas some doubts have arisen whether children got by any Englishman upon a Negro woman should be slave or free, *be it therefore enacted and declared by this present Grand Assembly,* that all children born in this country shall be held bond or free only according to the condition of the mother; and that if any Christian shall commit fornication with a Negro man or woman, he or she so offending shall pay double the fines imposed by the former act.

September 1667

Whereas some doubts have risen whether children that are slaves by birth, and by the charity and piety of their owners made partakers of the blessed sacrament of baptism, should by virtue of their baptism be made free, *it is enacted and declared by this Grand Assembly, and the authority thereof,* that the conferring of baptism does not alter the condition of the person as to his bondage or freedom; that diverse masters, freed from this doubt may more carefully endeavor the propagation of Christianity by permitting children, though slaves, or those of greater growth if capable, to be admitted to that sacrament.

September 1668

Whereas it has been questioned whether servants running away may be punished with corporal punishment by their master or magistrate, since the act already made gives the master satisfaction by prolonging their time by service, *it is declared and enacted by this Assembly* that moderate corporal punishment inflicted by master or magistrate upon a runaway servant shall not deprive the master of the satisfaction allowed by the law, the one being as necessary to reclaim them from persisting in that idle course as the other is just to repair the damages sustained by the master.

October 1669

Whereas the only law in force for the punishment of refractory servants resisting their master, mistress, or overseer cannot be inflicted upon Negroes, nor the obstinacy of many of them be suppressed by other than violent means, *be it enacted and declared by this Grand Assembly* if any slave resists his master (or other by his master's order correcting him) and by the extremity of the correction should chance to die, that his death shall not be accounted a felony, but the master (or that other person appointed by the master to punish him) be acquitted from molestation, since it cannot be presumed that premeditated malice (which alone makes murder a felony) should induce any man to destroy his own estate.

A defence of slavery from antebellum US (1854) by George Fitzhugh

The civilized man hates the savage, and the savage returns the hatred with interest. Hence, West India slavery, of newly caught negroes, is not a very humane, affectionate or civilizing institution. Virginia negroes have become moral and intelligent. They love their master and his family, and the attachment is reciprocated. Still, we like the idle, but intelligent house-servants, better than the hard-used, but stupid outhands; and we like the mulatto better than the negro; yet the negro is generally more affectionate, contented and faithful.

The world at large looks on negro slavery as much the worst form of slavery; because it is only acquainted with West India slavery. Abolition never arose till negro slavery was instituted; and now abolition is only directed against negro slavery. There is no philanthropic crusade attempting to set free the white slaves of Eastern Europe and of Asia. The world, then, is prepared for the defence of slavery in the abstract – it is prejudiced only against negro slavery. These prejudices were in their origin well founded. The Slave Trade, the horrors of the Middle Passage, and West India slavery, were enough to rouse the most torpid philanthropy.

But our Southern slavery has become a benign and protective institution, and our negroes are confessedly better off than any free labouring population in the world. How can we contend that white slavery is wrong, whilst all the great body of free labourers are starving; and slaves, white or black, throughout the world, are enjoying comfort? We write in the cause of Truth and Humanity, and will not play the advocate for master or for slave.

The aversion to negroes, the antipathy of race, is much greater at the North than at the South; and it is very probable that this antipathy to the person of the negro, is confounded with or generates hatred of the institution with which he is usually connected. Hatred to slavery is very generally little more than hatred of negroes.

There is one strong argument in favour of negro slavery over all other slavery: that he, being unfitted for the mechanic arts, for trade, and all skillful pursuits, leaves those pursuits to be carried on by the whites; and does not bring all industry into disrepute, as in Greece and Rome, where the slaves were not only the artists and mechanics, but also the merchants.

Whilst, as a general and abstract question, negro slavery has no other claims over other forms of slavery, except that from inferiority, or rather peculiarity, of race, almost all negroes require masters, whilst only the children, the women, the very weak, poor, and ignorant, &c., among the whites, need some protective and governing relation of this kind; yet as a subject of temporary, but worldwide importance, negro slavery has become the most necessary of all human institutions.

The African slave trade to America commenced three centuries and a half since. By the time of the American Revolution, the supply of slaves had exceeded the demand for slave labour, and the slaveholders, to get rid of a burden, and to prevent the increase of a nuisance, became violent opponents of the slave trade, and many of them abolitionists. New England, Bristol, and Liverpool, who reaped the profits of the trade, without suffering from the nuisance, stood out for a long time against its abolition. Finally, laws and treaties were made, and fleets fitted out to abolish it; and after a while, the slaves of most of South America, of the West Indies, and of Mexico were liberated. In the meantime, cotton, rice, sugar, coffee, tobacco, and other products of slave labour, came into universal use as necessaries of life. The population of Western Europe, sustained and stimulated by those products, was trebled, and that of the North increased ten fold. The products of slave labour became scarce and dear, and famines frequent. Now, it is obvious that to emancipate all the negroes would be to starve Western Europe and our North. Not to extend and increase negro slavery, *pari passu*, with the extension and multiplication of free society, will produce much suffering. If all South America, Mexico, the West Indies, and our Union south of Mason and Dixon's line, of the Ohio and Missouri, were slaveholding, slave products would be abundant and cheap in free society; and their market for their merchandise, manufactures, commerce, &c., illimitable. Free white labourers might live in comfort and luxury on light work, but for the exacting and greedy landlords, bosses and other capitalists.

We must confess, that overstock the world as you will with comforts and with luxuries, we do not see how to make capital relax its monopoly – how to do aught but tantalize the hireling. Capital, irresponsible capital, begets, and ever will beget, the 'immedicabile vulnus' of so-called Free Society. It invades every recess of domestic life, infects its food, its clothing, its drink, its very atmosphere, and pursues the hireling, from the hovel to the poor-house, the prison and the grave. Do what he will, go where he will, capital pursues and persecutes him. '*Hæret lateri lethalis arundo!*'

Capital supports and protects the domestic slave; taxes, oppresses and persecutes the free labourer.

Olaudah Equiano on his Middle Passage crossing (1789)

At last, when the ship we were in had got in all her cargo, they made ready with many fearful noises, and we were all put under deck, so that we could not see how they managed the vessel. But this disappointment was the least of my sorrow. The stench of the hold while we were on the coast was so intolerably loathsome, that it was dangerous to remain there for any time, and some of us had been permitted to stay on the deck for the fresh air; but now that the whole ship's cargo were confined together, it became absolutely pestilential. The closeness of the place, and the heat of the climate, added to the number in the ship, which was so crowded that each had scarcely room to turn himself, almost suffocated us. This produced copious perspirations, so that the air soon became unfit for respiration, from a variety of loathsome smells, and brought on a sickness among the slaves, of which many died, thus falling victims to the improvident avarice, as I may call it, of their purchasers. This wretched situation was again aggravated by the galling of the chains, now become insupportable; and the filth of the necessary tubs, into which the children often fell, and were almost suffocated. The shrieks of the women, and the groans of the dying, rendered the whole a scene of horror almost inconceivable. Happily perhaps for myself I was soon reduced so low here that it was thought necessary to keep me almost always on deck; and from my extreme youth I was not put in fetters. In this situation I expected every hour to share the fate of my companions, some of whom were almost daily brought upon deck at the point of death, which I began to hope would soon put an end to my miseries. Often did I think many of the inhabitants of the deep much more happy than myself; I envied them the freedom they enjoyed, and as often wished I could change my condition for theirs. Every circumstance I met with served only to render my state more painful, and heighten my apprehensions, and my opinion of the cruelty of the whites. One day they had taken a number of fishes; and when they had killed and satisfied themselves with as many as they thought fit, to our astonishment who were on the deck, rather than give any of them to us to eat, as we expected, they tossed the remaining fish into the sea again, although we begged and prayed for some as well we cold [sic], but in vain; and some of my countrymen, being pressed by hunger, took an opportunity, when they thought no one saw them, of trying to get a little privately; but they were discovered, and the attempt procured them some very severe floggings.

One day, when we had a smooth sea, and a moderate wind, two of my wearied countrymen, who were chained together (I was near them at the time), preferring death to such a life of misery, somehow made through the nettings, and jumped into the sea: immediately another quite dejected fellow, who, on account of his illness, was suffered to be out of irons, also followed their example; and I believe many more would soon have done the same, if they had not been prevented by the ship's crew, who were instantly alarmed. Those of us that were the most active were, in a moment, put down under the deck; and there was such a noise and confusion amongst the people of the ship as I never heard before, to stop her, and get the boat to go out after the slaves. However, two of the wretches were drowned, but they got the other, and afterwards flogged him unmercifully, for thus attempting to prefer death to slavery. In this manner we continued to undergo more hardships than I can now relate; hardships which are inseparable from this accursed trade. – Many a time we were near suffocation, from the want of fresh air, which we were often without for whole days together. This, and the stench of the necessary tubs, carried off many. During our passage I first saw flying fishes, which surprised me very much: they used frequently to fly across the ship, and many of them fell on the deck. I also now first saw the use of the quadrant. I had often with astonishment seen the mariners make observations with it, and I could not think what it meant. They at last took notice of my surprise; and one of them, willing to increase it, as well as to gratify my curiosity, made me one day look through it. The clouds appeared to me to be land, which disappeared as they passed along. This heightened my wonder: and I was now more persuaded than ever that I was in another world, and that every thing about me was magic. At last we came in sight of the island of Barbadoes, at which the whites on board gave a great shout, and made many signs of joy to us.

Capt. J. E. Alexander observes slave life in Guiana (1833)

The 'works' were visited, where I saw the steam-engine for crushing the canes; the five cauldrons for boiling the juice; the coolers in which it congeals and becomes sugar; the curing-house, where hogsheads on end allowed the molasses to drain from them; the still-house, where from the skimming of the cauldrons the rum is prepared; the trash-house, where under cover is kept the dry and pressed canes to be mind as fuel; the hospital, where every care and attention was paid to the sick negroes; and the negro-houses in two rows, with gardens round them, in which were pigs, poultry and culinary vegetables.

It was a holiday, and Quashee and Quasheba were lounging about in their gala dresses, and waiting impatiently for evening, to commence their festivities in the 'Great House.' The men were dressed in white vests and trowsers, and cloth jackets; and the women in printed gowns, with straw hats or handkerchiefs on their heads. Every where as we passed through the different groups in the garden, the white teeth were

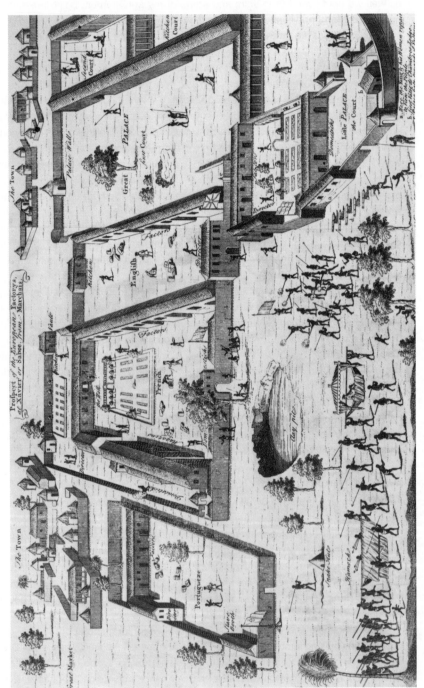

Study image 3 *Slave trading compounds on the African coast, 1746.*

displayed in a smile, and 'How de massa? ready for dance massa!' was heard. The piccaninnies, black and mischievous as monkeys, were 'scurrying' about, running between their parents' legs, laughing loud, and tumbling one another head over heels on the grass.

At last a drum is heard in the gallery, and the negroes take possession of the house; two or three musicians then seat themselves in chairs, and with fiddle, tambourine, and drum strike up some lively jigs, at the same time thumping the floor vigorously with their heels. Every one is alive; short cries of mirth are uttered by the men as they hand out their sable partners; and they lead one another up and down the lane of the country dance, with as much enjoyment as I have ever witnessed at a Highland wedding.

The little black urchins, boys and girls, are not idle round the room, whilst their parents are 'tripping it' in the centre, but copying their elders, they 'cut and shuffle' at a great rate; the mothers, with children at their breasts, alone quietly enjoy the scene. A worthless fellow who rushed in his chemise into the room, and attempted to join the well-dressed figurantes, was instantly expelled. Santa (sweet punch) and cakes, were handed round from time to time. Mulatta ladies looked in at the windows at the mirthful scene, but declined to join the negroes; and a few overseers and book-keepers 'whispered soft nonsense' in their ears.

Outside the house, in the moonlight, a musician seated himself with his drum on the grass, and commenced singing an African air, when a circle of men and women, linked hand in hand, danced round him with rattling seeds on their legs, and joined in the chorus.

Oh! how I wished that some of the kind ladies of Peckham could have contemplated for five minutes this scene of mirth! could have beheld what they are pleased to call 'the naked, starved, and oppressed negroes,' well clothed, plump, and full of glee: instead of shrieks of misery, could have heard shouts of laughter: and instead of the clang of the whip, could have heard the lively music of the fiddles, and the gladsome songs of the creole dancers. Surely, then, their feeling hearts would prompt them to look for more distressed objects nearer home on which to exercise their benevolence, would induce them to leave emancipation to be wrought out by slow and rational means, and not cruelly insist, that since the planters have had for so long time the use of their slaves, they should now give them liberty – forgetting that to the suddenly emancipated slave this boon immediately opens the door to licentiousness and misery. 'Vide ut supra,' see the preceding statement, and be convinced of your error.

Recommended Reading

Hilary Beckles, *Caribbean Slavery in the Atlantic World: A Student Reader* (London, 1999). A comprehensive collection of articles about all aspects of slavery in the Caribbean islands.

Ira Berlin, *Many Thousands Gone* (Cambridge, MA, 1998). An important book that shows how slavery, slave culture and experience, and perceptions of racial difference in North America developed during the colonial period.

Robin Blackburn, *The Making of New World Slavery* (London, 1997). Provides a survey of Atlantic slavery from its origins to the nineteenth century, exploring the experience of the colonies of the Spanish, Portuguese, British, French and Dutch.

Carl Degler, *Neither Black Nor White* (Madison, 1986). Examines the histories of slavery in Brazil and the United States, showing that a variety of cultural and economic factors caused the differing race relations.

Oscar and Mary Handlin, 'Origins of the Southern Labour System', *William and Mary Quarterly* 3.7 (1950). A seminal article that argues that racism developed after the slave labour system had gradually emerged in North America and that the use of Africans was only one choice out of a range of 'unfree' labour options.

Winthrop Jordan, *White over Black* (Chapel Hill, 1968). Contrary to the Handlins' work, Jordan explores how racial prejudice pre-dated the development of the plantation system in the New World.

Peter Kolchin, *American Slavery* (London, 1993). A student-friendly survey of the origins and development of the slave system in North America.

John Thornton, *Africa and Africans and the Making of the Atlantic World* (Cambridge, 1998). Shows that prior to the eighteenth century Africans were able to control the slave trade, and explains that in the story of the slave system Africans were self-conscious actors and not merely passive victims.

James Walvin, *Slaves and Slavery: The British Colonial Experience* (Manchester, 1992). Explores the development and decline of the slave system throughout the British Atlantic world.

TEST YOUR KNOWLEDGE

1 What biblical and pseudo-physiological reasons did Europeans use to justify using Africans as slaves?
2 Who started the African slave trade and who benefited from it?
3 Under what circumstances were white Europeans enslaved?
4 What arguments were used against Native Americans being used as slaves?
5 How were Africans who lived in Europe treated?
6 Does the use of the words 'slave' or 'servant' signify anything in terms of race?
7 Which came first, slavery or racism?
8 How did plantation slavery differ from other forms of slavery?
9 How do free blacks, people of mixed race and Native Americans fit into the traditional story of plantation slavery?

4   Exploiting the Atlantic: Trade and Economy

As previously explained, Europeans did not seek to colonize simply to expand their sphere of influence around the globe. Colonies were intended to bring valuable natural resources under the control of European powers, which then used this new-found wealth to either protect their borders or to challenge their enemies. At a time when water-borne trade was often a more direct and lucrative alternative to land routes, Europeans turned towards the land masses that bounded the Atlantic to increase access to diverse trade goods. This chapter's focus is on what these vital commodities were, the characteristics of trade routes and technologies, and the influence they exerted on policy and people.

Trade Heritage: Diverse Commodities and Appetites

When the Portuguese explored Africa in the fifteenth century, they encountered the west coast of a continent that already possessed a vibrant trading economy. Fairly quickly, they learned the lesson that conquest by force was far less certain and lucrative than peaceful trade. By the middle of the fifteenth century, the Portuguese had established their first *feitoria*, or trading 'factory', on the African coast. Soon to be followed by many more, these became centres for exporting African goods such as gold, salt, dyes and, of course, humans to be used in coerced labour systems. In return, Africans eagerly traded for horses, cotton cloth, copper, and kola nuts. The trade in kola nuts is of particular interest because it sheds light on an element of trade that often takes a back seat to the more arduous movement of goods around the Atlantic littoral. The Portuguese were valued trading partners for their ability to trans-ship merchandise – that is, move it from one coastal port to another – which was often more cost-effective and easier than moving the same items by land. Many Atlantic world cultures, including various Native American groups, the Africans themselves and, of course, Europeans, became active trans-shippers – that is, the movers of goods to markets via water, instead of the producers of them. Trans-shipment required smaller distances and less overall investment than transatlantic voyages. It also contributed to the consistent employment of numerous classes of working people tied to maritime industries. These ranged from coastal pilots who helped larger vessels navigate tricky coasts and waterways to West African mariners known as 'surfmen', who unloaded vessels and delivered the merchandise to points of sale. African coastal pilots, known as *grumetes*, were in great demand.

On the African coast, the mixing of local Africans and incoming Portuguese resulted in a distinct class of people. Known by the derisive Portuguese term *tangos-mãos* ('renegades'), these were a mixed-race creole people who had knowledge of both sub-Saharan African and European cultures. They could speak multiple languages, navigate the trading worlds of diverse cultures, and dressed and worshipped in both African and Christian styles. Neither wholly African nor wholly European, they were derided by representatives of both cultures as unsavoury. Yet they were also valuable for their knowledge, and served local leaders, economies, and their own families well.

In the sixteenth and seventeenth centuries, some African coastal towns boomed in population and commercial activity. Historian Ira Berlin describes this transformation as it unfolded along the so-called 'Gold Coast'. Between 1550 and the end of the eighteenth century, Mouri grew from 200 to perhaps as many as 6000 people. Another village, Axim, more than quadrupled its population between 1631 and 1690. These figures are particularly impressive in light of the mortality that was common for communities with ever-shifting, and often disease-importing, populations. These populations, of course, included European and African mariners, as well as enslaved humans brought to the coast for sale and export.

Traders were among the earliest Europeans to attempt to establish an Atlantic world base. They often followed closely on the heels of the explorers themselves. Many early Europeans were convinced that the interior land mass of the Americas harboured huge amounts of gold, easily discovered and harvested. But there were others who had been trading on the Atlantic's genuine bounty – fish – for decades, if not centuries. From the eleventh century, fishermen of various European nations, including the Spanish Basques, had been making landfall in the western hemisphere, setting up crude settlements and processing apparatus for their rich harvest from the sea. The codfish, which fed this industry, was known for its tastiness, the ease of the curing and preservation process, and its plenitude. In pre-Reformation, largely Roman Catholic Europe, much of the calendar consisted of feast and fast days requiring abstinence from meat. Fish was therefore consumed in massive quantities. The ability to both find the fish and preserve them well was considered vital.

The European appetite for sugar – a holdover from the Crusades – as well as economic stability in the wake of civil unrest and the disruptions wrought by the Black Death, influenced the conquest of the Atlantic islands off the coast of Africa. Though two weeks by water, the Canaries, Azores and Madeiras possessed rich soil which proved ideal for cultivating sugar. Though known for supporting the cultivation of other important trade items, notably lumber and horses, it was sugar that became the primary staple, first on the island of Madeira and then elsewhere. A labour-intensive industry involving advanced technical knowledge, sugar is seen by modern historians as giving rise to the dominant plantation systems of the Atlantic. Even in the fifteenth century, the sugar plantations of Madeira relied on the coerced labour of religious and cultural outsiders. Later, these practices would be exported across the Atlantic and take with them African slaves.

Some New World colonies were set up exclusively for the trade activities. The Dutch West India Company had no goals of spreading the glory of the Dutch Republic or its Reformed Protestant Christianity. The Dutch spread into Africa, the Caribbean, North and South America to become the Atlantic's pre-eminent traders – a role in which they retained their dominance well into the seventeenth century and beyond.

Despite some popular interpretations of the pre-Columbian western hemisphere, Indian cultures did not develop in complete isolation and independence. We know this in part from the archaeological record, which shows more or less conclusively that indigenous people throughout the Americas and Caribbean, with few exceptions, traded with one another. Some of these networks of trade were quite expansive. Seashells found only in Atlantic coastal waters have been excavated in the Midwest. Objects containing fibres from plants grown in the Mississippi region, where Native American cultures thrived for centuries, have been found in sites hundreds of miles away. Indians were in contact with one another, and their chief reason for interacting with other groups was trade.

In general, the Native peoples who survived the onslaught of European diseases were intrigued by European objects. Yet only a certain number were considered useful. Native peoples often pursued objects that made their lives easier. These desired objects included knives, guns and textiles. Less desirable objects were those that either limited mobility or encouraged Indians to pursue farming exclusively. As time passed, however, more and more groups that came into closer contact with Europeans adopted more sedentary ways. This often led to the accumulation of more items and, in some cases, dependency on the Europeans who crafted or imported them. Controlling the flow of trade goods sometimes led to conflict between Native American groups. The 1640s saw an escalation in violence between the Iroquois and their traditional enemies, the Hurons, over the flow of guns and furs in and out of the interior regions. The Iroquois supplied the Dutch, the Hurons, the French. In the 1640s, the more powerful Iroquois moved against their competitors and, through violent attack after violent attack, came close to completely obliterating the Huron people. While trade improved the lives and fortunes of some, it destroyed the livelihoods, and sometimes the lives, of others.

Mercantilism

Older histories that focus on a purely 'colonial' understanding of the Atlantic world speak of the importance of the so-called 'triangular trade'. In this construct of early modern trade systems, raw goods moved from the Americas back to Europe; Europeans converted them into finished goods, and shipped these goods to Africa; Africans and their European business partners shipped slaves to the Americas. Though variations of this network were indeed in action, they hardly tell the entire story. Rather, they were but one version of the many ways trade networks operated. In general, trade was multilateral rather than triangular, involving multiple ports, continents and commodities. Concerns such as the types of vessels carrying the commodities, winds and seasons, climate, and condition of markets in other parts of the Atlantic world influenced its complex workings.

In its simplest form, mercantilism posited that strong nations kept money and raw goods within their own borders. Nations were strengthened further still when competitor nations had to go through them to access the goods they needed. With such an arrangement, a nation could easily sell needed goods for a high price, or cut out its competitors altogether from goods they needed. Early modern people believed that the competition to exploit African and New World resources made such strategies necessary.

Competition between European powers and their trade offerings was keen and constant. For example, France strove to dominate certain areas of the sugar market by doing away with taxes in 1717. Decades later, the British likewise did away with duties on sugar imported directly to Britain from its Caribbean colonies. Still, the French maintained something of a monopoly on molasses, which they had to export in abundance, as French planters made more clayed, or semi-refined, sugar than their British counterparts did. Merchants in British America purchased this cheaper alternative to that being produced by their Caribbean countrymen. This option deprived the British crown of the revenue it demanded. As a response, it issued the Sugar Act of 1764, which confirmed the mercantilist principles of commodity control for the mother country's benefit.

Trade regulations set by the various mother countries were the all-important means of determining who traded with whom, and on whose terms. The English took a lead in this area with a series of Navigation Acts meant to ensure that New World products continued to feed Old World political interests. The first act came in 1651 in the wake of the end of the English Civil War and Oliver Cromwell's desire to restrict the rival Dutch from cutting into English trade. It prohibited the importation of goods from around the globe to England except by English vessels, and forbade ships of other nations to bring anything to English ports except goods manufactured in their own country of origin. Such restrictions were damaging to the Dutch, who were Europe's pre-eminent traders at the time, and the attempted enforcement of these regulations touched off the first of several Anglo-Dutch wars of the seventeenth century.

The impulse to control colonial trade was reasserted with the restoration of the English Stuart monarchy. Needing to raise revenue, the new king, Charles II, and the Restoration Parliament created the Navigation Act of 1660. The chief feature of this Act was the so-called 'enumerated list,' which stipulated that the commodities it specified – chiefly tobacco and sugar – could only be exported from an English colonial port in accordance with certain conditions. In short, enumerated goods could only be transported in ships owned by subjects of England or Ireland with a crew that was 75 per cent English, and could only be shipped either directly to England or through an English colonial port, where duties were collected. Later, the English would add rice, molasses, dye woods and naval stores to the list. They also restricted trade in white pine by forbidding locals to harvest them without a royal licence. Those that grew to the desired diameter were marked for the exclusive use of the British monarch. The addition of these trees to the enumerated items almost single-handedly illustrates the utility of mercantilism: the colony supplied the trees, which were reserved for the predictable use of the Royal Navy. The Royal Navy, in turn, continued to both protect and advance British interests in trade and cultivation of new markets. This, in theory, was meant to benefit everyone within the empire.

Obviously, the colonists themselves saw such regulations as prohibitive, and for more than a century contrived the means to circumvent them and trade as they pleased. Patriotism meant little in trade. New England Puritans, who so often set themselves up in opposition to everything that smacked of Catholicism, were still happy to trade in fish for Catholic Europeans to keep their Catholic feast days. Producers throughout the English New World colonies continued to devise loopholes in the Navigation Acts. And when a loophole was not to be found, they smuggled. America became a nation of smugglers in the first half of the eighteenth century, and remained that way until the English attempted to stem the haemorrhaging of trade revenue after defeating the French in 1763.

What did the rather dangerous art of smuggling accomplish? For one, it helped keep local prices down. Smuggling meant avoiding high prices on goods that were often the result of collusion by English merchants. It also meant getting a better price for items that were in high demand – and bypassing English merchant middlemen who, in taking their own percentage of the profits, deprived Americans of some of theirs. Smuggling was not always done under the cover of darkness, as might be thought. Instead, colonists brazenly left colonial ports and simply sailed to the destination of their choice. Others technically fulfilled the law by stopping at another English colonial port and, from there, sailing on to the market that gave the best price with the least investment. An enhancement to the Act in 1673 ended this practice, but colonists, and New Englanders in particular, continued to sell their goods in accordance with their own wishes – not the English king's or queen's.

Trade Bureaucracy

Europeans were quick to realize that trade and resource exploitation needed to be controlled, or 'regulated', in bureaucratic terms, for colonies to create revenue for their mother countries. Such regulations consisted of licensing, taxation and rules regarding the export of raw goods and creation and dissemination of manufactured ones.

This effort was underway quite early in Atlantic exploration. João II, Portugal's king from 1455 to 1495, established the Guinea Mina House to regulate trade with Africa. The House was charged with licensing ships for trade, storing the goods they returned with, and collecting the king's revenues of these transactions. Such activities later morphed into a Portuguese royal council, which performed much the same function but for trading and colonizing sectors of Africa, Brazil and Asia. By the mid-seventeenth century, this had become known as the Overseas Council. In Brazil, Madeira and São Tomé, its chief function was to keep the all-powerful sugar trade, and all its support trades, profitable.

Within a decade of Columbus's return from his first voyage, the *Casa de Contratación* (House of Trade) was established in Seville, for the purpose of assessing and regulating the flow of New World goods. By 1524, a larger agency, the Council of the Indies, was formed by Spain's Charles I to create colonial policy. Together, these agencies paved the way for many levels of bureaucratic trade and taxation that contributed to the notoriety of the Spanish Atlantic world presence. Some of these, such as the local *cabildo*, or town council, functioned on a local level to regulate trade and markets. Others reflected Spain's diffuse, far-flung empire, which could not be governed easily in a top-down way. Bureaucratic bloating and overlapping were common in the Spanish empire, paving the way for abuse of office, mismanagement and corruption. Still, the New World, with its silver mines and rich soils, enriched the Spanish crown beyond all expectation for generations.

France's early explorers looked towards pelts and codfish to supply a French fortune. New France (French Canada) was an unattractive option for many French people, though, and its population remained puny. Nevertheless, those who were there formed important partnerships for beaver fur, and by 1627 New France was sufficiently lucrative to require oversight from Paris. Armand de Plessis, Cardinal Richelieu, established the Company of One Hundred Associates to encourage settlement, trade and exports. The stakeholders in the colony were men known as *seigneurs*, who were granted large tracts of land that they could then rent to prospective settlers. But with few gains for common people, the colony still failed to excite interest. In 1663, the French king, Louis XIV, made the colony a royal province and developed a bureaucratic superstructure mirroring that of France. New incentives (including the export of willing women to marry male settlers and start colonial families), greater military security, and more resources to enhance the fur trade failed to bring waves of settlement, yet the colony persisted. Its failure to become a truly important pillar in the French economy, however, was apparent when, in 1763, the French bargained away its North American colonies in order to keep their more lucrative Caribbean ones.

England's James I hated tobacco. His 1604 treatise, *A Counterblaste to Tobacco*, asserted that smoking it was dangerous to the body and obnoxious to the senses. Yet, he and his successors would come to value the revenue that the 'stinking weed' produced, and the geographic spread of influence its cultivation encouraged. Virginia's stability, however, was repeatedly challenged by disease, mismanagement and conflict with the local Powhatan Indians, which in turn threatened to disrupt the flow of tobacco revenues. Impatient with the ham-fisted management of the Virginia Company, the crown revoked its charter in 1624 and converted Virginia into a royal colony, with direct control over the tobacco trade. With the growth of English influence and settlement came an increased need for management. In 1651, the English Lord Protector, Oliver Cromwell, issued the first Navigation Act, another pillar in Britain's trade structure. In 1673, Charles II created a subcommittee of his Privy

Council known as the Lords of Trade and Plantations (reorganized in 1696 as the Board of Trade), to manage England's colonies and ensure that trade regulations were followed. Eventually, the British Parliament also became involved in managing the extraction of revenue and taxes from its colonies – an event that would prove to be the major catalyst of the American War of Independence.

The Dutch Republic left much of the administration of its trading ventures in the hands of the companies that managed local affairs. Though many of their investors were Dutch government officials, the Dutch East and West India Companies both had broad powers to start colonies, create and equip armies to protect them, and even build their own warships. By the middle of the seventeenth century, the Dutch had a lean and lucrative New World trading empire that linked North and South America and the Caribbean in the West, and the Netherlands with Africa and Indonesia in the East. Trade towered above all other concerns, so much so that the New World Dutch cared little about who managed their colony, as long as trade remained lucrative. From this assumption comes the legend of Peter Stuyvesant, the Dutch governor of New Amsterdam who tried to rally local men to protect the settlement from English invaders. Upon assurances from the English that their trade interests were safe, the Dutch simply surrendered their arms without firing a shot. Now living in English territory, the Dutch merchants and their descendants were subject to English trade regulations, which became tighter and tighter.

Money

The use of currency fluctuated tremendously throughout the Atlantic world, with currency forms ranging from gold to cowry and clam shells. As mining in Mexico and Peru developed, it increased the amounts of valuable metals in circulation. As Alan Taylor notes, by 1650 the Spanish had exported 16,000 tons of silver and 181 tons of gold from the New World. But this new mineral wealth created problems as well as solving them. For one, it hastened the development of the military in the Spanish New World system, which was itself costly and difficult to maintain.

Creating coinage from raw mineral wealth created a convenient way to make such wealth diffuse, mobile and easily deployed in the settlement of a debt. Indeed, coinage is an ancient system of exchange that had been in use since the sixth century BCE. The mixing of peoples and economies along the Atlantic rim created a greater need for comprehensible currency systems, in which the value of one nation's coin could be understood in the terms of another nation's. Given the profusion of Spanish mineral wealth, and Spain's primacy in the New World, the Spanish dollar (the classic 'piece of eight' of pirate lore) became a standard measure of value that even those outside the Spanish empire could comprehend. Spanish dollars mingled in colonial English cities such as New York and Boston alongside British and local pounds, French *livres*, Dutch guilders and Iroquois wampum. Coins were manufactured in various ways. Some were cut from cobs, or long rolls of metal, with a stamped image. But such coins were sloppy and fragile, and soon lost their value. More time was invested to create coins with milled edges that prevented 'clipping', the practice of shaving off the edges to reduce the weights and true values of the coins. Unscrupulous people could then make new coins from the clipped fragments, thus increasing their buying power without increasing the amount of money spent.

Much of the real value that flowed through the British Atlantic world took the form of bills of exchange. Many throughout the Atlantic world relied on this form of credit, mostly from European banking houses and merchant establishments. Bills of credit were frequently used in place of currency. They were used in transactions between Americans, who wanted to procure English goods more quickly and efficiently. Bills of exchange (also called bills of credit) allowed them to do so at a convenient time. In the meantime, a debt against the purchaser was drawn up by the English merchant, who would then receive either goods or payment that equalled the debt. This enormously complicated system is difficult to understand, yet it was an important part of life in early America, where 'cash and carry' transactions were but one of many. In general, wealthy American consumers spent money before they had it, making them chronically indebted to their English trading partners.

On a local level, and especially outside cities and market towns, barter – the acceptance of one item in exchange for another item – remained common. There were large regions populated with people who rarely, if ever, used coins or bills of exchange for purchases and most other transactions.

Port Cities

Thanks to ever-growing and more complex trade networks, the Atlantic world's port cities became a showcase for the world. Merchants in Africa's port cities sold goods of European manufacture; Europeans and Americans alike seasoned food with spices and other ingredients imported from Africa and as far east as modern-day Java. Coffee, a plantation staple of parts of South America and the Caribbean, became a common beverage not just for the urban elite, but for people of more modest means as well. Tea also travelled more than halfway around the globe for consumption in European and American households, at times served with lavish ceremony, including serving apparatus that came all the way from China.

First and foremost, port cities were points of access for ships, allowing them to either anchor safely or pull up to a large quay to unload their cargo. Humans who manned or travelled on the vessels also needed access. The most successful port cities, such as New York, Havana, London, Seville and Philadelphia, had deep water to allow for the easy passage of ships, and surrounding land masses to shelter the vessels from the ocean's punishing elements. But nature could also be the undoing of great harbours, as Seville would learn: the silty soil of the Guadalquivir River eventually blocked access to shipping and caused the port's decline.

Port cities were necessary, but they all came with disadvantages and dangers (real or perceived) to contemporary society. Chief among these were bored and potentially unruly sailors, whose desires for women and alcohol led to bustling sex trades and a proliferating number of grog shops. Sailors, stowaway vermin, and microbes in cargoes could import disease, insects or invasive species of plants. The great outbreak of venereal syphilis in major European port cities in the wake of Columbus's first New World voyage led to centuries of speculation that that disease was Indian in origin. Other diseases, including yellow fever, cholera and smallpox, were spread by the close quarters and constantly shifting populations of early modern port cities.

In some corners of the Atlantic, certain trades were also suspect and unwelcome. The book trade, for example, presented some challenges, as not all port communities welcomed the messages appearing in print literature on the other side of the Atlantic. Boston Puritans, for example, went to great lengths to keep undesirable reading material out of local bookshops. The Inquisitorial offices of the Spanish colonies likewise attempted to root out heresy, brought to their communities by the texts of Enlightenment thinkers imported from overseas. Port cities were also the gateways for people who professed Enlightenment principles to import these ideas to the New World. One of these, the Spanish-born botanist José Celestino Mutis, ran afoul of the Inquisition in Bogotá, Colombia, for teaching the heliocentric theory of the Polish astronomer Nicolas Copernicus. This is not to suggest, however, that the Spanish were determined to squash all new lines of enquiry. Helped in part by new learning brought by books and migrating intellectuals, Mexico in particular witnessed a flowering of scientific ideas that celebrated new discoveries while maintaining Catholic orthodoxy. The movement of news across the Atlantic also influenced new attitudes. In Spanish America, newspapers and journals brought items of scientific and social interest to their readers. In some cases, powerful church leaders objected; in others, they worked to integrate new ideas into colonial religious life.

Inhabitants of port cities also feared the constant influx of new peoples, from new regions, into their communities. Even healthy sailors were considered a threat to the local population. Drinking and raucous behaviour disturbed the peace. Mainstream houses of worship attempted to counteract the perceived lack of religion of the seafaring life. They also stood in opposition to the persistence of 'occult industries' that relied on the superstitions of the maritime world to sell their charms, spells, fortunes, horoscopes and good-luck charms tailored to those who made their living on the sea. Even Olaudah Equiano, a Christian minister and a particularly zealous one at that, availed himself of the services of a fortune teller when he was in port in Philadelphia.

The inhabitants of port cities were often the first to suffer in times of economic crisis. When war, weather, international economics or downturns in agricultural production threatened trade, work dried up. Those in the cities who made their living off the world of seaborne commerce had few options. Whereas people in the country could turn to alternative, subsistence forms of production, hunting and gathering, city dwellers lacked access to land, and often the skills and tools, to patch their personal economies. Particularly vulnerable were the port cities of British and French North America, where trade patterns were seasonal and winters often long and hard. Sailors were often the hardest hit, followed by small manufacturers of maritime goods and, if they had any, their employees.

Still, as Alan Taylor points out, fewer than five per cent of all the people in British North America lived in port cities. With riches lying elsewhere (chiefly in cultivated fields and forests), none of these cities exceeded 30,000 inhabitants by the time of the American Revolution. By 1776, only four – New York, Philadelphia, Boston and Charleston – had more than 10,000 people.

The buildings of trade encompassed many different types of structures that eventually evolved over time. The cityscapes they were part of existed in their own variations, but they also provided clear visual and cultural links for those who travelled within them.

The specific trade of any given region could require buildings that dominated the skyline. The port cities of coastal Africa were often distinguished by their trading castles. With high walls fortified with cannon, these buildings were forts that both kept both hostile competitors out and, eventually, enslaved humans within. Castles of significant size and breadth became common sights on the sub-Saharan African coast by the seventeenth century, and many European groups erected them, including the Swedes, Dutch and Portuguese. Others, such as the Danes, English, French and Dutch, seized well-developed castles from trade and political enemies whenever they could. Elmina Castle in Ghana, which still exists, was constructed by the Portuguese in 1482, and came to contain a network of dungeons for detaining the captured Africans, fortified walls, trading spaces, open-air yards, barracks, and eventually a chapel. The trading coasts of British North America were linked with wharves, warehouses, ropewalks and the businesses of maritime tradesmen. Communities with deep-water ports built networks of wharves and docks, which allowed for easy connections between vessels and land and facilitating the loading and unloading of peoples and goods, as well as other outfitting and repairs. Wharves were therefore human-made extensions of dry land that allowed maritime workers to bring the things they needed to ensure a smooth voyage right up to the vessel itself. The deeper the port, the larger the vessels it could accommodate. Those with shallower water had to rely on a small navy of smaller boats to move goods and people beyond nature's roadblocks in order to fill vessels with cargo. Wharves, however, were often choked with structures and barrels holding the highly flammable products that made maritime transport possible. An accident that resulted in fire could spell disaster of immense proportions for an entire port city. This was the case when a defective stovepipe in a hat shop on Nantucket became a factor that sealed the island's economic fate: when the fire spread to warehouses full of highly combustible oil and the oil-soaked wharves, it destroyed the economic infrastructure that had taken the island's Quaker merchants a century to develop.

The cities of Latin America also teemed with commercial activity. More often than not, they also teemed with colonial administrators, who kept close tabs on the activities of the urban populations. Administrative buildings therefore commonly went hand in hand with commerce, the more lucrative ends of which were also protected by arms. One of the chief maritime enterprises of the Spanish was the regular Atlantic crossings of the 'treasure fleet', a flotilla of small and large ships moving gold and silver across the ocean. Large and lumbering ships carried the precious metals;

smaller, fleeter, armed vessels protected them as they travelled through pirate-infested waters. The gold exporting centre of Portobelo, on what is today Panama's Atlantic coast, was heavily fortified to protect the city and its important contents from hostile predators, especially pirates. Though they bustled with commercial activity, the coastal towns of Central and South America were poor places to live. Like other port towns, they were plagued by disease, attackers and unruly behaviour. But they also endured heat, humidity and threatening weather, including hurricanes. For those who could live there, cities such as Mexico City, Lima, and Salvator da Bahía in Portugal were more attractive choices. Close to mining and other resource centres such as Zacatecas and Potosí, they were also thriving trading and cultural centres. Their streets were paved and, in the case of Mexico City, their water was fresh, thanks to a feat of Aztec engineering pre-dating the Spanish conquest. They had religious institutions, schools and universities. Building was a booming industry, and the arts flourished. The local economies of Latin America thus supported many diverse industries, nourishing body, soul and intellect – at least for the well-placed in society. They were also the homes of enslaved Africans and Indians, and the urban poor, who lived in cramped quarters and worked at uncertain jobs. In between was a tremendous variety of skilled labourers and tradesmen – blacksmiths and silversmiths, bakers, painters, weavers, caulkers, builders, tailors, shoemakers and shopkeepers – whose skills often provided them with opportunities to accumulate at least some personal wealth. Certainly their employment was steadier than that of the poor, and their goods and services were often available at the large marketplaces that were the centres of so many of the major communities of Spanish and Portuguese America.

Shipbuilding was another trade that dominated the skyline of many port cities. As vessels grew in size and sophistication, their construction in dry dock overtook other landscape features. A well-known print of the building of a warship in Joshua Humphries' Philadelphia shipyard in 1800 shows the bow of the vessel towering over the nearest landmark, Gloria Dei church. Ships needed outfitting (the stocking of a vessel with the materials that allowed for the boat to sail and support a crew), which spurred a whole array of related industries. The maritime powerhouses of British North America consisted of an array of buildings that supported seaborne enterprise, whose function was easily recognizable by their exterior dimensions. Ports often had ropewalks, and extremely long, narrow buildings (some were more akin to elongated covered sheds) that were used for laying out and twisting hemp into rope. Maritime industry ran, in part, on rope, and huge coils of it could be found in the rigging, attached to the anchor, and in the hold in just about any vessel that transported goods or people at any distance. Rigging lofts, which resembled tall, waterfront barns, allowed for the assembly of long and heavy lines of rope.

Some of the largest buildings were those that housed commodities between arrival and distribution. Warehouses were common features in all port cities, and were at times its largest structures, next to churches. Often built of the most durable building materials and secured against thieves, these could be turned to other purposes in times of stress. Sugar houses of prominent New York merchant families were used by the British Army to detain patriot prisoners of war during the American

Revolution. Thus a structure that had come to represent the freedom to accumulate was turned to the ironic means of depriving American patriots of their freedom altogether.

Plantations

In its period understanding, 'plantation' simply meant large farm. It could also mean new colony, as it did with the original name for Rhode Island, 'Providence Plantations'. As agriculture developed, plantations specifically became commercial farms that produced crops for markets, which could rely on any number of labour systems to make them productive. The cultural connotation of the word 'plantation' – a large farm owned by southern North American elites that was highly dependent on human bondage – is also deeply associated with the Atlantic experience. The suggestion that slavery 'made' many elite families throughout the Atlantic world is not far-fetched.

The plantation crops of the Atlantic world required tremendous human effort. With technology primitive by modern standards, every step of the process somehow involved human hands. Individuals were relied upon to plant, weed, hoe, water, remove destructive pests from, harvest, and process all crops for market. Labour needs drove relationships between colonists. The lucky few – 'planters' as they came to be known – owned the land and benefited from just about everything it produced. Working for them were various levels of managers, who kept the hardest labouring – slaves and indentured servants – 'on task'. Some planters also had tenants, who farmed land the planter owned and were often obliged to sell their crop to him. The planter usually set the terms of this relationship, which underscores that there were frequently distinctive characteristics between the powerful and those with less power, in the Atlantic world. Still, tenants and indentured servants had rights that the enslaved almost universally lacked. Chief among them was the potential to rise within colonial society. A difficult road by any standard, it was still a possibility, provided the ambitious survived illness and weathered enough financial downturns to build up a little capital. The ability to rise in some planter societies had the capacity to influence relationships between European nations. This was the case with Jamaica, which was controlled by Spain until 1651. Religious wars gave England's Oliver Cromwell the pretext he needed to seize control of loosely settled Caribbean islands claimed by Spain. When Jamaica came under English control, however, it conveniently provided a place for English colonists of Barbados, where arable land had grown scarce and expensive, to develop new plantations. When Jamaica filled up as well, new would-be farmers moved to the coast of North America to the new colony of Carolina.

Many plantation crops required not only arduous labour while they were still in the ground, but also extensive processing, preserving and packing once harvested. Even a bumper harvest and uneventful processing was not a guarantee of profits. The reliance on transatlantic movement, with its often unpredictable outcomes and the lag time in communication across the Atlantic, could mean that a planter sent out his harvest with one expectation – only to have the sale of the crop return a very different one.

Like other merchants, planters moved in a world of credit. Many of them lived in remote locations, far from neighbours and towns. They used their incomes, and even occasional trips to Europe, to acquire the fashionable goods and luxuries they wanted. Many, like George Washington, for example, dealt with a London trade facilitator (called a 'factor') to whom he shipped his crop and gave instructions for making purchases with the proceeds. The factor then shipped across the Atlantic the goods the planter wanted. This relationship was fraught with difficulties. British North American planters, such as Washington and others, often suspected their factors were not giving them the best prices for their crops or were dishonest in their claims of damage in transit and other issues that kept the planters from receiving maximum profits. And while bad faith in these transactions was common, dependence on the sea made them worse. Goods that were in perfect condition when they left London were subject to all sorts of hazards in transit, leading American planters to conclude that their factors had purchased shoddy goods for them yet charged them a high price. At times, travellers to the Americas with their fashionable clothes and sense of fashion and refinement, coming directly from London, confirmed planters' worst beliefs about their trade relationships.

Planters in British North America might have been men of local importance, but on an Atlantic scale they lacked the clout and status that Britain conferred on its great men at home. Caribbean planters, however, commanded more regard and respect in their mother countries. The difference is explained in terms of their importance to colonial trade, which delivered more net benefits to Europe than any other region of the Atlantic world. As Jan Rogoziński notes, 'By the early 1770's, Jamaica, Barbados and the Leewards … supplied about 24 percent of all goods imported into Britain and took 13.4 percent of all British exports.' These were markets of huge importance, making the people who ran them very important men and women. Sugar profits led to enormous personal fortunes. Planters who established productive plantations were quick to leave the Caribbean and establish themselves and their families back in England. As landowners, they therefore had access to political power. By the 1760s, as Rogoziński states, there were 40 members of Parliament whose fortunes were tied to the Caribbean. This explains in large part why the British Caribbean refused to join the Americans in their bid for freedom from the constraints of the British empire – the wealthiest among them actually *did* possess a political voice back in England, and were therefore assured that their interests were steadily set forward in creating trade policy for the empire.

Manufactures

The objects produced in Europe, purchased by planters such as Washington as well as people of lesser and greater means, were the products of Atlantic movement – and, in many ways, its reason for existing. Before the Industrial Revolution, largely identified as having happened in Britain in the eighteenth century and in the new United States in the nineteenth, there was the 'Industrious Revolution', a term coined by historian Jan de Vries. This period lacks the distinctive leaps in mechanical processes associated with the Industrial Revolution, such as the spinning jenny. Instead, it was something more of an 'attitude' towards work that affected European people of the seventeenth century. Most common among the English, Flemish and Dutch who lived either in small towns or in close proximity to cities, the 'industrious revolution' was categorized by a drive to do piecework for an employer, or for farming people to supplement their income by making goods for local markets. In addition, the money they earned had greater and greater utility, which inspired common people to seek more of it. This apparently sparked the drive not just to create from the market, but also to buy: it is no coincidence that many people of the late seventeenth and early eighteenth centuries owned more household goods than their near predecessors.

Increasingly in the eighteenth century, people throughout the Americas turned to Europe to provide them with textiles, ceramics, books, foodstuffs, tea, wine, decorative arts and luxury goods. Planters even imported complete carriages, as well as fashionable tailored clothing from overseas purveyors. In cities and larger towns, these items were offered for sale by shopkeepers, who often paired up with ship-owning partners to bring in these imports.

Other merchants were engaged in provisioning: that is, connecting the Caribbean plantation colonies with the foodstuffs they needed. With most of the arable land in the Caribbean turned over to the production of plantation crops, planters, workers and colonial bureaucrats needed to import most of their food. This often came from North America where 'provisioning plantations' produced surplus food to be shipped to the islands. The merchant-provisioners of the eighteenth century were particularly skilled in preserving and transporting food. While milk, in the form of a hard-rinded cheese, would keep well, butter would not. It was therefore patted down with heavy salt before being packed into barrels. When it reached its destination, the butter was washed of its excess salt and ready for use. Eggs were cleverly transported suspended in small barrels of honey, the viscosity of which insulated the eggs from the intense heat and kept the delicate shells from breaking. They too often arrived safely even from hundreds of miles away. In Carolina, some early settlers accumulated large herds of cattle. They slaughtered the surplus, salted and packed it in barrels, and sold it in the Caribbean sugar islands for a substantial profit.

With almost every arable acre of the Leewards and Barbados turned over to sugar farming, planters relied on these Atlantic connections to also feed their slaves, importing huge quantities of North American grains and preserved meat and fish. North American producers were therefore frequently *not* the self-sufficient farmers of colonial lore: in their eagerness to improve their station in life they produced what surplus they could for markets outside of their local communities. A healthy percentage of this surplus found its way to the Caribbean. In addition, it undermines the mythology that the so-called 'North' of what is now the United States had always been a region that embraced freedom and relied on free labour. Not only were many labourers not free (they were held to their work by a contract, and slavery was definitely present), but many of the producers for markets elsewhere were making income off the institution of slavery. The same can be said for New England ironworks that fashioned objects ultimately used in the slave trade, or the producers of ironware naval stores, whose tar, pitch, hemp and sailcloth made the functioning of slave ships and the movement of slave-produced commodities possible. It is no coincidence, therefore, that a port such as Newport in Rhode Island rose to prominence in the transatlantic slave trade. It had all the means to build and provision its ships, to man them, and to subdue the human cargo that would soon be taken on board.

Native Americans: Trade Variations

Logistically, trade often followed topographical 'lines of least resistance'. Interiors that linked Europeans with Native American trading partners often relied on waterways, which promised smooth passage downstream and facilitated the growth of local communities. More challenging were the return trips, but if these could be accomplished by either a light current that offered little resistance to paddling, or a trace (a footpath on the water's edge), it made strategically placed trade centres all the more important. This relative ease of passage contributed to the growth of communities such as Albany (known to the Dutch as Fort Orange), near the confluence of the Hudson and Mohawk rivers. The Hudson River was (and remains) relatively easy to navigate, and the Mohawk River, despite some obstructions, brought goods for trade far into the interior while providing easy access for shipment back to Europe.

The Native Americans who came into contact with Europeans were often eager to trade for items they themselves could not manufacture. The fur trade of North America relied almost exclusively on Native American partners. French and Dutch fur traders (called *coureurs des bois* and *beslopers*, respectively), traversed the woods and borderlands, building contacts among the Hurons and Iroquois, who received household goods, tools, and at times guns, all of European manufacture, in exchange for furs. Unfortunately, this led to serious conflict between the Iroquois, who traded primarily with the Dutch, and the Hurons, who were French trading partners. The Iroquois were more numerous and their access to guns more dependable, and in 1649 they came close to wiping out their trade rivals.

Similar contests happened on the borders of Carolina, where the trade in deerskins was lively and most successful when enacted with the help of Indian partners. The very guns the Yamasees, Creeks and other Indian groups traded for, however, often contained the seeds of their undoing: as they ran out of deer to pursue in their own areas, they invaded the territories of neighbouring groups, creating greater competition for the commodity and often all-out war. But guns needed repair, gunpowder and shot, and Europeans were likely to guard these avenues of trade very carefully. When one partner started to lag in the production of skins, it would be denied these critical items. A new group, with fresh access to deer, would then be armed with European weapons for hunting and warfare – often at the expense of the original partners, who lost land and lives in ensuing conflicts.

In Latin America, indigenous peoples and free people of colour were often involved in the movement of goods. They drove oxen and mule teams to move trade goods across challenging landscapes. Those who created carting businesses at the busiest trade crossroads could make handsome fortunes. But they also exposed indigenous people to bandits, hostile enemies and unscrupulous Europeans who, in cheating and stealing from Indians, were rarely prosecuted.

The French who traded with Native Americans sometimes did so with an eye to converting them to Catholic Christianity. Some of the goods they offered in trade, or as presents, were religious in nature (at least to the Europeans). Writing in 1676, Jesuit Jean Enjalran advised his priest-comrades to be aware of the importance of trade and gift-giving to the conversion process, and advised them to bring with them 'medals, small crucifixes a finger in length, or smaller still; small brass crosses and brass rings, also some in which there is the figure of a saint, or the face of Jesus Christ or the Blessed Virgin; wooden rosaries, … [and] knives'. The inclusion of 'knives' suggests that objects that were beautiful and useful were equally desirable. The discovery of the ship *La Belle*, a vessel in René Robert Cavalier's 1685 expedition to claim the mouth of the Mississippi for the French, underscores the point. When the wreck was excavated from its underwater location in Texas's Matagorda Bay – far off Cavalier's mark of the Mississippi, explaining in part why the expedition was ultimately a deadly failure – one of the many items recovered was an intact box of trade goods, both religious and useful in nature, that were to be used to build alliances between the French and Indians throughout the Mississippi Valley. This is one more example of how trade furnished both the motive and the means to expand across the Atlantic.

Local-level Economies

As a general rule, many of the manufactures produced on the western Atlantic littoral stayed on the western Atlantic littoral. Locally produced furniture, clothing, tableware and foodstuffs were often purchased locally. Much was imported, but comparatively little in the way of finished goods was exported.

With the advent of the Consumer Revolution, American producers of finished goods could copy English models with greater accuracy. Families of cabinetmakers, such as the Quaker Townsends and Goddards, made pieces for local buyers that drew inspiration from the work of English craftsman Thomas Chippendale. Artists such as Benjamin West and John Singleton Copley created portraits of exquisite beauty that clearly evoked European styles, again for wealthy clients.

The backbone of local trade was the shop, a general store of sorts that could be found in most well-developed communities. Shopkeepers sold imported items such as coffee, tea, printed calico and sugar. But they also carried locally produced items such as hardware, pottery, tin goods and baskets. Shopkeepers were people of commercial wealth. As people who worked with their hands (versus the genteel classes, which by definition did not), they were on a lower rung of the social order. Yet they were also well versed in the availability of goods, the new trends and styles in Europe, and the tastes of their wealthy patrons. A good shopkeeper did not have access to high society, but he often knew what elites would want in advance of them knowing themselves.

Some popular items were produced and consumed locally, including certain popular forms of alcohol. While rum was produced and shipped throughout the Atlantic world, other alcoholic beverages reflected the region's most available botanical products and were enjoyed near to the means of production. In Mexico, local haciendas produced much of the *pulque*, a beverage made from the agave cactus, for regional consumption. This ancient drink was an invention of the Aztecs and restricted in its ceremonial and class-based uses. After the Spanish conquest, however, it was widely disseminated and became a favourite of the lower classes throughout Mexico. West Africans had long enjoyed a fermented palm wine, but trade with Europe and the western hemisphere brought in wine and distilled beverages. Though Muslim Africans in general adhered to strict religious prohibitions of alcohol use, non-Muslims used imported alcohol for ceremonial purposes. New England and New France's orchards made hard cider and perry, an alcoholic beverage made from fermented pears, regionally popular. So were stronger spirits, which some considered necessary for survival. One traveller to early Canada professed that one needed 'blood of brandy' to survive a Canadian winter. Grain producers throughout North America obliged the cold, sick and thirsty by producing whiskey in their own small stills, retaining some for their own needs but sending the rest to market.

New Englanders enjoyed their liquor, but they also were careful to determine who sold it, and under what circumstances. The same was true for many communities: limiting retailing of liquors to a licensed few controlled both the number of people selling this potentially disruptive product, and also the circumstances of its sale. Licensing for 'ordinaries' (taverns) and inns was likewise common.

Moving Goods on Land

Much of the western hemisphere lacked what modern observers would consider 'good' roads. Paving with stones (often surplus ballast from transatlantic vessels) was fairly common in settled areas throughout the Americas and even the Caribbean. Underwater archaeological investigations of Port Royal, Jamaica, which was sent tumbling into the sea by an earthquake in 1692, revealed that the town had at least some paved sections. But with expense, maintenance and responsibility all at issue, paving was rare to non-existent on longer stretches of road. Most roads linking population centres consisted of the packed earth of the region only. When they threaded through low ground, they could easily turn to mud for weeks and months of the year. High use and saturation often took away soil, leaving roads pock-marked and all but impassable for carts or carriages. Even good roads – level and on high, dry ground – could be made impassable to carts by a falling tree or lack of maintenance. In short, reliance on roads for the movement of goods could be a tricky business, and one had to know any given road's seasonal characteristics before relying on it too heavily. More ambitious communities, however, augmented the desirability of their location by maintaining their road locally, sometimes coerced. Though inhabitants were often not keen on the forced 'volunteering' of either themselves or their workers, they often appreciated the resulting boost in local trade. But the fact that they were not well made or maintained does not detract from their basic utility. Many interior roads were based on Indian trails, pioneered by Native peoples as they travelled seasonally to hunt, fish and gather. They were also based on topographical lines of least resistance and linked important features on the landscape. Many colonists throughout the Americas relied on the paths through this new geography based on the knowledge of those who passed before them.

There were also commonly used alternatives for producers and buyers who needed to move goods without the benefit of waterways. Pack animals were important to the transportation of goods. The Spanish introduced ox teams to the Americas. These sturdy animals were capable of pulling heavily laden wagons across relatively flat surfaces. The more mountainous the terrain, the more traders relied on pack mules, which were quicker and more sure-footed than oxen. In Peru, sure-footed and resilient llamas were the animals of choice.

Travel was often limited by changes of climate and season. Certainly, trade entre-pôts bustled with more than usual fervour during the planting and harvest seasons, when the need for additional goods was greatest and new goods were available for sale. For Catholic New France, the times surrounding major feast days, such as All Saints' and Pentecost, were a time for travel for both the French colonists in the hinterland and Catholic Native American trade allies. It was during these times that Natives, such as the Wabanakis of Maine and Nova Scotia, met with colonial leaders to report news and negotiate other dealings. But the celebratory atmosphere of religious festivals was also a time for bringing goods to market, and using the proceeds of their sales to stock up on new items for themselves.

Wherever possible, goods were moved by water. But this, too, had its challenges once one left the Atlantic littoral and headed into the interiors. Rivers and creeks might be navigable stretches, but most also had challenges of rocks, rapids, waterfalls and shallows. Atlantic peoples dealt with these obstructions by *portaging* around them – that is, walking from one navigable stretch to another. This was common, but also onerous. Making river travel still more difficult was the fact that most have currents that run in one direction, which made travel against the current long and fatiguing.

Consumer Revolution

In most of the Americas and in the Caribbean, complete self-sufficiency was virtually impossible to achieve. While farming families throughout most of the Atlantic world could produce enough food and textiles for regular use, they clearly needed to trade for other items. Metal tools and household goods such as axes, saws, kettles and butchering equipment, at the very least, were produced elsewhere and needed to be purchased. As the eighteenth century wore on, however, many were able to purchase upgraded goods that added refinement to their lives. For the very wealthy, the shift in available goods was profound. The changes in the goods available are collectively known as the 'Consumer Revolution'.

In British North America in particular, this shift in availability and consumption of goods was shaped by several factors. Firstly, decades or centuries of crossing the Atlantic had rendered what was once an unpredictable venture into one that was far more likely to be successful. Larger trade vessels, and larger masts and sails to propel them, resulted in faster Atlantic crossings. Goods were unloaded and consigned to merchants for sale; new cargos loaded; and then the vessel was once again at sea, seeking a new harbour and the hopeful profit that lay beyond.

Shops proliferated, and so did the variety of goods that they sold. In 1761, Boston merchant Samuel Abbot advertised the finished goods imported from London and from as far away as India that graced his shop's shelves:

> a great variety of linnens of all sorts, cambricks, lawns, gauzes, &c. a fine assortment of calicoes, chinces, patches, diapers, table cloths, dimoties, thicksetts, &c., cutlery ware, earthen & glass ware by the crate or box, starch by the cask, best of the French indigo, Kippen's snuff by the cask or dozen, spices of all sorts, dry casks, &c. with too many other articles here to be enumerated.

Similar advertisements at times listed four or five times the number of items that Abbot included in his notice.

For the very wealthy, the Consumer Revolution meant a major transformation in their lives, affecting not only the goods they accumulated but the spaces that housed them. Towards the end of the seventeenth century, most inhabitants of England's North American colonies still lived in relatively modest structures with few luxury goods. Furniture was scant and functional, and its Dutch-inspired, chunky 'William and Mary' style, though not unpleasing, could be thick, heavy and seemingly better suited to a medieval home than a late seventeenth-century one. The combination of Old World and New, however, resulted in a flowering of new styles, techniques and materials to turn into domestic products.

The availability of fine consumer goods and more reliable methods of transporting them led to the rise of 'gentility' among wealthier colonists. Throughout French, British and Spanish America, colonial elites adopted the styles – and with them, methods of behaviour, social interaction and education – normally reserved for the hereditary wealthy back in their mother countries. These ideas were fed by new Enlightenment philosophies of the self-worth and dignity of the individual, and the propriety of self-control and proper manners.

For many colonial elites, their homes became showplaces for both their array of fashionable goods and the rather theatrical impulse to demonstrate to others that they knew how to use them properly. The personal theatre of gentility was augmented by changes in domestic structure. With its emphasis on harmonious proportions, symmetry, light and space, Georgian architecture could be found throughout British America, and even made some inroads in colonial New France. One of the key features of the homes of the elites was the rise of 'personal' versus 'public' space. In the seventeenth century, even the most elite homes lacked space for dedicated tasks. Parlours often doubled as spaces for sleeping; the kitchen room housed many other, non-food-related domestic crafts. Privacy was very limited. In short, however, Georgian buildings on a grand scale did away with the old seventeenth-century version of omnipresent flexible space. Instead, the home's inhabitants – often a nuclear family alone, with perhaps some additional family and, of course, servants – reserved chambers for their own personal use. Many visitors would never see the family's personal space, which was often on a second storey.

Still, observers could see the family at their genteel best, if they wished. Georgian houses often displayed a second new trend – lavish use of glass-paned windows – which allowed observers to peek within to witness the full effect of eighteenth-century gentility. Inside, houses glistened with pewter, silver and china. Panelled walls were painted brightly. Those who could afford mirrors hung as many as possible in their houses. Vanity notwithstanding, mirrors were practical household items that, thanks to their polished reflective surfaces, multiplied the strength of candles. Fewer candles and more mirrors meant fewer hazards (fewer candles to watch and manage) and greater light. Evening entertainment did not have to end when the sun went down, and could consist of dancing, cards and conversation – all enjoyed under the glow of ample interior light.

Patterns of consumption and expressions of gentility varied according to wealth, status and the society one kept. One of the remarkable innovations of the Atlantic movement was that anyone with means, no matter how humble their family origins, could remake themselves through the world of goods. Wealth opened the door for acquiring goods, and economic opportunities provided ever-increasing means of accumulating more. By the middle of the eighteenth century, American elites of French, Spanish, English and Dutch origin for the most part looked and acted like their counterparts in Europe. Some were wealthy enough to afford the refinement of the highest classes – those who, for the most part, were wealthy and powerful thanks to family heritage rather than commercial wealth. Nevertheless, European observers often found the aspiring classes of the eighteenth-century world ridiculous, and poked fun at their inability to get all the details of gentility right. In short, they were still provincials of merchant wealth, even if they dressed and acted as though they were products of 'the better sort' one would find in London, Madrid or Paris. Though they welcomed valuable trade connections with Atlantic world colonists, the elitism of those who had stayed in Europe in lieu of migrating was palpable.

This Euro-elitism led some in British North America to consider European imports wasteful. When hostilities between Britain and its American colonists heated up after 1763, some colonists unleashed their frustrations and patriotic fervour on the imported trade goods they had valued so much. What had been the mark of civility was now converted into a badge of Toryism, as Americans sought to damage Britain through boycotts and demonstrations aimed at overt signs of England's perceived cultural superiority. This is particularly evident in the Boston Tea Party and its copycat incidents.

● **UP FOR DEBATE** Land of opportunity?

Scholars have traditionally interpreted the Americas as a land of opportunity. Other scholars, however, have noted that the transplantation of Old World hierarchies closed off opportunity for many. Take a side on this issue, and back up your position with evidence.

Types of Work

In the context of a world bounded by a huge ocean, it was the merchant – often well educated, with connections on multiple continents – who took a leading role in harnessing the sea in lucrative and inventive ways. Merchants were found chiefly among the Atlantic world's upper classes. As their fortunes increased, they often sought to enhance that standing further still by marrying themselves or their children into elite families, engaging politically and buying land. This was certainly the pattern in Mexico, where merchants of means diversified their holdings through purchasing plantations and producing textiles.

Most Atlantic world merchants relied on the sea for their success. The sea shipped the goods they dealt in; it brought finished goods that they could sell, as well as letters of credit and new potential consumers. But a run of bad luck – the loss of a ship or the ruin of a ship's cargo, the failure or death of a valued business partner – could easily rob one of success, or even bring about ruin. Merchants did what they could to mitigate the hand of fate by keeping scrupulous accounts of their investments and transactions. When they had the means to do so, they expanded their enterprises in other directions, a move that softened the blows the sea might bring to business.

Extended family played a key role in building fortunes throughout the Atlantic world. Merchants needed colleagues who were trustworthy, honest and could think on their feet. Merchant families of fathers, sons, brothers, nephews and cousins fanned out throughout the Atlantic world to guard family interests. One family, the Philipses of New York, had family overseeing diverse interests in London, Barbados, New York City and New York's Westchester County. Boston merchant Ebenezer Storer encouraged his sister Mary, who lived near Montreal, to send one of her sons to work in the family business in New England. The fact that the boy had connections in both New England and Canada and spoke French was no doubt a potential asset to family fortunes. Other merchants and businesspeople sent representatives to open up bases of operation in their name throughout the Atlantic world. Benjamin Franklin was one such entrepreneur, maintaining offices for his printing establishment in both Philadelphia and the Caribbean.

Religious networks were also important to trade relationships. Quaker and Jewish merchants throughout the Atlantic world used well-developed trade routes to look after one another's business interests across the ocean. They also supported one another for moral reasons and to see their co-religionists thrive. Indeed, the children of these merchant families often intermarried, transforming religious sympathizers into literal family.

Though merchants tended to be well educated, and were definitely elites on the local level, they were often disparaged as 'men of commercial wealth' in Europe. Their successes could allow them to retire to a life of rest, contemplation and discreet leadership. Yet in England, France or Spain, they could never aspire to meet the highest societal standards occupied by the aristocracy and, in England, hereditary landowners.

Farmers could be found on every level of Atlantic world society, and great fortunes were made in agriculture. Wealthy planters were, of course, ostensibly farmers, but their landholdings and the commodities they produced allowed the owners to live as gentlemen. Similarly, New Spain's *encomederos* claimed huge parcels of land from the crown, as well as the right to compel labour or exact tribute from the Native people who had hitherto occupied the land. This grossly unjust system created huge family fortunes and deprived many Natives of their autonomy and self-determination. The elites this system created were often politically and socially active, influencing policy, setting trends and demanding deference from their 'inferiors'.

Most farmers were of more modest means, and they never escaped the need to work with their hands. Some had the labour of their children for support; others hired servants or, if they had the means, purchased one or a few slaves. For farming families, the cycles of work were fairly constant. Seasonal steps needed to be taken, year after year, to optimize planting and growing cycles. Their livestock needed constant care even during the period of lowest agricultural demand, from January to March. Even so, there were different types of farming, and each demanded different knowledge of the soil and climate, or insects and optimal harvesting, and of storing and preserving. Spring, summer and autumn saw many small farmers consumed with work in their planting fields, day after day. Rising early, they tended to animals, and then to more systematic crop-related work. Other critical tasks involved building fences, making repairs to tools and outbuildings, and the arduous task of clearing new fields. Farmers were on constant guard to product their livestock from marauding animals. Crops required constant protection, from insects while in the field, and from pests and vermin once harvested.

Subsistence farmers had small landholdings and produced just enough on an annual basis to feed their families, with little surplus to sell for cash. More prosperous farmers grew enough for comfort, plus surplus for key purchases and some luxuries. The Dyckmans of northern Manhattan, New York, are an example of this class of farmer. By the late eighteenth century, they were farming almost 400 acres, including many of apple and cherry trees. They also kept livestock. Their home, though modest, was well built and fairly large. The American Revolution temporarily ended the family's prosperity: a detachment of Hessians camped on their land for years, and the British occupied their abandoned house, only to burn it upon evacuation. The Dyckmans, however, rebuilt, and devised new ways to use their property to produce income. They built a new house, which they ran as an inn for about a decade, and also rented pasturage to drovers who moved herds from nearby Westchester County to the slaughterhouses in lower Manhattan. Eventually, they remodelled their modest home to conform more closely to genteel standards. And while some of their sons remained as farmers, others pursued careers in medicine, business and law.

Women were producers throughout the Atlantic world. The Europeans who first observed Native American women of the north-eastern woodlands complained that the men treated them as drudges, expecting their wives to do the hard, physical work as they themselves engaged in the pleasurable pursuits of hunting, fishing and relaxing. Women were traditionally the agriculturalists in most North American cultures, and seemed to mind little that their work was more consistent than that of their spouses (which, as many Europeans failed to mention, had its busy seasons). Still, women on both sides of the Atlantic had much in common in terms of the world of work. While many juggled this work with bearing and caring for children, they remained fundamental to the economic success of their families.

As Laurel Ulrich has described her, Beatrice Plummer of Newbury, Massachusetts, engaged in baking, cooking, brewing, slaughtering smaller animals, creating and tending the fire (no small task), pickling and cleaning, among other things. Another woman documented by Ulrich – the Maine midwife Martha Ballard – not only tended to a busy household but also found the time to deliver hundreds of babies over a decade-spanning career. Though Martha never described the 'presents' made to her in exchange for medical care as income, it is clear that she contributed to her family's material success. It was not only the women in culturally English colonies who worked to support their families. *Casta* paintings from seventeenth- and eighteenth-century Mexico illustrate women of modest means engaged in various tasks, including rolling cigarettes, spinning yarn and selling prepared food in public.

If possible, families sought to marry particularly desirable children into better families than their own, thus raising the status of their child in society and providing venues for siblings to meet equally desirable spouses. Thus education for elite females, which is often considered 'ornamental' at best, was actually anything but. Women who showcased desirable skills of music, dancing, public refinement, sewing and grace only enhanced their natural beauty in the eyes of potential suitors. This in turn could lead to a better marriage, in socio-economic terms, than the generation before had enjoyed, raising family prestige and facilitating important connections. In Latin America, innocence and purity were highly desirable virtues, which led to young women being shut away from much of the world to focus on pious pursuits and 'womanly' arts. Any hint of scandal or impurity could ruin a daughter's chances of making a good marriage for herself and alliance for her family. Thus young women and girls of marriageable age sometimes became commodities in and of themselves – to be shown around for the best offer, and the best connections to the family a marriage could afford. The *tangosmãos* of the sub-Saharan African littoral saw their children intermarry, which in turn kept the power of trade within the hands of certain families. The *tangosmãos* often faced ostracism because of their mixed-raced ancestry, yet their continued intermarriage and control of family resources meant that real economic power remained concentrated in their hands.

Children too were part of the family economy, assisting families in feeding themselves and, if fortunate, achieving material advantages. Older children in households of more modest means helped parents tend and harvest crops; preserve food; take care of animals; produce textiles, soap, candles, cigars and leather goods; and run small businesses. In the homes of skilled artisans, adolescent sons often learned the crafts of their fathers and helped in their shops. Some went to sea, even enlisting on whale ships at an early age. Younger children freed up the hands of their busy mothers by relieving them of the burden of watching even smaller siblings – sometimes with tragic results. Children learned to use the tools of various trades, even those that by the standards of today would be considered highly dangerous. They worked knives, sickles, hammers and guns, and performed household tasks that involved kettles of boiling hot fluid, barrels of scalding lye, and open flames.

Much of the mercantile world touched at least in some way on enslaved labour. It was thoroughly integrated into sugar production, a commodity that, due to decreased fertility after years of planting, became profitable again only through new technologies and more working slaves. Still, not all enslaved Africans worked in agrarian settings. In the Dutch North American colonies in particular, enslaved Africans filled a labour void left by a shortage of labourers from Europe and constituted a significant percentage of the workforce.

Then as now, a servant is someone who is in the service of another. Such a relationship conjures up ideas of inequality, and in particular, slavery. But while all enslaved people were, in one way or another, servants, not all servants were enslaved. Many had rights protected by law, and their duties and restrictions on their uses were governed by either a contract or a raft of basic rights. Protecting those rights was another issue: abuse of servants was common, those who had no status in society being the most vulnerable. In Latin American society, these were often women who lacked male protectors such as husbands, fathers and brothers. The most obvious of these were often young unmarried women working for others. Throughout the Atlantic world, those living on plantations far from other neighbours were similarly vulnerable. Still, the threat of abuse, or even death (court cases involving servant murder were tragically common), did not stop early modern people from embracing the potential advantages of temporary or permanent servitude. These incentives ranged from tools and clothes to set oneself up as a farmer in one's own right to promises of education. Servants were integral to making a farm, shop or even home productive. A passing phase of life for many, it sometimes provided the poor and friendless with important experience and, if lucky, friends in higher places than their own. For some, liberation from servitude could signal the right to rise. The key to rising in Atlantic world society was one's capacity to gain access to, recognize and successfully exploit economic opportunities.

CHAPTER CHRONOLOGY

1324	Ruler of Mali, Mansa Musa, goes on pilgrimage to Mecca, spending so much on luxuries and slaves that he upsets local economies.
1482	Portuguese crown establishes the *Casa de Índia* (known by other names, including the Guinea Mina House), to regulate spice trade with Africa.
1524	Charles I of Spain establishes the Council of the Indies.
1545	Spanish start mining for silver at Potosí.
1602	Dutch East India Company founded.
1610	Tobacco cultivated in Virginia for the first time.
1624	New Amsterdam established by the Dutch: it will become a major trade entrepôt on the Hudson River.
1627	The French establish the One Hundred Associates to encourage trade and settlement in New France.
1649	The Iroquois Indians destroy their rivals, the Hurons, to achieve dominance in the fur trade with Europeans.
1660	Charles II of England's First Navigation Act applies trade parameters to certain New World commodities.
1663	England's Second Navigation Act closes off most direct trade between English colonies and Europe.
1673	Third Navigation Act closes loopholes that had allowed North American colonists to trade duty free.
1675	England established the Lords of Trade to regulate and oversee, among other things, colonial trade.
1717	By reducing taxes on sugar, the French attempt to corner the market on the commodity.
1733	The Molasses Act aims at curbing smuggling between New England and the Caribbean.
1750	Paper money issued in Virginia.
1763–74	A series of policies aimed at taxing Britain's North American colonies propels the region towards revolution.

■ PRIMARY SOURCES AND STUDY IMAGE

'Diario' of Christopher Columbus (1492–3)

Being at sea, about midway between Santa Maria and the large island, which I name Fernandina, we met a man in a canoe going from Santa Maria to Fernandina; he had with him a piece of the bread which the natives make, as big as one's fist, a calabash of water, a quantity of reddish earth, pulverized and afterwards kneaded up, and some dried leaves which are in high value among them, for a quantity of it was brought to me at San Salvador; he had besides a little basket made after their fashion, containing some glass beads, and two blancas by all which I knew he had come from San Salvador, and had passed from thence to Santa Maria. He came to the ship and I caused him to be taken on board, as he requested it; we took his canoe also on board and took care of his things. I ordered him to be presented with bread and honey, and drink, and shall carry him to Fernandina and give him his property, that he may carry a good report of us, so that if it please our Lord when your Highnesses shall send again to these regions, those who arrive here may receive honour, and procure what the natives may be found to possess.

'Commercial Orders to Governor Andros, Royal Governor of New England' (1686–7)

Sir,

Having notice that under colour of a trade to Newfoundland for fish, great quantities of wine, brandy and other European goods, are imported from thence into his Majesty's plantations, particularly New England, on an allegation, that the said New Foundland is accounted as one of the said plantations. To which purpose, it is now become a Magazine of all sorts of goods brought thither directly from France, Holland, Scotland, Ireland and other places, which is not only contrary to law, but greatly to the prejudice of his Majesty's Customs, and to the trade and navigation of this Kingdom. To the end, therefore, that so destructive and growing an evil may be timely prevented, we desire you, for his Majesty's service, to give public notice to all persons concerned within your government, that the New Foundland is not to be taken or accounted a plantation, being under no Government or other regulation, as all his Majesty's plantations are. But that all European goods, imported from thence, will be seized, together with the ships importing the same, as forfeited by the act of trade, made in the 15th year of his late Majesty's reign, and his said Majesty's Proclamation pursuant thereunto. And you are strictly to give in charge to all his Majesty's officers, that they be very careful not to suffer any European goods, other than what are by the aforesaid law and Proclamation accepted, to be imported into New England …

We are

Your most humble Servants,

T. Chudleigh.

Ch. Cheyne

D. North.

Jo. Wenden

J. Butler.

Buckworth

The General Advertiser (New York, 22 October 1767)

HENRY BREVOORT,

At the sign of the Frying-Pan, in Queen's-street,/ between the Fly-Market and Burling's Slip, has/ lately imported and will sell on the lowest terms,/ wholesale and retail;/

A neat and general assortment of ironmongery,/ viz, iron pots, kettles, skillets, dogs, and cart/ boxes, brass kettles, Dutch and English tea kettles,/ copper, brass, and iron chafing dishes, chamber and/ common bellows, brass and iron candlesticks, brass/ and steel snuffers and stands, Dutch and English/ chimney backs, sheet iron, hearth tiles, best blister'd/ and faggot steel, bar and sheet lead, frying pans,/ gridirons, saucepans and coffee pots, brass and iron-/ headed tongs and shovels, smoothing irons and/ warming pans, buck and bone table knives and forks,/ cuttoes and penknives, scissors and shears, brass and/ iron door locks, long and square brass nob'd [sic] latches,/ brass and iron spring bolts, stock locks, padlocks,/ chest locks and hinges, brass and iron H hinges,/ HL do [ditto], strap hinges, cross garnet dovetail and but [sic] do,/ hooks and hinges of many sizes, brads, tacks, clout/ and sharp trunk nails of all sizes, hob nails, 4d,/ 8d, 10d, 12d, 20d, and 24d nails, carpenters/ hammers, axes, augers, and gimblets, chissels, gou-/ges, rools [sic] and compasses, awl blades, tacks, pin-/cers, nippers, size sticks and shoe knives, files and/ shovels, ditching ditto; an assortment of pewter/ plates, platters and basons [sic], very best Scotch snuff,/ redwood, slates and pencils, round and side sweep-/ing brooms, hand brushes, cloth and shoe do, round/ and long rubbing ditto, hatters and buckle brushes,/ house-bells, springs and carriages, fine sailmakers[sic]/ sewing twine, with many other articles in the iron-/mongery way.

Study image 4 *'Tobacco Production, French West Indies', from Jean Baptiste Labat, Nouveau voyage aux isles de l'Amerique (Paris, 1722), vol. 4.*

Recommended Reading

David Birmingham, *Portugal and Africa* (London, 1999). Explores the parameters of this critical encounter in Atlantic and global history.

C. R. Boxer, *The Dutch Seaborne Empire, 1600–1800* (New York, 1995). Describes the rise and fall of the Dutch as a major maritime player, with special attention paid to technological and trade innovations.

T. H. Breen, *The Marketplace of Revolution: How Consumer Politics Shaped American Independence* (Oxford, 2005). Argues that although the colonists of Britain's North America colonies shared little else, they spoke a common language of commerce and upward mobility that shaped the American Revolution.

Philip Curtin, *The Rise and Fall of the Plantation Complex* (Cambridge, 1998). Collection of essays considering the global impact of American plantation systems, from their evolution through their decline in the nineteenth century.

David Hancock, *Oceans of Wine: Madeira and the Emergence of American Trade and Taste* (New Haven, 2009). An important entry in the literature on the history of specific commodities, examining, in this case, the manufacture, trade and social dimensions of Madeira wine.

Sidney Mintz, *Sweetness and Power: The Place of Sugar in Modern History* (New York, 1985). One of the first commodity histories, it explores, among other things, the transforming effects of sugar in Atlantic and global history.

David Ormrod, *The Rise of Commercial Empires: England and the Netherlands in the Age of Mercantilism* (Cambridge, 2008). Examines the factors that led to the pre-eminence of two Protestant powers in manufacture and trade.

Anthony Pagden, *Lords of All the World: Ideologies of Empire in Spain, Britain and France, c.1500–c.1800* (New Haven, 1995). An exhaustive comparative treatment of the three major European powers in the Americas.

Ian Steele, *The English Atlantic, 1675–1740: An Exploration of Communication and Community* (Oxford, 1986). Demonstrates the effectiveness of communications and movement of people and goods between various English spheres of influence.

James D. Tracy, *The Rise of the Merchant Empires: Long-Distance Trade in the Early Modern World, 1350–1750* (Cambridge, 1991). Explores early modern trading empires, and argues that Europeans did not dominate global trade.

TEST YOUR KNOWLEDGE

1 What was the connection between early Atlantic exploration and the drive to trade?
2 How did Europeans attempt to regulate trade within their own nations and spheres of influence?
3 How did mercantilism reinforce this control?
4 What was the so-called 'Consumer Revolution'? What factors affected its development?
5 What were some of the challenges involved in moving goods from point of production to point of sale?
6 What role did agriculture play in various Atlantic economies?
7 What were some of the specific attributes of port cities? How did a good port enhance the wealth of an Atlantic community?
8 How did trade and business concerns affect Atlantic families?
9 What specific work did merchants perform? On what other industries did they rely?

5 Atlantic Religion: Beliefs and Behaviours

As historian Carla Gardina Pestana has noted, 'European religion, especially Christianity, invaded the Atlantic World and was dramatically transformed in the process.' Indeed, Pestana speaks of changes to European Christianity that had been evolving for centuries. The experience of Atlantic encounters was one more element of this evolutionary process.

It is a mistake to view the story of Atlantic encounters as either a triumphal or a tyrannical story of Christian conquest. The peoples of the Atlantic world were by no means all Christians nor, of course, did they all eventually become Christians. If anything, the Atlantic experience *challenged* Old World Christianity as much as it reinforced it by creating many more possibilities for travellers to encounter the religious 'other'. Furthermore, non-Christians seized upon new opportunities to leave oppressive religious environments to preserve their own practices. In addition, peoples of the Old World and the New, specifically Africans and Indians, had little or no exposure to Christianity and cherished their own beliefs. And it cannot be forgotten that exploration of the Atlantic World unfolded against a backdrop of Europeans' own wrestling to figure out what it actually meant to be a Christian. This chapter explores topics related to the remarkable flowering of religious belief in the wake of Atlantic encounters, with special attention paid to topics of convergence, influence and transformation of this truly dynamic force in the lives of many Atlantic people.

Converging Religions: Belief at the Time of Encounter

By the fifteenth century, Europe was home to Muslims, Jews, Orthodox Christians, and practitioners of nature-based spiritual systems, among others. The dominant religion, however, was Catholic Christianity. But soon, the rise of a new Christian form would topple Catholicism's primacy.

This is known historically as the Protestant Reformation. The first critical event of what would become the Reformation happened two years before the Mexican mainland was invaded by the Catholic Spanish, and the flowering of Protestantism unfolded against the same backdrop of Atlantic exploration by Europeans. When Martin Luther, an Augustinian monk, challenged the Catholic Church directly in 1517, he touched off a chain of events that would have profound consequences for people of the developing Atlantic world. Luther's numerous complaints against late medieval Catholicism were not entirely new; within western Christianity reformers had been calling for change for centuries. Addressing Luther's criticisms, however, required more than just changes to Catholicism: it required separation from the old faith. With Protestantism's birth, Europe's Christianity's inextricable ties to politics saw newly identified Protestant and Catholic monarchs viewing religious difference as pretext for conflict and competition.

Reform movements inspired religious change from Scotland to Poland, Scandinavia to southern France. Most Christians in Spain, Portugal, Italy and pre-conquest Ireland retained their association with Catholicism. France eventually had a sizeable Protestant population and, at one time, a Protestant-born monarch (Henry IV, who converted to Catholicism to inherit the throne). The Lowlands were split, with some parts emerging heavily Protestant (largely today's Netherlands) and others heavily Catholic (modern Belgium). Various German principalities were also split. By the mid-sixteenth century, so was Scotland, with Lowland Scots of the south adopting Protestantism, and Highlanders often retaining ties to Catholicism. Scandinavia was largely Protestant, and England became so as well. The Holy Roman Empire, a political structure holding a sizeable chunk of Europe in uneasy alliance, attempted to enforce Catholic solidarity, but as with France, significant Protestant communities could be found within its borders and, of course, the Lowlands, over which it asserted its power. But such generalities tell only part of the story. In every region of Europe, even places as seemingly homogeneous as Italy, people discovered – and were attracted by – Protestant ideas.

Persecution of the religious 'other' was common, forcing the truly committed to find ways to hide their beliefs. Some Protestants in Catholic territories practised in secret; others were found out and prosecuted as heretics. In England, believers known as 'recusants' retained their Catholic identity and received the sacraments, often from priests who travelled incognito and hid in 'priest holes', or cupboard-like chambers buried in the walls of the houses of wealthy Catholics.

Because Protestantism broke with the Pope, the head of the Catholic Church in Rome, its theorists were free to develop their understandings of Christ's teachings away from the oversight of a centralized power. This freedom, however, soon spurred new theological insights and charismatic leaders. Luther's followers became innovators in their own right. The most influential of these was John Calvin, whose doctrine of predestination insisted that nothing a believer could do in this life would influence their fate in the next. This might seem like a recipe for despair for the deeply religious, yet many found it a liberating challenge to spend their lives looking for signs of their salvation. In England, these particular Protestants came to be known as Puritans. Although most were still communicants of the official Church of England while they remained in the mother country, emigration to the New World allowed them to develop religious communities in accordance with their principles and away from the prying eyes of Church of England leaders.

Responding to Protestantism's reorientation of Christianity and the population it attracted, Catholicism experienced its own Reformation. This collection of reforms has long been called the 'Counter-Reformation', which reflected a common belief that the remainder of Catholicism redefined itself in opposition to Protestantism in all ways. More recent scholars such as R. Po-Chia Hsia, however, argue that Catholicism's reforms were much more complex and far-reaching, and even at times progressive, affecting doctrinal changes, politics, social and cultural interactions, and Catholicism's response to the religious and cultural 'other'. Some of the most important innovations to the story of the Atlantic world came in the form of new Catholic religious orders, or groups of men and women who had taken vows to live in religious communities and abide by their laws. Enthused with new ideas that took religious people out of the monastery and into the world, men and women became missionaries, nurses and educators who performed worldly services while spreading the word of God. Many, it turned out, would view the lands across the Atlantic as an outlet for their zealous energies.

It was tragically common for officials or rank-and-file believers of one Christian form to persecute the religious 'other' in their midst. Christian-against-Christian violence reached horrific peaks in incidents like France's Saint Bartholomew's Day massacre of 1572, where thousands of French Protestants, called Huguenots, were slaughtered by Catholic neighbours. A legacy of distrust, and memories of persecution, crossed the Atlantic with Europe's immigrants and frequently influenced events on the ocean's western littoral.

The Spanish and English defined themselves as Catholic and Protestant colonizers, respectively. The Spanish were deeply determined to convert Indians and spread Catholicism, and by the end of the sixteenth century, the English became aware of the need to check Catholic growth in the New World. Thus the rhetoric of religion became a powerful tool for knitting would-be colonizers together in common purpose. And, as will be seen, the French and the Dutch presented different models of the religious dimensions of exploration, encounter and settlement, thus complicating the idea that all colonizers viewed the Atlantic world with the same ideas of religious conquest in mind.

By the end of the sixteenth century, both Protestantism and Catholicism had redefined what it meant to be Christian. This extended even to religious art, which was largely rejected by Protestants and subject to new guidelines for Catholics. Many Catholic missionaries would eventually conclude that their forms of worship had parallels with Indian ones, and would use them to give Catholicism a toehold in Native American life. Europeans who sought to extend Christianity's influence to Africa encountered a different set of realities and challenges.

Like Europe, the fifteenth-century African continent was home to several significant faith systems that were frequently in competition with one another. Islam predominated in the north and some of the sub-Saharan regions. Christianity already had a long history along Africa's Mediterranean rim, with saints of African origin, most notably Augustine, Cyril of Alexandria and Athanasius, playing important roles in its early development and spread. The Portuguese traders of the fifteenth century brought their Catholicism with them down Africa's western coast, building churches and missions. When powerful African coastal families intermarried with the

Portuguese, new generations of culturally mixed children were raised in ways that integrated both traditional African beliefs and Catholicism. The vast majority of West and West Central African people practised diverse forms of animism, a set of beliefs that venerated the spirits of living things, the souls of one's ancestors, and compassionate and malevolent supernatural beings. Many of these cultures, however, and in particular those between the Senegal and Gambia Rivers, had contact with Islam and appropriated some of its practices. Others, such as the various coastal peoples of West Africa, invested water with deep spiritual meaning and made offerings to its numerous spirits. Still others were pantheists with gods who corresponded with plants, animals, topographical features and natural phenomena. Still others, particularly those in the Kingdom of Kongo, adopted some form of Catholicism. John Thornton notes that partial responsibility for the ensuing religious bonds comes from the fact that both the Kongolese and Catholics believed in the power of revelation through dreams. Kongolese rulers harnessed this compatibility by building Catholic churches and inviting their clergy to proselytize to the local people. Nevertheless, the conversion process remained slow and, by Christian standards, incomplete. When Queen Njinga professed Christianity in 1655, Christians regarded this as a miracle. The Queen, however, attributed her conversion to the intervention of her ancestors, who spoke to her through the intermediary of a *xingula* (medium) and urged her to become a Christian. What followed for the Kongolese people was, as Thornton observes, the merging of local spirits and deities with Catholic angels and saints. This pattern of syncretism – the blending of two belief systems in equal measure to form something new – would become a hallmark of the religious trajectory of enslaved Africans.

The people of the pre-contact Americas were as religiously diverse as their contemporaries in Europe and Africa. Creation stories emphasizing the role of a god or gods in the creation of the world and of humanity, such as the Mayan *Popol Vuh* and the Iroquoian story of Sky-Woman, were common to groups throughout the Americas. For some Europeans such as Jesuit missionaries, the similarities these religious elements bore to their own sacred text, the Bible, convinced them that the convergence of Indians and Europeans was part of God's divine plan.

Like Europeans and Africans, powerful Native American empires organized some of their cultural features around key religious traits. The Mexica of the Aztec empire, for example, believed they were a chosen people whose duty it was to honour their god, Huitzilpochtli, with human blood. At its height, worship of Huitzilpochtli demanded tens of thousands of victims. The supply of sacrificial victims for Mexica worship centres was replenished through nearly constant warfare, which had become a central organizing principle for the Aztec empire. Also sacrificed to the Aztec pantheon of gods were children, who were believed to supply tears to the rain god, Tlaloc. These ceremonies horrified European observers (who, ironically, were not above killing religious rivals in the name of God), but they served as a powerful force for binding the Mexica together in a common identity and for common purposes.

Like the Catholic and Protestant powers that vied to control the Americas and the Caribbean, the Mexica used religion as a tool of empire. Children were educated in the ways of Mexica religion and warfare in schools. Young boys from prominent families received their education at the *telpochcalli* ('house of youth'). The sons of families at the highest stratum of Mexica society were further educated in the *calmecac* ('priests' house'), where they were prepared for their futures as priests, imperial administrators and warriors.

Spiritual beliefs among Caribbean Indians were local in nature, reflecting their lives in smaller island communities. These belief systems were often ravaged along with their populations, as disease and war left few survivors to preserve religious traditions. Still, they survived in other forms, and appeared in new post-encounter forms when they merged with Christianity and African religious practices to form new faiths, including Vodou ('Voodoo') and later, Obeah.

In contrast, the religious beliefs of many of North American Indians operated on a local level. Most faith systems were based in the belief that the world was infused with spirits, present in all things throughout the natural world. Animals and plants were thus linked to the same spirit world as humans and were therefore handled with respect. People drew guidance from legends and allegorical stories that spoke of their origins, which had been handed down orally from generation to generation.

For eastern woodland people, religious ceremonies were the demesne of a shaman. Usually male, shamans healed the sick and gave blessings to warriors on their way to battle. In early Virginia, shamans tended temples that housed the bones of deceased leaders and statues representing powerful deities. As the figures within Native bands who wielded supernatural powers, they were of special interest to invading Jesuit missionaries, who sought to unseat them by undermining their powers in public.

Encounter and Atlantic Movement

Many Christians were inspired to move into the broader Atlantic by conditions at home. Major changes in Europe's religious balance of power affected the lives of believers in profound ways.

In both Moorish Iberia and medieval Portugal, Jews, Christians and Muslims were more or less free to pursue business and scholarly interests. This created a level of interfaith toleration that was rare for its time in Europe. The fifteenth century and the Spanish *Reconquista* in particular, however, signified the beginning of the end for such tolerance. The Spanish Catholics who emerged from centuries of fighting religious outsiders increasingly viewed religious diversity not as an ideal, but as a danger to their newly achieved victory. The Reformation added yet another justification for Spaniards who longed for religious and cultural purity, and the ensuing brutal persecution of Jews, Muslims and suspected Protestants within the Spanish empire became a hallmark of Spanish life in the sixteenth century. This sense of urgency to control religious belief within its sphere of influence was turned outward during the age of encounter. Believing in the importance of religious purity for a well-managed society, Spanish conquistadors, as well as many of the Catholic clergy directed to bring

Catholicism to the Indians, turned to extreme measures to force Indians to convert. Others used Christianity more cynically by claiming that those who rejected conversion were free to be enslaved – or worse. These perverse tactics were described by Bartolomé de Las Casas, a Spanish colonist who renounced worldly goods to become a Dominican priest. His *Short Account of the Devastation of the Indies*, published in Spain in 1552, recounted these raw abuses of religion and power. Though they unfolded slowly, Las Casas's arguments eventually had an impact on the way the Spanish crown managed settler–Indian relations, resulting in orders that disallowed physical abuse of Natives, theft of their possessions, or violation of Native American women. Such directives might have become official, but in an empire as diffuse and distant as Spanish North America, enforcement was impossible.

The Spanish attempted to transplant the Catholic Church, with all its structures, to the Americas. The New World's challenges – of distance from the mother country, dispersed population, numbers of non-Catholics, and willingness of Catholic clergy to leave Europe for New Spain – left the transplanted church with a reduced leadership structure. In Portuguese Brazil, the clergy, and specifically Jesuit missionaries, clashed almost from the beginning with Portuguese planters, who resented the priests' attempts to halt the enslavement of local Indians and their capacity to acquire land and possessions. For the Indians themselves, life in the missions was almost as undesirable as slavery. Indians throughout New Spain and Brazil often had few other options beyond living at Jesuit *reducciones* and farming, creating handicrafts, and maintaining the mission's structures and animals. Though not slaves per se, Indian people from Paraguay to California were treated harshly if they tried to leave these missions, and their labours made the Iberian Jesuit missions very wealthy.

As they did in other parts of the Atlantic world, the Caribbean's Christian settlers transplanted their faith to the New World. Yet the Caribbean remained, in many ways, virtually the least Christian area of the Atlantic world. In part, planters of both the Catholic and Protestant variety lived lives that were poor examples of ideal Christian behaviour. Fearful of Christianity's potentially radical message (a fear that was upheld by the clear Christian dimension to almost every major slave insurrection), the planters forbade the local clergy to attempt to convert enslaved Africans, who in some places comprised 90 per cent of the population. Until the nineteenth century, mainstream Christianity was often confined to towns and administrative centres, where there were high concentrations of white Christians. In the countryside, where enslaved Africans far outnumbered whites, African religious practices survived and thrived with little Christian interference.

Christianity spread through North America slowly, in part because the numbers of Europeans were comparatively small. In addition, Europeans often recognized that their colonies would succeed only if they maintained respectful trade partnerships with Indians. Indians themselves were often unimpressed by the Christians they encountered and saw no reason to renounce their own beliefs for those of the newcomers. Furthermore, the newcomers themselves (such as those at Jamestown) were often more interested in exploration and trade than spreading religious influence. They allocated few resources to Christian evangelization, the term used for attempting to gain converts for a specific religious vision.

As the consequences of European invasion became clear, however, Native American attitudes towards Christianity changed over time. Traditional communities lost numbers and became fragmented, and new beliefs and alliances with Christians became more attractive. Some were drawn to the new religion by its seemingly magical elements. Another group adopted a syncretic approach, embracing those elements of Catholicism that complemented Native American belief systems. A final category of converts found in Catholicism the means to protect their souls and bodies in ways their original religious beliefs seemed to lack. An example of this impulse is the story of Catherine (Kateri) Tekakwitha, a Mohawk Indian who, according to her Jesuit biographer, fervently embraced Catholicism's deep respect of female virginity to avoid marriage with an uncle.

Nevertheless, many aspects of Christianity remained puzzling and contradictory. A lack of religious concepts such as sin and hell within the Indian world view sometimes put Indians on a collision course with the missionaries, who saw it as their job to incorporate a sense of shame, guilt and desire for forgiveness into the beliefs of their neophytes. When Native leaders sought to reassert traditional community religious practices, they sometimes encountered brutal repression. These circumstances led to the Pueblo Revolt of 1680. Organized by a charismatic shaman named Popé, various Pueblo groups laid aside their differences and overthrew the repressive local Spanish civil and religious leaders with great violence. It took more than a decade for the Spanish to reassert control, and when they did, the missionaries who came to the region were considerably more respectful of Pueblo ways.

For Catholics, the Atlantic provided a conduit for encountering Protestants, and vice versa. Though levels of tolerance varied and coexistence was extremely rare, religious diversity was present even in its earliest stages. By 1644, a French Jesuit priest, Isaac Jogues, was saved from ritual torture from the Iroquois by Dutch Protestant trappers, who took the wounded man to New Amsterdam for treatment and passage back to France. While recuperating among the Dutch, Jogues wandered the city at will, remarking on its variety of peoples, languages (he counted 16) and cultural traditions. The spirit of Jogues's observations was captured in 1687 by royal governor Thomas Dongan. Himself a Catholic, Dongan identified many of the sects that combined to create New York's religious pluralism: 'Here bee not many of the Church of England; few Roman Catholicks; abundance of Quakers preachers men and Women especially; Singing Quakers, Ranting Quakers, Sabbatarians; antisabbatarians; Some Anabaptists; some Independents; some Jews; in short, of all sorts of opinions there are some, and the most part [are] of none at all.' The groups Dongan described cohabitated peaceably, yet the religious climate in Europe often dictated the levels at which diverse religions would be tolerated. The years to come would find the radical Dutch Calvinist Jacob Leisler in control of the colony. He and his followers claimed to do so to protect Protestants in New York from 'Popish Doggs & Divells', and went about arresting other colonists on suspicion of being Catholics. Though Leisler's Rebellion was short-lived, fears of a Catholic conspiracy against

New York arose several more times in the coming centuries. A notable outbreak of anti-Catholic hostility came in the wake of a feared conspiracy among the city's slaves, Irish colonists and black Catholic Spanish sailors. One of the casualties was John Ury, an itinerant teacher whose knowledge of Latin suggested he was a priest and responsible for inciting the violence. Ury's case, and that of the slave uprising in general, underscores one of the chief concerns of the Atlantic world: the reliance on seaborne trade brought mariners and travellers of all faiths into ports where, because of religious differences, they might or might not be welcome. Certainly the New York uprising fears of 1741 underscore the extremes to which fears of the religious 'other' could go.

In colonial inland towns from New England to New Spain, outward religious conformity was to a degree enforceable. Less settled regions – the English colonies' northern and southern frontiers, undeveloped coastal communities, and port cities – were more difficult to control. The people attracted to these areas were often either religiously out of step with the communities from which they came, or indifferent to religion altogether. In these borderland spaces, people from all backgrounds often encountered new religious traditions, which at times fostered interfaith cooperation and, in some cases, converts. A particularly vivid example was seventeenth-century Maine, where Puritan nonconformists intermingled with Baptists and Quakers, two denominations unwelcome in the more settled regions of New England. All these Protestants came up against nearby Catholics in the form of the French and Wabanaki Indians.

And what of Native American beliefs? Most, as described by contemporary observers, can be labelled syncretic. The Native Americans who were baptized en masse by Spanish Dominicans and Franciscans might have accepted the sacrament and attended Mass, feasts and holy days, but many continued to cling to elements of the faith they had known before the invaders. The retention of these beliefs can be seen even in the present day in *La Dia de los Muertes*, a celebration of dead loved ones with pre-Christian origins that is celebrated on the Catholic All Souls' Day. While some saw the retention of these beliefs as threatening and subversive, others saw in them a confirmation that Indians were children of God who had, through isolation or perhaps the defects of their ancestors, fallen away from true religion. This was the attitude of Jesuit Sebastien Rale, who lived at a mission on Maine's Kennebec River. The mission's chapel was decorated with traditional crafts by the resident Wabanaki Indians, who also taught the priest to make candles for liturgies out of local berries. Rale himself found Indian culture so appealing that he claimed to see, hear and speak 'only as an Indian'.

Despite tradition and popular narratives that link the development of nations with 'pure' religious ideologies, few places throughout the Atlantic world avoided religious mixing. In many places where multiple religious traditions came together, no single religion could claim the upper hand. In some of these cases, syncretic religions developed to create new faith altogether. Forcing belief systems on others was a common and sometimes deadly component of Atlantic encounter. But for others, the Atlantic provided the means to escape religious persecution and preserve cherished beliefs.

Women and Atlantic World Religion

Religious people – Protestant ministers, priests, nuns and preachers – were often the most literate and learned in Atlantic world. As such, many preserved their conviction that they were making history by keeping voluminous records of their actions and encounters. Many of these chroniclers were men, but their chronicles document the roles women played in the New World's nascent societies. Though these works were meant to inspire others to adopt appropriately gendered concepts of piety and power, they also illustrate for modern readers the range of possibilities for the Atlantic world's women, some of which were facilitated through religious innovations.

The Protestant Reformation and its aftermath created new avenues for Christian women and closed off others. Most Protestant denominations taught that the celibacy practised by Catholics in monasteries and convents was self-indulgent and contradictory to God's will. For women, Puritanism in particular raised the role of wife and mother to a higher, holier level. While men were revered as the head of household, claiming the same relation that God had to Creation, they were also expected to share major decisions and management of their households and children with their wives. Sex within marriage was a holy act, one that, given the sizes of their families, Puritans clearly valued. Puritans believed that physical attraction and fundamental compatibility were essential to a durable marriage and were, in and of themselves, godly expressions.

In addition, Protestantism's focus on literacy for believers meant that Protestant women were more likely to be able to read than Catholic women. Protestant women seized religiously sanctioned opportunities to seek education and pursue a wide variety of intellectual interests. As Natalie Zemon Davis has shown, Dutch evangelical Maria Sibylla Merian, who lived in the colony of Surinam for several years, drew strength and professional guidance from her commitment to Protestantism. Puritan writer Anne Dudley Bradstreet clearly had access to a large body of both pious and classical literature, and was trained by her father to read and understand it.

Gender equality in Protestantism's many variations was a more complicated matter. With a theology that insisted on the equality of all souls, and the encouragement of women to speak in religious meetings, Quakers were particularly aggressive on the issue and would become more so over time. These attitudes can be contrasted to some Virginia Anglicans, who were witnessed by an eighteenth-century observer debating whether women had souls or not. And though women were more likely than men to apply for church membership in New England, they were not offered the same ministerial functions as men, nor did they have access to a college education. Early Massachusetts Bay Puritan Anne Hutchinson ran afoul of colonial authorities when she presumed to interpret scripture for congregations of women and men: she was eventually banished from the colony for subverting the colony's leadership. Protestant women also lacked the alternative of the convent, a place where Catholic women who did not or could not marry could lead respectable lives. For most Protestants, marrying and bearing children was the lone alternative. Women who did not marry, therefore, occupied a very low place in society and within their own families, on whom they remained dependent.

There were some exceptions to this marriage paradigm in some of Protestantism's more radical sects. An example is the Shakers, who practised a variant of Quakerism and required celibacy of all their members. Their founder was an Englishwoman called Ann Lee. Abused and abandoned by her husband and with her children all dying in infancy, Lee knew well the hazards and heartbreak that women potentially faced when marriage and motherhood were their only options. Known as Mother Ann to her followers, she advocated hard work and innovation, the equality of souls, and ecstatic dancing to relieve pent-up energy and draw the faithful closer to God. Crossing the Atlantic shortly after the American Revolution, the people known as Shakers developed communities that pledged to keep these ideals.

Catholic women throughout the Atlantic world lived lives bounded by many of the same issues as Protestants did. They were expected to be pious, patient and submissive helpmeets to their spouses, and to bear the indignities of life with a bad marriage partner. There were, however, some significant differences. Firstly, married Catholic women (as well as for Protestant Dutch women, who were not bound by the gender-based exclusion from public life of English common law) could inherit from their parents and retain exclusive title to their property throughout their lives, a liberty that allowed the particularly pious to support their favourite religious institutions and causes with their own money.

In addition, Catholic women had the example of the Virgin Mary, whose near-universal veneration among Catholics promoted a forceful model of female piety. In the Catholic Atlantic world, the Virgin Mary was esteemed as a local protector, who interceded with her son to guarantee a given colony's safety. The Virgin Mary was even credited with direct intervention in repulsing English attacks on Quebec in 1690 and 1711. The Stono rebels, who were largely from the Catholic Kingdom of Kongo, operated in the same spirit when they rose up against their Protestant owners in 1739. As Mark Smith has shown, they evoked their native Afro-Catholicism by launching their attack on the Feast of the Nativity of the Blessed Virgin Mary, using ritualistic elements of devotion to the Virgin Mary that were common in Africa.

The concept of sacred virginity attracted some Native American women, particularly those who came from groups where daughters of the powerful served as diplomatic pawns and were 'given' in marriage to potential allies. This was the case with the aforementioned Catherine Tekakwitha, a Mohawk convert to Catholicism. Catherine's life was recounted by Jesuit missionary Claude Chauchetière, who was pleased by the convert's extreme piety. But when Catherine and her followers began to demonstrate their devotions through acts of severe physical deprivation, Jesuit observers became alarmed and forbade the women from founding their own religious order. Tellingly, European religious women had been engaging in similar practices for centuries, and were generally admired for their stoicism and virtue.

Life in a convent as an alternative to marriage was an important advantage Catholic women claimed over their Protestant contemporaries. Women's religious orders in South America could be wealthy and powerful, and received support from local elites who often sent their daughters to be educated by nuns. At more prestigious institutions, nuns from elite families enjoyed peaceful contemplation and abundant leisure.

Some had suites of rooms where they entertained family in comfortable surroundings, or spent their time decorating their cells and their habits (religious garb) with ribbons and gems. Women with intellectual interests often had no other place to indulge them than in a convent. Without children or husbands to compete for their attention, and with more books than a lay female colonist might see in a lifetime, convents provided a few lucky women with a life of the mind. The convent of the Ursuline nuns of Quebec boasted the city's largest library. Peru's notable colonial poet, Sor Juana Inés de la Cruz, found the cloister to be the perfect place for her to practise her literary arts.

Many convents were also schools for girls. In convents throughout the French, Spanish and Portuguese New World, nuns taught girls of varied social backgrounds to read, sew, pray and, depending on the status of the student, pursue music, decorative arts and handicrafts. In their own way, they also became cradles of cultural syncretism. In Quebec, for example, girls often learned the Native American technique of embroidering birch bark with stained porcupine quills. In Peru, the daughters of elites might learn *briscada*, the New World technique of fashioning wire and beads into flowers and symbols of piety.

Catholic women who were wives and mothers found ample opportunities to celebrate their faith publically in the numerous saint's days and other feasts, such as Carnival and Lent, which marked the Catholic calendar. Organizations of pious laywomen in French, Spanish and Portuguese territories organized public religious processions, raised funds for their communities, cared for the sick, and developed ministries for societal outcasts. Women of all races and ethnicities could be found in these groups, which often chose patron saints whose racial or ethnic backgrounds mirrored their own.

When moved to embrace Christianity of any kind, women of colour were often vigorous advocates of their new faith. The enslaved Bostonian Phillis Wheatley showed through her collection of verse, *Poems on Various Subjects, Religious and Moral*, that she was better versed in the principles of Christianity than many of her white neighbours. On the Virgin Islands, mulatto Rebecca Protten left the Dutch Reformed Church to join the Moravians. She was one of the architects of an evangelical revival on the island, before leaving to continue her work in Europe and Africa. In early nineteenth-century New York City, Zilpah Montjoy, an emancipated slave who attended Methodist and African Methodist Episcopal churches, was known as a healer and mystic to a group of diverse supporters.

Atlantic Religious Encounters: Diverse Experiences

Jews were integral members of some of the Atlantic world's earliest explorations. The explorations themselves were possible because of innovations in nautical astronomy that rested on the work of Arab and Jewish scholars, scientists and translators. Jewish scholars were warmly received in Portugal, a country that encouraged their migration from Castile in Spain, which was becoming increasingly hostile. Nevertheless, though local authorities often turned a blind eye to aggressive prosecution, laws and customs in many other parts of western Europe restricted the liberties of Jews. And in Spain, the practices of restriction became increasingly intense.

Jewish communities were found throughout the Atlantic world. Most were Iberian in origin. In 1492, the Spanish monarchs Ferdinand and Isabella issued an edict demanding that all Jews either convert to Catholicism or leave Spain. Though some remained, as many as 8000 families left to practise their faith openly in North Africa and Turkey. Those who stayed behind and converted faced the task of demonstrating their sincerity. Called *conversos* or *Cristianos nuevos* ('New Christians'), they were always suspected of retaining their old faith. Falsely accusing New Christian neighbours of being *marranos*, or secret Jews, was common, and could subject the accused to prosecution by the Inquisition. Their families suffered as well: the young Teresa of Avila, who eventually became a nun, abbess, mystic, saint and doctor of the Catholic Church, was forced to endure humiliating public acts of penance because her Jewish *converso* grandfather, Juan de Toledo, was an accused *marrano*. Eager to escape persecution, Jews were among the first groups to seek opportunity across the Atlantic. Still, even the New World's distance could not save all Jewish immigrants from the highly structured oppression of the Old. Tomas Treviño de Sobremonte and Luis de Carvajal were both victims of the Spanish Inquisition, the long arm of which reached all the way to Mexico to root out *marranos*.

Other Jewish migrations out of Iberia were forced, including one that transported 2000 forcibly converted children to the African island colony of São Tomé. Tragically, few of these children survived the new diseases they encountered there. Those who managed to survive often took African life partners, and in the process created a society of Jewish *mulattos* on São Tomé.

Expulsion on such a massive scale had unforeseen consequences. Among them was a high degree of cultural preservation. The Jews who left Spain for a less hostile cultural climate continued to celebrate important days, maintain regular rituals, and retain other cultural elements much as they had on the Iberian Peninsula. Music in particular crossed the Mediterranean and made its way to Amsterdam and London, and survived Atlantic crossings. Sephardic Jews often sang in Ladino, a language specific to Iberian Jews that blended Hebrew, Aramaic and Old Castilian.

Fleeing persecution, Sephardic Jews already described themselves as a nation. Therefore, scholars theorize, common religion, heritage of persecution, traditions and customs continued to link the New World's Jewish communities across geographical and national boundaries. To elaborate on this link, historian Erik Seeman investigated deathways common to Jews throughout the Atlantic world. His work concludes that, despite issues of distance and other cultural differences, Jewish communities tended to treat the bodies of the deceased and remember the dead in similar ways. In doing so, they followed the centuries-old dictates of Jewish law as a guide to direct the handling of the deceased, regardless of the part of the Atlantic world in which they found themselves.

By the beginning of the eighteenth century, Jewish colonists could be found throughout the Dutch colonies of North America, the Caribbean and Africa, with communities in Senegal, Curaçao, Suriname, New York, Newport, Rhode Island, Barbados, Jamaica and Halifax. Their arrival in English North America, as historian J. H. Elliott has noted, 'added yet another distinctive piece to the patchwork of creeds and cults that was beginning to cover the north Atlantic seaboard'. When the Dutch briefly seized part of Brazil, the colony attracted Jews from many backgrounds, including New Christians and immigrants from Europe, the Atlantic Islands and Africa. Some of these migrants possessed important sugar-processing technology, which they brought with them to the new colony. During this period, a few became elite planters in their own right, joining the ranks of the *senhores de engenho*. The return of the Portuguese in 1654 ended the regional aspirations of these planters. As a result, many migrated to the burgeoning English colonies as well as to Dutch Curaçao. Jews would eventually comprise more than 30 per cent of the island's colonial population. Built in 1732 in Punda, Curaçao, the Mikvé Israel-Emanuel synagogue remains the oldest Jewish house of worship in continuous use in the western hemisphere.

Still, many faced persecution in the New World as well as the Old. Peter Stuyvesant, the last Dutch Director-General of New Netherland, openly disparaged the settlement's Jews. Anti-Semitism lurked under the surface even of communities with a long-entrenched Jewish community, as was seen in Barbados when, in 1739, a Bridgetown mob responded to news of a Jewish colonist brawling with a Christian by destroying the local synagogue. As non-Protestants, North America's Jews fell into roughly the same category as Roman Catholics, whose ability to participate in colonial civic life had been severely restricted in all but Pennsylvania, Rhode Island and, for a time, Maryland. In most places, neither Jews nor Catholics could hold government office or vote. The American Revolution did not clarify where these minority religious groups stood within the new order, and they remained in an ambiguous situation until well into the nineteenth century. Members of both groups placed their lives, fortunes and sacred honour on the line for the patriot cause. This prompted some prominent Americans to speak in support of full civil rights for religious outsiders who were also of Judeo-Christian origin.

Almost all the Africans who came to the western hemisphere did so involuntarily. Captured in Africa, they were marched to its coast, detained in the dungeons and courtyards of trading castles, and then loaded on to ships bound for the west. The ensuing horrors of the Middle Passage led to what Jon Butler terms 'the African spiritual holocaust'. In their determination to break the spiritual and cultural bonds of their human cargo, workers on slave vessels embarked on a programme to destroy any connection to their traditional beliefs. Their goal was to replace the central role of these beliefs in the lives of slaves, with the slave master as the ultimate master and arbiter of their fate. Such programmes of cultural annihilation, however, could not destroy discrete African spiritual practices. Evidence of their survival has been found wherever enslaved Africans passed their days: in farmhouses on Dutch Long Island, in Maryland, in refuse pits in the Caribbean, and in racially segregated burying grounds in Dutch and English Manhattan. Nevertheless, it was nearly impossible to transfer complete African religious systems across the Atlantic. The stress of the Middle Passage, the enslavement strategy of keeping captives with common cultural and linguistic bonds separate, and dispersal throughout the Atlantic world severely curtailed the communal nature of these practices.

For the most part, the introduction of Christianity to enslaved Africans was slow and done with great trepidation. Slaveholders feared that slaves would latch on to Christianity's more radical messages. To combat this possibility, Anglican missionaries were careful to impart an 'approved' Christian message to converts, one that emphasized obedience to masters and the rewards of the afterlife. Africans who converted could expect few advantages. In the early decades of slavery in Virginia before the institution was strictly codified, slaves who became Christians were sometimes accepted as near-equals. This was the case of Anthony and Mary Johnson, the proprietors of 'Tony's Vineyard', a small plantation in Maryland. Anthony came to the colony as 'Antonio, a Negro', suggesting he had a previous connection of some sort with Catholic Europeans. His wife, Mary, came to the colonies without a connection to Christianity. Nevertheless, the couple outlived enslavement, married, and baptized their children in local Anglican churches. When jostled by bad fortune, they received additional considerations from white neighbours. By the end of the seventeenth century, however, emancipation and Christian conversion were specifically uncoupled in Virginia law.

In contrast, Spanish and Iberian Catholics were aggressive proselytizers to enslaved Africans. Some priests cared little if their converts understood and embraced Catholicism as long as they outwardly conformed to it. African converts were frequently suspected of retaining pre-conversion religious ties while outwardly conforming to Catholicism – a sentiment that echoed Iberian Catholicism's determination to persecute Catholic converts who continued to covertly practise Judaism. Thus women of colour were more likely than their white co-religionists to be accused of witchcraft and other anti-Christian subversive activities than whites, who might be engaging in similarly misunderstood folk practices.

The Moravians, a Pietist sect originally from the Protestant German states, were important early missionaries to the Atlantic world's enslaved Africans. They proselytized in the British North American colonies of Georgia and the Carolinas, and various Caribbean islands. As Jon Sensbach and Katherine Carté Engel have shown, the Moravians were some of the most committed, determined and enthusiastic missionaries of the eighteenth century. Nevertheless, in a complicated justification of slavery meant to allow missionaries to preach to slaves while mollifying white fears of enslaved Christians, some Moravians also kept enslaved Africans and thus supported the very system they claimed to abhor.

Most of the English people who moved throughout the Atlantic world considered themselves Anglicans, or followers of the Church of England. Though the early modern form of Christianity retained many liturgical and hierarchical connections with the Catholicism from which it separated, it privileged liturgy in English, relied heavily on the *Book of Common Prayer*, and called the English monarch, as advised by the Archbishop of Canterbury, its spiritual leader.

In North America, Anglicans could be found in every colony, at virtually every time. Though they suffered the dislike of the Massachusetts Puritans, they were sufficiently confident of their favour with the English monarch to lobby for control of nearby New Hampshire and early Maine. In Virginia and Carolina, they were dominant. In Virginia, settlers of all faiths paid annual taxes in support of the Anglican Church until after the American Revolution. Anglicanism was likewise established in the Anglo-Caribbean colonies. Both mainland and island churches had their own distinct Atlantic world difficulties. Colonies like Virginia were subdivided into parishes that covered vast areas. Coupled with a culture that privileged personal honour over religious principles, such an arrangement undermined the community life of Anglican parishes. In the geographically limited world of the Caribbean islands, Anglican ministers were often powerless to censure the social intrigues and sexual abuses of slaves and others that often characterized the lives of the great planters. For the most part, colonial Anglicanism also lacked the complete hierarchical structure of the faith they had left behind. As late as the end of the seventeenth century, colonists who wished to be ordained as Anglican ministers could only do so back in England, which entailed a risky and expensive round-trip voyage.

As the eighteenth century wore on, Atlantic world Anglicanism faced many challenges. Most of these came from within Christianity, and even within Anglicanism itself. Chief among these was the so-called Great Awakening, a spirit of evangelical revival that swept through many parts of the Protestant Atlantic in the mid-eighteenth century. A second wave crested along the Atlantic a century later and was called by the rather uncreative title, the Second Great Awakening. The earlier version coincided with many factors, including the introduction of new Enlightenment ideas that marginalized religious matters in philosophical and public discourse, and a terrible smallpox epidemic that ravaged the colonial world. A new generation of preachers focused on redemption and 'heart religion': that is, belief that relied on an emotional form of Christianity that privileged conversion and repentance. The movement relied on masterful preachers, whose skilful use of metaphor drove their audiences into ecstatic responses. A master of this style was George Whitefield, an English Anglican minister and associate of John Wesley. Whitefield travelled through English America preaching to audiences of various Protestant denominations. He drew huge audiences and had fans from diverse corners (even Benjamin Franklin appreciated his style). Whitefield is remembered today largely as a founder of Methodism.

Puritans, who followed John Calvin's interpretation of Protestant Christianity, were a sizeable yet disliked minority in early modern England. Still, they remained members of the Church of England and advocated for reforms that swept away any vestiges of Catholicism. Other Puritans, believing it was impossible to purge the Church of England, became Separatists and opted instead to split off from the Church of England and form their own denomination, founded on Calvinist principles and stripped of the liturgical elements. One such group was the Brownists, a group so named for their following of the writings of the Puritan thinker Robert Browne. Persecution of dissenters in the England of James I made life difficult, and the Brownists left England for the more tolerant city of Leiden in Protestant Holland. More than a decade in the Netherlands, however, convinced the Brownists that Dutch society was *too* tolerant. When they learned that the Plymouth Company of Virginia, a joint-stock company composed of merchant adventurers who wished to make profits from the New World, needed colonists for a voyage, the Leiden Brownists (together with some co-religionists they had left back in England), offered their services. The situation seemed like a good one to them: in exchange for harvesting New World resources to make the company profitable, they would be able to construct their own colonial society according to their own practices and standards.

The state of affairs between England's royalists and reformers deteriorated rapidly in the 1620s with the accession of a new king, Charles I, whose Catholic queen, Henrietta Maria, was a powerful player in her husband's court. Persecution in England forced many Puritans to leave the country. Like the Brownists before them, English Puritans migrated to New England to escape laws that restricted their practices and movements, and customs that disadvantaged them economically. Still, they refused to break with the Church of England altogether, preferring instead to purify from within. Removal to the New World, however, created a split for them. As many scholars see it, the term 'Puritan' became a proper noun to describe English reforming Calvinists who set up churches using the congregational model only with the migration to North America.

The New World's Puritans craved freedom of worship and self-determination for themselves, not for others. Yet they were not hypocrites. Like many other Atlantic world Christians, they were vocal enemies of religious plurality, and argued against the idea that all faiths were equal and deserved to be protected under the law. Such ideas of religion are far more modern, post-dating the founding of the American Republic. Modern beliefs that all Christians who are not tolerant are hypocrites often distorts our understanding of who the Puritans actually were and how they lived their lives. Popular nineteenth-century treatments by writers such as Nathaniel Hawthorne paint a grim picture of these reformers, casting them as dour, cold and severe, aloof from spouses and children, and determined to preserve their godly societies – even if that meant public executions of presumed criminals convicted with little proof. Victorian stereotypes contained their own, romanticized version of the Puritans aimed to make them more picturesque and compatible with period values. Many of these writings recast the Puritans as sexless teetotallers. Both these literary traditions, however, created a historically inaccurate picture of these people as meddlesome, overbearing, unkind, and indifferent to human sufferings and pleasures of any kind, all in the name of God.

In reality, Puritans were as likely as any European colonists to be affectionate parents and concerned neighbours who enjoyed the company of family and friends and the occasional public celebration. As demonstrated by the size of their families, many enjoyed sex as well, provided it was kept within appropriate confines. They produced, consumed and enjoyed alcoholic beverages; though they prosecuted drunkenness, Puritan towns regularly granted licences to ordinaries (taverns) and independent retailers of liquor.

But they were not tolerant people. Nor did they think religious tolerance was a good thing. Virtually no Puritan community was ever composed exclusively of Puritans. Nevertheless, it was the Puritans who were determined to build godly societies, and it was their laws that prevailed. Church attendance was required, dancing and the celebration of Christmas forbidden and certain social behaviours of little consequence in England were penalized in New England. Puritans hoped conformity to proper codes of godliness would be voluntary, but if they could not make the religious outsiders in their midst share their beliefs, they would do their best to ensure at least the appearance of assent with Puritan beliefs.

Into their midst marched the Quakers, who caused the Puritans much chagrin. Also called the Society of Friends, Quakerism was one of the many new religions born of a burst of religious enthusiasm during the English Civil War and its aftermath. Many early Quakers were found among the most extreme antinomians, who carried their religious principles to radical extremes. Groups such as the Diggers, Ranters, Levellers and Fifth Monarchists turned these beliefs outwards, practising revolutionary beliefs in public in ways that more conventionally religious English women and men found unseemly. The founder of Quakerism, Englishman George Fox, espoused the belief that all people possessed what he termed an 'inner light', which guided their conscience and dictated their actions towards their fellow human beings. Quakerism was radical for its use of inclusive language, belief in the gender equality of souls, simplicity of dress of its members, and refusal to bow to the established hierarchies of English society. In addition, it began as an evangelical religion whose members enthusiastically proclaimed their beliefs in public. After the restoration of the Stuart monarchs, the Quakers tried to deflect suspicion of their practices by renouncing violence and adopting pacifism as a central idea of their religion. Post-Interregnum Quakers, however, continued to face oppression at home in England. Chief among these was William Penn, a Quaker convert whose father, Admiral Sir William Penn, had been a royal favourite of Charles II.

Penn had good reasons to found a colony that welcomed his fellow Quakers. Oppression of the sect had spread throughout the Atlantic world wherever Quakers settled and proclaimed their ideas. Quakers in Massachusetts met with particular trouble, especially when they attempted to evangelize the local Puritans. Warnings, public punishments and banishment ensued; but when a Quaker preacher named Mary Dyer refused to be deterred, she and three co-religionists were executed in 1660. In other areas they were reviled and harassed. Emerson Baker has described the ordeal of Quaker tavern owner George Walton and his family, whose neighbours on Great Island, New Hampshire, tormented them for months, disguising their mischief as the work of malevolent spirits.

After observing the failures and hypocritical behaviours towards Native Americans of other European colonists, the early Quakers vowed to operate differently. Penn insisted on dealing fairly with the local Lenape Indians, trading for land and ensuring understanding of what the transaction entailed. His egalitarian ways and sincerity earned him the nickname 'Brother Onus' ('Brother Quill', a pun of Penn's surname). Later generations of Penns would not be so diligent. William Penn's heirs inherited leadership of the colony and managed it for income and prestige, drifting away from its original Quaker mission and identity.

Atlantic crossings also created conditions that were favourable overall to Quakerism's survival. Friends bonded with one another through common beliefs and hardships. Leaving England created conditions for Quaker communities to thrive and prosper.

Quaker merchants in London, the Caribbean and North American cities such as Philadelphia and Portsmouth, New Hampshire, sought out business connections among the Friends. Such preferences for building business connections among co-religionists would be followed by other oppressed religious minorities and disliked newcomers, including a home-grown American sect that came to be known as the Mormons.

The evolution of the Catholic Church in most parts of the New World happened in the wake of the Catholic Reformation, a powerful series of internal reforms aimed at reinvigorating and spreading the faith. These reforms fostered development of new religious orders for males and females. Groups like Ignatius of Loyola's Society of Jesus and Angela Merici's Company of Saint Ursula took the devout out of monasteries and cloisters and into greater public engagement, including schools. Male religious orders preached and educated; those of women educated and ministered to the sick and needy. Given the need to build new societies that replicated the best of Europe and incorporated new peoples, these religious orders found ample opportunities to flourish and improvise in the New World.

The Atlantic world's Catholic people were a diverse lot. Coming from both Europe and Africa, they blended with the people of the western hemisphere through partnerships that produced ethnically and racially mixed people. Generations of intermixing and cultural refinement created distinctly new people such as the *Métis* of Canada, who viewed themselves in equal parts as Indian and French, with a cultural mix that blended Native American customs and Catholicism in equal measure. Most mixed-race people in Spanish and Portuguese territories also associated with Catholicism, though they were sometimes viewed as second-class citizens, especially if they retained traditional beliefs that could be seen to challenge prevailing religious norms. In areas dominated by Spain and Portugal, adherence to Catholicism set the pace of public and private life. As colonies matured and transportation improved, Iberian Catholicism grew more entrenched, with fine buildings, monasteries and convents, and clergy (almost all of European heritage) who were born in the Americas.

The new United States got a strong dose of Catholic diversity in the wake of the Haitian Revolution. Surviving white planters, their slaves and free people of colour who did not support the Revolution fled to major cities on the East Coast. Some went to francophone French Canada and Louisiana; others went to traditionally Protestant-dominated North American cities such as Philadelphia, Newport, New York, Charleston and Savannah. These refugees were welcomed into pre-existing Catholic congregations, though many of the blacks among them were forced to sit in segregated galleries or worship in specially timed Sunday liturgies.

Some of the Catholics who crossed the Atlantic were from Scotland. The Highland Scots were mostly farmers and came as tenants of large landowners. Some settled on the lands of William Johnson, an Irish Anglican who also served as the British king's superintendent of Indian affairs for the northern colonies. Once there, they intermingled with Catholic and Anglican Mohawks, a convergence that shows the possible varieties of Catholic experience in the New World.

Most Scots, however, were Presbyterians, who had had their own Reformation under the influence of the Calvinist reformer, John Knox. Scotland and England have a legacy of conflict, and their competing views of Protestantism had their share as well. Nevertheless, the English of the Atlantic world made common cause with the Scottish Presbyterians when it suited them. In times of peace and growth, inter-denominational strife was not uncommon.

The Atlantic world's economic opportunities allowed Europe's religious outcasts to seek a better environment for themselves and their children. One of the largest groups to seek their fortunes in the Atlantic world was also Presbyterian, the so-called Scots-Irish. The Scots-Irish were chronic migrants. Originally Scottish Lowland Presbyterian farmers, they were encouraged by their English overlords to migrate to Ireland. The English planned for these newcomers to create a buffer between them-selves and the hostile Irish Catholics; they hoped they would numerically overwhelm them and perhaps adopt the Protestantism of their peers. Instead, the two peasant groups clashed violently. The Scots-Irish also resisted harsh taxes imposed on them by the English. When the chance to leave arose, many seized the opportunity.

The Scots-Irish are interesting to consider within the context of the Atlantic world because they were one of the peoples who were quick to turn away from it. Upon landing in the New World (the largest numbers in Pennsylvania), they quickly divorced themselves from colonial society and set out for the frontier regions. Considering themselves abused by those in power, they were determined to move beyond their reach. Once on the frontier, they settled (or squatted) on the best farm-land they could find. They also did not shy away from protecting their goods or well-being – with guns, if necessary. Their list of enemies included colonial officials and local Indians, on whose lands they often encroached. Determined and independent, the Scots-Irish were slow to rebuild the religious institutions they had left behind in Europe. An Anglican minister named Charles Woodmason who travelled among them in the 1790s wrote of these borderland people as unruly, licentious and unchris-tian in their beliefs and habits. Though Woodmason's assessment was likely an exag-geration, it was indeed logical to assume that the distance the Scots-Irish put between themselves and the Atlantic littoral made it difficult to establish the institutions and tools of faith that bound Europeans to their religious origins.

In contrast, other groups retained their transatlantic ties, and used them to attract new settlers and build their communities. One of the largest groups consisted of German Protestants, who began to arriving in Pennsylvania almost as soon as the colony was founded. They eventually numbered close to 120,000, and their exodus to North America persisted well into the eighteenth century. Many were followers of new expressions of Protestant reformed Christianity collectively known as Pietism. Pietist beliefs often emphasized 'heart religion' over the conventional pious practices and structured liturgies of established churches. Formal institutions of learning and spiritual interpretation were less important than family and commu-nity. The chief theorist of Pietism was a Lutheran pastor named Philipp Jacob Spener. His *Pia Desideria* (The Piety We Desire) called for all Christians to experi-ence a renewed personal piety. Pietist ideas influenced the founding of some radical sects of religious mystics, including Johann Conrad Beissel's Ephrata Cloister and Johannes Kelpius's Woman in the Wilderness, a sect that revived the ancient practices of a group called the Rosicrucians, who looked for divine messages in numbers and symbols.

Pietists left Germany to escape Lutheran and Catholic prejudice and the conscription of their sons into the armies of various German princes, who often sold their forces to their fellow European allies. Many came to America to found utopian communities based on their principles. Some groups, like the Schwenkfelders and Hutterites, eventually fell apart or were absorbed into other churches. Other groups, like the Mennonites and Amish, proved far more durable and persist to this day.

It is important to remember that Pietism was a method of practising Christianity, not necessarily a distinct denomination in its own right. As such, it influenced mainstream Protestant practices and contributed to the Great Awakening. The connection between conventional denominations and the new beliefs that influenced them is evident in the work of Count Nikolaus Ludwig von Zinzendorf. Zinzendorf spent two years in America, during which time he helped set up the Moravian community in Bethlehem, Pennsylvania, and also acted as the pastor of a Lutheran church. A believer in ecumenism (interfaith cooperation), he advocated interdenominational synods and studied the pious practices of other faiths.

Many German immigrants – Pietists, conventional Protestants and Catholics alike – renewed their community numbers thanks to the work of *neulanders*, or immigration 'agents', who crossed the Atlantic pairing would-be immigrants with passage and finding them work. Thus German communities were continuously refreshed with new arrivals, which through their more recent connections reinforced German culture.

● UP FOR DEBATE   The role of religion

Some historians view religion as the prime motivating factor in Atlantic exploration and colonization. In contrast, others regard religious motives as convenient pretexts to achieve non-religious goals. Which side do you take? Explain your answer.

Conversion

The Reformation left a legacy of conversion among Europeans – that is, the practice of willingly breaking away from one religion to embrace another. Catholics became Protestants, and Protestants became Catholics, non-Christians adopted Christianity, and Christians occasionally became apostate from Christianity, throughout the Atlantic world. In the Atlantic world's communities, these changes came about through a variety of means. One possible avenue to another faith was the simple lack of a worship space or clergy of one's own. With religious toleration discouraged in many places, and the practices of certain faiths outlawed, the devout often had little choice but to adhere to the established local religion. The fact that religious outliers were penalized for not attending religious services added another compelling reason for conversion. Furthermore, in some places, conforming to the established religion was a way to worldly success. Sometimes, however, such affiliations proved temporary. This was the case of Philip English, an English-speaking Anglican Channel Islander who found his way to Essex County, Massachusetts. A successful merchant with important business connections in New – and old – England, English worshipped at their local Puritan church. After his family was swept up in the Essex County witchcraft crisis, English returned to his old denomination and worshipped at Salem's new Anglican Church.

During the 'wars of empire', captives of frontier warfare sometimes adopted the Catholicism of their Indian and French captors. For women especially, conversion to Catholicism provided an opportunity for full engagement in French Catholic society through holy orders. One such woman was Esther Wheelwright, a great-grandniece of Puritan radical Anne Hutchinson. Born in frontier Maine in 1696 and taken captive in 1703, Esther lived in a Jesuit mission to the Wabanaki Indians for six years. She was eventually ransomed to New France and brought to live in the household of the royal governor. Plans were made for her exchange, but by that time Esther had decided to remain among the Ursuline nuns, who had been educating her, and eventually became the order's superior.

Liberation from the Old World allowed the spiritually curious new venues to explore their interests. Without family ties or expectations, New World travellers were exposed to new religious perspectives. Some of these conversions were in behaviour only, however: while still clinging to traditional religious labels, the religiously motivated adopted new pious practices. This was especially common in the waves of religious fervour brought about by the Great Awakening. The late eighteenth and early nineteenth centuries witnessed significant growth in evangelical denominations such as the Methodists and Baptists.

Less common, but still in evidence, was when a Christian adopted Native American religion. This conversion, however, is difficult to track, in large part because of Christianity's influence on Indian beliefs. Captives such as Freedom French and Eunice Williams of Deerfield adopted Native American modes of living, as well as the syncretic Catholicism they practised. A more clear-cut case of apostasy from Christianity to adopt Indian ways completely is seen in the far earlier example of Étienne Brûlé, a young Frenchman and trader who lived among numerous western Indians including the Hurons, who killed him in 1633.

Occult Practices, Non-Believers and the Religious Material World

Even orthodox Puritans demonstrated beliefs in the supernatural. Signs, wonders and portents were constantly being identified and analysed. With fear of God's displeasure omnipresent, Puritans were keen to read the signs and correct themselves. Some of these practices reflected pre-Christian beliefs common to so many early modern English people, Puritan or otherwise. Fear of the Christian devil was rife. Yet belief in malevolent forces capable of actively shaping daily existence linked believers across confessional, geographical, ethnic and racial lines. The witchcraft crisis of Essex County in 1692 showed the power of these beliefs to infect even pious

Puritans, who claimed to reject superstition of any kind. Still, Puritans believed, much as other Christians did, that the Devil and his followers were capable of walking among them and destroying lives and fortunes. They sometimes protected against his malevolence, and also preserved good luck, by reverting to occult practices that pre-dated the Reformation, and even Christianity. Seventeenth-century New England homebuilders were known to carve hex symbols in houses on obscure sections of beams and sills, and to bury coins beneath the posts that situated the structures. The 'Eye of Providence', a solitary eye suggesting the overarching gaze of a divine being that for eons has been in use among many diverse cultures and is still seen on American paper currency, was often the solitary decoration of Puritan meeting-houses. Atlantic world Catholics also saw ample evidence of the divine and the demonic at play in the New World. Pious practices mingled with occult beliefs, and churches were filled with objects called ex-votos that were left as tokens of thanks to the Virgin Mary and the saints for answered prayers. Wax ex-votos of body parts that were healed and crutches no longer needed still line the walls of Saint Anne de Beaupré, a shrine north of Quebec.

The excesses of the French Revolution had the ironic consequence of linking, in a limited way, New World Catholics and Protestants against a common threat: deism. During the eighteenth century, many thinkers embraced deism – a belief that God created the world and set it in motion, yet remained aloof from human affairs. The idea of a personal God was rejected by professed deists, who sidelined religious issues in favour of scientific, philosophical and political ones. These ideas were articulated for transatlantic audiences by the deistic Thomas Paine in *The Age of Reason*.

Records on atheists are scant, perhaps a reflection of how professing such views might harm one's professional and social aspirations. Some modern writers have attempted to equate deism with atheism, yet evidence to do so is scant – professed deists frequently evoked God's name and protection, and some, such as Benjamin Franklin, considered religious belief a positive good to society. Yet atheists, or perhaps more accurately, people who behaved in ways that were impugned as atheistic, were sufficiently known to inspire works that spoke against them. Sermons, tracts, and even several poems by Phillis Wheatley challenged and excoriated perceived non-believers. After the American and French revolutions, however, atheism became more of a spoken reality. Celebrated American revolutionary Ethan Allen had views on religion that can only be described as atheistic. The works of Voltaire, the French philosopher and writer, were sharply critical of Christianity and conventional expressions of faith in God and were both admired and condemned by Atlantic world readers.

Many Old World Christians hoped to convert the non-Christians they encountered. In both Africa and the Americas, missionaries attempted to bring the new peoples they met to their conception of the one true faith. Some tried by force. The early Spanish in particular were notorious for forcing their faith on others at the point of a sword. But as the Spanish New World presence evolved, some missionaries developed a more subtle approach. Spanish colonial art reflected the attempts of religious orders to integrate Christian principles to new realities. In the cathedral in Cuzco, Peru, for example, one can still view a depiction of Christ's last supper where the apostles dine on guinea pig and avocado, along with bread and wine. In Mexico, Hernando Franco, the first *maestro* of the cathedral, composed several *chanzonetas*, or hymns, to be sung in Nahuatl, the pre-contact language of the Mexica. Later composers infused baroque music, an imported European style, with Nahuatl and other languages to create syncretic masses and oratorios.

Catholic missionaries, especially the Jesuits, blended Native American languages and metaphors with the European melodies for Catholic holidays and feast days. A particularly vivid example of Atlantic world syncretic religious music is Jesuit Jean de Brébeuf's 'Jesous Ahatonhia', which combined Huron folkways and language with the basic contours of the Christmas story. Set to the French melody 'Une Jeune Pucelle', 'Jesous Ahatonhia' contains Native American and European elements in equal measure:

> Within a lodge of broken bark
> The tender Babe was found,
> A ragged robe of rabbit skin
> Enwrapped His beauty round;
> But as the hunters brave drew nigh,
> The angel song rang loud and high

In Massachusetts, Puritan minister John Eliot earned the title 'Apostle to the Indians' through active evangelization and by translating the Bible into Natick, the language of the local Wampanoag Indians. Few other Puritan ministers, however, went to such lengths to bring Indians to Christ.

The Atlantic Ocean was a conduit for religious beliefs. In crossing the Atlantic, believers imported religious systems to new places and peoples, where it encountered unforeseen challenges. In the process, it also transformed them, and even morphed into new forms of expression. Those already living on the Atlantic littoral witnessed similar spiritual transformations. Often imposed or even forced, they were at times embraced and even integrated into resurgent ideas to create distinctive new forms of belief.

CHAPTER CHRONOLOGY

1494   Catholic papacy issues the Treaty of Tordesillas, splitting Spanish and Portuguese claims.

1517   Martin Luther produces his Ninety-Five Theses against the Roman Catholic Church, sparking the Protestant Reformation.

1631   English Puritans found Providence Island in the Bahamas.

1689   England's 'Glorious' Revolution replaces Catholic Stuart king James II with his Protestant daughter and nephew, William of Orange and Mary.

1724   Founding of convent for Indian women in Mexico.

1783   In the wake of the American Revolution, Jewish congregants of the Philadelphia Synagogue petition for full civil rights.

1831   The popularly titled 'Baptist War' slave rebellion breaks out in Jamaica.

PRIMARY SOURCES AND STUDY IMAGE

Letter from Father Sébastien Rale, S.J., Missionary of the Society of Jesus in New France, to Monsieur his nephew (1722) [excerpt]

The Village in which I dwell is called *Nanrantsouak*; it is situated on the bank of a river, which empties into the sea thirty leagues below. I have built here a Church which is commodious and well adorned. I thought it my duty to spare nothing, either for its decoration or for the beauty of the vestments that are used in our holy Ceremonies; altar-cloths, chasubles, copes, sacred vessels, everything is suitable, and would be esteemed in the Churches of Europe. I have trained a minor Clergy of about forty young Savages, who, in cassocks and surplices, assist at divine Service; each one has his duty, not only in serving at the holy Sacrifice of the Mass, but in chanting the divine Office at the Benediction of the blessed Sacrament, and in the Processions – which are made with a great concourse of Savages, who often come from a great distance in order to be present at them. You would be edified with the good order which they observe, and with the reverence which they show.

Two Chapels have been built, about three hundred steps from the Village: one, which is dedicated to the most blessed Virgin, and in which her statue in relief is seen, stands at the head of the river; the other, which is dedicated to the Guardian Angel, is below, on the same river. As they both are on the path that leads either to the woods or to the fields, the Savages never pass them without offering prayers therein. There is a holy emulation among the women of the Village regarding the best decoration of the Chapel, of which they have care, when the Procession is to enter it; all that they have in the way of trinkets, pieces of silk or chintz, and other things of that sort – all are used for adornment.

The many lights contribute not a little to the decoration of the Church and Chapels; I have no need to economize in wax, for this country furnishes me with abundance. The islands of the sea are bordered with wild laurel, which in autumn bears berries closely resembling those of the juniper-tree. Large kettles are filled with them and they are boiled in water; as the water boils, the green wax rises, and remains on the surface of the water. From a minot of these berries can be obtained nearly four livres of wax; it is very pure and very fine, but is neither soft nor pliable. After a few experiments, I have found that by mixing with it equal quantities of tallow, – either beef, mutton, or elk, – the mixture makes beautiful, solid, and very service-able candles. From twenty-four livres of wax, and as many of tallow, can be made two hundred tapers more than a royal foot in length. Abundance of these laurels are found on the Islands, and on the shore of the sea; one person alone could easily gather four minots of berries daily. The berries hang in clusters from the branches of the shrub. I sent a branch of them to Quebec, with a cake of wax, and it was pronounced excellent.

Flushing Remonstrance (27 December 1657)

Right Honourable,

You have been pleased to send up unto us a certain prohibition or command that we should not receive or entertain any of those people called Quakers because they are supposed to be by some, seducers of the people. For our part we cannot condemn them in this case, neither can we stretch out our hands against them, to punish, banish or persecute them for out of Christ God is a consuming fire, and it is a fearful thing to fall into the hands of the living God.

We desire therefore in this case not to judge least we be judged, neither to condemn least we be condemned, but rather let every man stand and fall to his own Master. Wee are bounde by the Law to Doe good unto all men, especially to those of the household of faith. And though for the present we seem to be unsensible of the law and the Law giver, yet when death and the Law assault us, if we have our advocate to seeke, who shall plead for us in this case of conscience betwixt God and our own souls; the powers of this world can neither attack us, neither excuse us, for if God justifye who can condemn and if God condemn there is none can justify.

And for those jealousies and suspicions which some have of them, that they are destructive unto Magistracy and Minssereye, that can not bee, for the magistrate hath the sword in his hand and the minister hath the sword in his hand, as witnesse those two great examples which all magistrates and ministers are to follow, Moses and Christ, whom God raised up maintained and defended against all the enemies both of flesh and spirit; and therefore that which is of God will stand, and that which is of man will come to nothing. And as the Lord hath taught Moses or the civil power to give an outward liberty in the state by the law written in his heart designed for the good of all, and can truly judge who is good, who is civil, who is true and who is false, and can pass definite sentence of life or death against that man which rises up against the fundamental law of the States General; soe he hath made his ministers a savor of life unto life, and a savor of death unto death.

The law of love, peace and liberty in the states extending to Jews, Turks, and Egyptians, as they are considered the sonnes of Adam, which is the glory of the outward state of Holland, soe love, peace and liberty, extending to all in Christ Jesus, condemns hatred, war and bondage. And because our Saviour saith it is impossible but that offenses will come, but woe unto him by whom they cometh, our desire is not to offend one of his little ones, in whatsoever form, name or title he appears in, whether Presbyterian, Independent, Baptist or Quaker, but shall be glad to see anything of God in any of them, desiring to doe unto all men as we desire all men should doe unto us, which is the true law both of Church and State; for our Savior saith this is the law and the prophets. Therefore, if any of these said persons come in love unto us, wee cannot in conscience lay violent hands upon them, but give them free egresse and regresse unto our Town, and houses, as God shall persuade our consciences. And in this we are true subjects both of Church and State, for we are bounde by the law of God and man to doe good unto all men and evil to noe man. And this is according to the patent and charter of our Towne, given unto us in the name of the States General, which we are not willing to infringe, and violate, but shall houlde to our patent and shall remaine, your humble subjects, the inhabitants of Vlishing.

Written this 27th day of December, in the year 1657, by mee
Edward Heart, Clericus

Study image 5 *'Sinners in Hell' from The Progress of Sin (1744).*

'You Men', by Sor Juana Inés de la Cruz (1651–95) [excerpt]

Silly, you men – so very adept
at wrongly faulting womankind,
not seeing you're alone to blame
for faults you plant in woman's mind.

After you've won by urgent plea
the right to tarnish her good name,
you still expect her to behave –
you, that coaxed her into shame.

You batter her resistance down
and then, all righteousness, proclaim
that feminine frivolity,
not your persistence, is to blame.

When it comes to bravely posturing,
your witlessness must take the prize:
you're the child that makes a bogeyman,
and then recoils in fear and cries …

Recommended Reading

James Axtell, *The Invasion Within: The Contest of Cultures in Colonial North America* (Oxford, 1985). Groundbreaking study of competing Catholic and Protestant missionaries in New France and New England.

Jody Bilinkoff and Alan Greer (eds), *Colonial Saints: Discovering the Holy in the Americas, 1500–1800* (London, 2002). Collection of essays examining new contexts of sainthood in the Americas.

Jon Butler, *Awash in a Sea of Faith: The Christianization of the American People* (Cambridge, MA, 1990). Explores the transformation of belief, and the persistence of older religious cultural practices and beliefs, in English North America.

Juan and Ondina González, *Religion in Latin America: A History* (Cambridge, 2002). A general treatment of the ranges of religious experience, as well as religious hierarchy and order, in various Latin American countries.

Allan Greer, *Mohawk Saint: Catherine Tekakwitha and the Jesuits* (Oxford, 2005). Examines the complex world and life choices of Kateri Tekakwitha, who was promoted by Jesuit missionaries as a paragon of Native American Catholicism.

David Hall, *Worlds of Wonder, Days of Judgment: Popular Religious Belief in Early New England* (Cambridge, MA, 1990). Demonstrates the complex interior lives, beliefs and practices of New England Puritans.

R. Po-Chia Hsia, *The World of Catholic Renewal, 1540–1770* (Cambridge, 2005). A reinterpretation of the Catholic response to the Protestant Reformation, as renewal and reinvention as well as retrenchment.

Barry Levy, *Quakers and the American Family* (Oxford, 1992). Explores how Quakerism developed in English North America, and affected lived lives and family structure.

Mark Noll, *The Old Religion in a New World: The History of North American Christianity* (Grand Rapids, MI, 2001). Looks at multiple Christianities and their growth, transformation and creation in North America.

Jon Sensbach, *Rebecca's Revival: Creating Black Christianity in the Atlantic World* (Cambridge, MA, 2006). A microhistorical treatment of the story of Rebecca Protten, an enslaved African who became a Moravian missionary and preacher on the sugar island of St. Thomas.

TEST YOUR KNOWLEDGE

1 What were the chief religious motivators underlying Atlantic exploration?

2 What was Christianity's connection to Africa?

3 What strategies did Europeans use in an attempt to convert Native Americans to Christianity?

4 What special conditions influenced the movement of Atlantic world Jews and Quakers?

5 What is religious syncretism? What are two examples of syncretic religion to come out of the Atlantic world?

6 What effect did race have on the spread of Christianity?

7 Violence provoked by religious difference was a frequent occurrence among Atlantic peoples. Identify several examples.

8 Who were the Puritans? What were some of the hallmarks of their complex movement?

9 How did the experience of Atlantic travel and settlement shape religious exploration?

6 Lived Lives and the Built Environment: Cultural Transfer in the Greater Atlantic

Atlantic peoples shared some common basic needs and experiences which transferred with them across the Atlantic, or changed due to the arrival of new people. All needed shelter and food; most had families and communities they valued. They expressed their joys and sorrows in life through shared experiences, communal activities, sports, games and social rituals. Their cities and towns reflected not only their climates but tastes, preferences, religious expressions and types of work. Some lived among diverse populations in terms of race, religion and ethnicity. Almost all would have lived among animals. In this chapter, these commonalities will be considered comparatively, showing how certain cultural elements developed the way they did and what factors influenced this development.

Shelter: a Universal Need

People throughout the Atlantic world were linked by similar physical and personal needs. To protect themselves from weather, the sun, animals and each other, all required some form of shelter. Throughout the Atlantic world, newcomers adapted shelters in accordance with available building materials and in response to new climates. Though they often harboured preconceived ideas of what a house was and how it was supposed to function, they grafted new ideas onto pre-existing ones to create wholly new forms.

The Atlantic world over, most agrarian people had few needs for a home that extended beyond basic protection from any particular region's climate. The homes of European peasants, coastal Africans, and numerous indigenous groups throughout the Americas resembled each other in key ways. At the heart of these similarities was functional simplicity. Families needed places to sleep and (if necessary, indoors) to cook and manage the temperature for maximum human comfort. Furnishings, textiles and household goods were few in nature and often had more than one practical use. Access to a means to grow or hunt food, drinkable water and burnable resources were also common necessities. Structures were frequently built close together, which provided security, resource-sharing and companionship. Finally, they were arranged to allow for the cultivation and processing of food.

For Indians on the Atlantic littoral, housing was extremely varied in form, yet certain elements were common to many groups, including the use of animal skins, tree bark and supple young trees. In Virginia, the Powhatan Confederacy's homes consisted of oval frames constructed of young trees. Bark and woven mats covered the frame, and a hole in the roof allowed smoke to escape. Similar designs were used by the Wampanoags and Pequots of New England. The homes of the Seminoles, in modern Florida, featured pitched thatched roofs and often no walls at all. In the Caribbean, Indians such as the Taino built huts of cane and palm fronds. In contrast, Mesoamerican Indians of today's Mexico and Central America built sturdier homes, using a sophisticated combination of gravel flooring, stone, clay and wood walls, and thatched roofs. Most of these cultures were organized on village or city models. They contained a mixture of domestic structures, civic buildings and temples, and agricultural fields.

The first waves of Europeans to arrive in the New World did not immediately make homes on dry land. Out of necessity or security, they often continued to live aboard the ship that brought them. This was true of the Plymouth separatists, who spent a harrowing winter on board the *Mayflower* before identifying a promising location for their settlement. Life aboard ship came with its own discomforts and dangers, which did not diminish simply because a vessel safely reached land. Close quarters continued to breed disease, and ignited hostilities among shipmates. It has even been suggested that a depressed Dorothy Bradford, the wife of Plymouth's first governor, committed suicide by casting herself off the deck of the moored *Mayflower*.

The first houses that Europeans built often borrowed from local building practices and, of course, needed to use local materials. Simple in their outlines, construction and planned functions, they were meant as shelter and not necessarily to last. Still, there were many regional variations to the structures themselves. For the English, communities in the New World could be modelled on those they knew back in England. The English New World migration was highly regional in nature. New England Puritans, for example, came from East Anglia, parts of the West Country, and the north of England. The tiny, one- or two-room houses they built followed patterns that had been established long before in English villages. They were arranged in clusters along central thoroughfares, with farmsteads radiating out and beyond, a style similar to that used in East Anglia. Seventeenth-century houses were small and pragmatic, based more on necessity than a sense of family comfort, and were hastily constructed to protect newcomers from challenging new climates. Average houses consisted of at most two rooms on the first floor (known traditionally as the 'hall' and 'parlour'), and a loft above. Both the hall and the parlour were what are nowadays called 'flex spaces' – places with no dedicated use, where a variety of work was done. Families often slept together in one of these spaces, crowded onto mattresses and, at best, one bed.

The same was the norm for families of modest means throughout Anglo North America and the Caribbean. Virginians retained these simple models but, consistent with their regional origins, tended to build houses that were less sturdy than those of the New Englanders. They too used the 'hall and parlour' model, but the Virginians and Marylanders drove the vertical elements for their homes directly into the ground. This might have reflected the perceived non-permanence of the Chesapeake's early settlers: many needed a place to stay while they made their fortune, but then hoped to return to England. Under such a presumption, a more elaborate house was unnecessary.

The relationship of these early houses to one another reflected any given group's concerns, strategies for survival, and plans for resource use. New Englanders clustered their homes together, waiting decades to spread to isolated farmsteads. Planting fields and dependencies (buildings that supported the work of the home or farm, such as barns and work sheds), radiated outward from the cluster of houses. The little villages also contained a blockhouse, a type of fort to keep watch for ships and enemies on land and sea. Tobacco cultivation dictated a different pattern for the Chesapeake, where planters were more interested in the ability to move their product to market than building a community. The houses and outbuildings of seventeenth-century planters and their dependants clung to the banks of waterways for ease of movement. This plan was good for business but poor for defence, as demonstrated twice in the early century, when war with Virginia's Powhatan Indians resulted in many burned plantations and dead colonists who, lacking easy access to one another, were unable to raise the alarm until it was too late.

Though they adopted a similar system of waterfront access, the French in Canada chose a different strategy that addressed that shortcoming. They organized themselves along the banks of the Saint Lawrence River in *rotures*, or ribbon farms. These long, thin farming plots provided access to the river yet left ample space for agriculture. French colonial houses were therefore in close proximity to one another, and settlers could pass on warnings and rally the militia with ease. The designs and building techniques of French houses reflected those of France. As the main Canadian commercial centres of Montreal and Quebec developed, the French were careful to institute strict building regulations to prevent the constantly burning fires that the harsh winters required from igniting large-scale fires and destroying their cities.

As the colonies evolved, many newcomers built sturdier houses with a more dedicated sense of space within. It is in these houses – some of which still exist – that the English models truly emerge. As with food, clothing, education and other cultural essentials, people on the western rim of the Atlantic world copied the styles of those on the eastern rim as soon as they had the means to do so. In British North America, this transition in housing began around 1660; in the Chesapeake, it happened somewhat later. Many homes in New England retained a 'core' structure to which later rooms and floors were added, yet retained small windows and large fireplaces. This created a hotchpotch effect in many New England houses, which grew haphazardly as the family acquired the means to expand.

Climate dictated house architecture in the eighteenth-century Chesapeake. Rooms needed to be light and airy, with high ceilings and good ventilation to provide respite from punishing summer weather. Such domestic luxuries, however, could be enjoyed only by the wealthy. Houses in both regions reflected a renewed interest in architectural symmetry, or evenness and balance between architectural elements. Based on ancient principles of harmony and numerology, these design adaptations came to be called 'Georgian', in honour of the Hanover kings of England. Yet the impulse for symmetry crossed the Atlantic quickly: the Sherburne House in Portsmouth, New Hampshire, was enlarged in 1728 by builders who attempted a symmetrical design, though they unfortunately fell short of their goal.

As with British North America, homes within the Spanish sphere of influence ranged from humble to grand. Building techniques reflected local availability and climate as well as Old World forms. Many larger houses were wood, adobe and tile, and organized around a central courtyard, with fountains and plantings to maintain at least the illusion of coolness. These elite forms could be found from Brazil to New Orleans. The houses of the poor and middling folk were often also mud brick and stucco, with thatched roofs. Such building materials were indeed humble, but they helped to insulate the inhabitants from extreme heat. They were also cheap and easily available. Homes of Caribbean elites also reflected British styles to the best of the ability of local builders. Yet even more than the builders in the Chesapeake, they adapted houses to suit the climate. Common features included ventilating shutters, high ceilings, and large and airy entryways. Houses were built with large porches and steps that created entries on higher floors, which were ideally placed to catch cooling breezes. Later innovations in both the Spanish and British Caribbean included fanciful wrought iron grillwork, grand and shady arcades, and brightly coloured stucco, such as can still be seen in places like Bermuda, Barbados and Havana.

Encounters with Europeans and the development of the slave trade left their marks on coastal Africa. Slaves left Africa from castles, hybrid buildings that blended European-style fortified coastal structures with West African building techniques and materials. By the late seventeenth century, the majority of the Caribbean's inhabitants were enslaved, and lived in wretched conditions in terms of their dirt floors, crowding, lack of ventilation, and proximity to dangerous insects and animals. Eighteenth-century slave houses in Ocho Rios, Jamaica, were thatched and stuccoed, but clearly raw within. Despite the trauma of their importation, however, enslaved Africans brought with them their own architectural traditions and adapted New World styles as well. Some of these homes could be disassembled by their owners and moved to a new location. The 'chattel houses' of Barbados grew out of the island's transition from enslaved to wage labour. No longer bound by law to inhabit their masters' plantations, workers of colour could move from job to job while taking this form of collapsible architecture with them for reassembly at a new site. The use of light wood for slave quarters was common in the American South as well. The earliest specimens were houses made of puncheons, roughly split timbers that followed the basic lines of English structures. As Peter Wood suggests, the packed dirt floor of slave cabins might have suited the enslaved as well as owners who refused to invest in anything better. In parts of Africa, such floors were commonly viewed as naturally cooling and, when carefully swept, were actually very clean.

The farther north one moved up the Atlantic coast of North America, the less likely one was to find slave quarters. Instead, slaves lived in their homes of their owners, often occupying attic or kitchen spaces. Though the circumstances were potentially a bit more comfortable than the crude cabins that many others knew, enslaved Africans were forced to live in greater intimacy with those who compelled their labour, instead of among their own family and friends.

The Consumer Revolution of the early eighteenth century brought changes to domestic life in its wake. So did Enlightenment thinking, which contributed new philosophies of personal space and dignity. These ideas filtered into domestic structures through the drive to subdivide interiors and designate spaces for specific uses. Typical seventeenth-century houses had few spaces with specific functions. Cooking, performing domestic work, eating, sleeping – all the functions of a family took places within these spaces. In the eighteenth century, changing philosophies and the importation of new styles from Europe brought change to homes, particularly those who had the means to enlarge their houses or build new ones from the ground up. Georgian architecture became increasingly important, and, for elite families, so did new distinctions of ceremonial and private space. Whereas parents, children, visitors, servants and slaves commonly occupied domestic spaces all together in the seventeenth century, wealthy and even middling people increasingly sought more privacy for dressing, sleeping, eating and entertaining during the eighteenth century.

Birth, Family and Social Hierarchy

When Europeans crossed the Atlantic, they brought with them a social structure based on monogamous relationships (at least for women), which had been legitimized by a civil or religious power. Ideally, such relationships precluded romance outside of marriage, and lasted until one of the partners died. On one hand, Atlantic migration spread these ideals; on the other, it created circumstances and temptations that severely undermined them.

Chief concerns for Europeans were illegitimacy and bigamy. In the seventeenth century, many Europeans came to the Americas and the Caribbean as single men and boys, who joined expeditionary forces to the New World colonies for glory, financial opportunities, adventure or lack of gainful employment in Europe. The all-male first colonists to the French North American colonies of Acadia and Quebec are but one example. As the population of females began to rise, so did illegitimate babies. As late as the mid-eighteenth century, a third of the population of French Canada were soldiers, who were temporarily sent to the colonies or joined colonial units. Many of these men returned to France when their enlistments were up, where they married and started families. Canada's church officials, however, complained that many left illegitimate children (called 'enfants naturelles') behind. Children born out of wedlock to French soldiers and Canadian mothers brought the stigma of fornication to families and concern to colonial officials, who feared these children would become public charges.

Illegitimate children faced life with varying degrees of ease or difficulty, which depended on the status and situation of one or both parents, community laws governing such children, and what they themselves managed to achieve in life. Certainly colonies throughout the English Atlantic world gave these children more opportunities than they would have had in Britain, with its highly stratified society and reliance on lineage. For evidence, one needs look no further than the life of Alexander Hamilton. Born out of wedlock in 1755 or 1757 (records referring to his birth conflict), Hamilton rose through his own intellect and will to become the first Secretary of the Treasury in the new United States. He also married the daughter of a prominent landowning family, the Schuylers, and enjoyed an adult life of comfort, prestige and political power.

Illegitimate children in Spanish colonial America often faced bleak futures. In a culture that thrived on honour, the legacy of one's blood and virtue in females, the birth of an illegitimate child to an unattached female could diminish her honour, as well as that of her family. Yet betrothed women – even elite ones – could and did become pregnant by their intended spouses before the actual marriage took place. Such cases were not as scandalous or damaging as one might think, as it proved the fertility of the prospective bride. If the marriage took place before birth, the child was legitimate; if not, it was legally legitimized. As Susan Socolow has noted, single women with children 'tended to be poorer and darker than the population of women in general'. These women headed their households and could claim few rights in the eyes of the law or civil society.

Puritans did much to discourage illegitimacy. Fornication was vigorously punished, and when unmarried women officially 'swore a child' on a man, the father was obliged to pay for the child's upkeep or, preferably, marry the mother. Popular perceptions assume that, due to punishments such as these, Puritans were prudish and sexless. In actuality, Puritan brides towards the end of the seventeenth century were almost as likely as non-Puritans to be pregnant at the time of their marriage. Robustly healthy babies born five months after their parents' marriage were clearly conceived in advance of the union, and the guilty parents were fined and sometimes publicly humiliated for fornication. But this phenomenon also highlights the fact that the conferral of marriage differed. Marriage for Puritans was a civil, not a religious event – betrothal came before the actual marriage, which was a small affair presided over by a civil official called a magistrate. After that, the bride remained with her family for weeks, her husband coming by only occasionally to spend nights, until the bride was ready to join her spouse in their new home. 'Going to housekeeping' was as much a right in early New England as the marriage ceremony itself, and carried the greater significance of separating the young bride from her family. Though the generations sometimes reconvened under the same roof (with ageing parents now moving in with children so that they could be provided for in old age), 'going to housekeeping' marked a woman's transition into full partnership in marriage, which included its commitments to husband, future children and household economy.

Modern stereotypes of the innate decency (or repression) of early American people tell us that, with the near-impossibility of divorce, marriages were stable and built upon respect and mutual economic need. While the durability and legal indissolubility are accurate, it must be noted that existing court records from throughout the English Atlantic world demonstrate that marital harmony was far from unanimous. Sexual activity between unmarried people was one issue; adultery was another altogether, and a far more serious offence against God and community that resulted in severe punishments for both men and women who engaged in it. Still, indictment for adultery alone was not enough to dissolve a marriage, and many couples persisted in states of union that were no doubt far from blissful. More than one colonial marriage devolved into violence, with wives and children hauled into court for plotting against a despised spouse and father. Puritans recognized the importance of contentedness in marriage and, given its civil basis, were more likely to dissolve unions where spousal abuse and cruelty were rife. In the Chesapeake, where Catholic and Anglican settlers considered marriage a sacrament ordained by God, the raising of a hand against a husband or father was considered an act of treason.

With divorce rare, the people of the Atlantic world often dealt creatively with the problems of unhappy marriages or long separations that deprived husbands and wives of each other's physical comfort. For many, the only way to dissolve bad marriages was escape or death. Others, not content with their options, took a more creative approach. One such strategy was bigamy, a persistent problem present in most colonies. Officially forbidden and actively prosecuted, local administrators went to great lengths to prevent mostly men from having more than one wife – that is, a woman to whom he was legally and, in the case of Catholics, sacramentally married. This did not prevent many married men from forming sexual relationships with additional women once they came to the colonies. Hernan Cortés and Malintzen's son, Martín, was born while his father's first, Spanish wife still lived. In a practice that extended well into the nineteenth century, New Orleans's creole men of standing and women of mixed racial heritage (enslaved or free) entered into common-law marriages despite the man's married status. This system, called *plaçage* or *la main gauche* ('left-handed marriage'), was so common that the relationship was spelled out by lawyers, who created contracts based on the lifestyle the *placée* (the woman in the union) could expect from her lover, and made provisions for any future children who might be born of the relationship. These children subsequently formed the core of New Orleans's community of free people of colour. Concubinage, or the practice of a man keeping one or several lovers, often when married to another, was also common throughout Mexico, Brazil and other areas of the Iberian Atlantic world. According to Susan Socolow, most of the concubines were widows and working women drawn from the lower rungs of society. Some were Spanish, others Indian. Some were women who simply never got around to formalizing, through marriage, their relationship with a male who was technically free to marry.

Wives throughout the Spanish and French New World knew that their husbands had lovers, and often whole second families. With a world of carefully circumscribed norms governing wives' actions to their husbands, many no doubt bore this reality with stoicism. Others were deeply resentful, and abused their husband's mistresses and children whenever possible. In the American South, where slave owners routinely raped or seduced servants and slaves, their legitimate wives had power over these offspring in the eyes of the law, and could take out their jealousy and frustrations at will.

Mixed-race relationships, some of which closely resembled conventional marriages, were also found in the British Caribbean and Saint Domingue, with similar consequences. Children born of unions between white men and women of African or mixed-race descent frequently became free people of colour in their own right. Often legitimized and recognized as rightful heirs by their white families, such children might be pampered at home, or sent to Europe to be educated. This common phenomenon was satirized by English writer William Makepeace Thackeray in his 1848 novel *Vanity Fair*, where one of the pupils in the English school attended by Becky Sharpe and Amelia Sedley is the pampered mulatto daughter of a Caribbean planter.

People living on the fringes of the Atlantic world often created relationships that were unorthodox by the standards of European Christians. French *coureurs de bois* – the fur-seeking forerunners of the fabled 'mountain men' of western lore – often had one or more Indian wives. If monogamous, and the bride a Christian, these unions received the blessing of a priest, if one were available and sought out. As Susan Sleeper-Smith has shown, Indian women of the Great Lakes region who married French men were often the agents of religious orthodoxy, who used their own kinship networks, religious beliefs and ties to the French to ensure the security of their communities and support their roles in the lucrative fur trade.

Another small, but important, percentage of French North America's population was comprised of captives from New England. These one-time Puritans were often taken from their New England frontier communities during the various 'wars of empire' that frequently rocked New England and New France between 1688 and 1763. Though many of these captives were ransomed and returned, others never came back. Instead, they converted to Catholicism, married French or Native American Catholics, and became subjects of the French king or members or tribal members. The actions of these unusual intercolonial migrants had the odd consequence of grafting Catholic branches onto Protestant family trees. Many reconnected with their New England families later in life. Mary Storer, who through captivity, conversion, marriage and naturalization spent the rest of her life as Marie Saint-Germaine, even visited her family in Boston. Afterwards, she continued to exchange letters with her brother, merchant Ebenezer Storer, for years.

Indentured servants of the seventeenth-century English North American colonies were often forbidden from marrying during the terms of service spelled out in their contracts. Women who became pregnant during the course of their contracts had to account for any unproductive time they spent in pregnancy and childcare by adding extra time to the endpoint of their indenture term. Still, women, even servant women, were valued in the Chesapeake colonies. The severe rate of death left many young widows, widowers and orphans. Remarriage was not simply desirable, it was virtually unavoidable – especially for young widows with property.

Increased barriers to economic success, the lack of available partners, and high mortality rates among newcomers meant that many servants who survived their term of servitude never married. Some, however, crafted some sense of a home life with members of their own sex, setting up households, sharing incomes, and leaving their worldly goods to each other, as would any life partner.

Many West and West Central Africans lived in extended family groups. In these cultures, a man demonstrated his prosperity through multiple marriages and families. These extended polygamous families lived in extended units within African villages, where wives and half-siblings intermingled and even worked cooperatively. The enslavement and forcible separation of African families altered these dynamics, yet preserved the spirit of broadly construed inclusion. Slavery destroyed families, but slaves themselves found ways to reconstitute them. Their ability to form new bonds was fostered by 'fictive kinship', in which adults cared for and loved unrelated young people as their own, which created a web of bonds that emulated an extended family. The ability to create and transfer loving familial bonds was, scholars believe, an important technique for coping with the loss and separation common to slavery.

Throughout the Atlantic world, the very old, the very young and the infirm faced the most profound challenges to their survival. Even New Englanders, whose climate was long considered to be the healthiest throughout the Atlantic world, suffered shockingly high childhood mortality rates. This led previous generations of historians to conclude that New England Calvinists resisted bonding with their children until the parents could have some reasonable assurance of their survival. New historical perspectives, however, suggest that even the most accepting of God's will were distressed by the deaths of the very young. An example of this is Samuel Sewall, a Boston-based Puritan minister, who wrote in his extensive diary of his sorrows for every young life lost, especially those of his own children and grandchildren. In addition, New World work demands followed patterns of child and family labour already deeply entrenched among the poor and middling classes in Europe. In colonial households, these often put children in harm's way. Often supervised by siblings not much older than themselves, toddlers were particularly vulnerable, with drowning or burning to death tragically common.

New Englanders in particular routinely sent their children to live among other families, a practice that, as historian Edmund Morgan suggested, kept Puritan children from being spoiled by their parents, and also helped them learn a trade, develop new household skills and meet eligible marriage partners. This change of abode provided children of both sexes with new opportunities to meet other young people under the watchful eye of their extended families. This practice continued in many parts of North America well into the nineteenth century.

Perhaps because Indians preferred to keep their children close, and did not demand much labour from them, Euroamericans considered the Indians they observed to be excessively attached to their children. Huron Indians were baffled and horrified when their children died from European diseases and suspected that baptism by Jesuit missionaries was the cause of death. Many therefore resisted European attempts to baptize their children or place them in schools. When European or African microbes devastated Native American communities, some responded by either seizing or inviting members of other groups to join their own. Though the process of adoption pre-dated the arrival of Europeans in the Americas, it increased considerably in their wake and, in some cases, contributed to 'mourning war' in which some captives were taken for adoption while others were earmarked for ritual torture.

Modern ideals of marriage privilege stability and monogamy. The upheaval of Atlantic explorations shows in sharp relief how much this ideal varied historically. Among the Spanish, men who had wives back home still pursued unions with Indian women. While women of low status were sought for sex (consensual and forced), stable relationships with elite Indian women often cemented alliances and eased the cultural integration of both conquerors and the conquered. The culturally mixed, Catholic daughters of Indian–Spanish unions were frequently married to further family fortunes even more. Other daughters became nuns in Latin America's new convents, creating important alliances with the Church as well. The destinies of Doña Isabel Monctezuma and Inés Yupanqui illustrate this point. Both women were 'given' to conquistadors in order to cement the alliance between the invading Spaniards and elite Aztecs. The women converted to Catholicism, bore their Spanish lovers children, and saw their offspring, male and female alike, married into elite families and well placed in prestigious religious institutions. They later went on to marry other, high-ranking Spanish men.

By the late seventeenth and early eighteenth centuries, children in elite Euroamerican households throughout the Americas and the Caribbean benefited from transforming views of the nature of childhood, as well as a burgeoning consumer culture and stabilization of colonial life. In the Caribbean, wealthy planters who could afford to leave their properties in the care of managers went to live either in Europe or on the American mainland, where the climate was healthier and the threat of slave revolt hundreds of miles of away. Though they no longer had daily interactions with those they owned in slavery, they continued to profit handsomely from their labour. Their children likewise benefited, enjoying the proximity to the highest echelons of English gentry society.

Sons of wealthy families sometimes returned to Europe for their education. This was the case of William Byrd II, the son and heir of a wealthy Virginia planter family with deep colonial roots. As a child, Byrd was placed in the care of an uncle to be educated back in England. This established a pattern that governed the rest of his life, during which Byrd travelled frequently to London, enjoying the city's sophistication and pleasures and importing fashionable goods back to Virginia.

In Protestant New World families, the oldest son inherited the bulk of his father's property. Younger sons might inherit livestock or money; daughters received house-hold goods and, occasionally, cash. In French, Spanish and Dutch colonies, however, estates were often split among all children, regardless of sex. Ultimately, daughters throughout the Atlantic world were subject to different standards than their brothers. Still, it does not necessarily follow that they were either uneducated or undereducated, or that they were deliberately restricted from living fulfilling lives. This may have been less the case for elite women in Iberian societies, whose families often saw public restrictions as an absolute necessity for preservation of virginity and family honour. Mostly educated by their mothers in domestic and maternal responsibilities, such women were expected to be largely innocent of the ways of the world. The lack of exposure with the world was intended to lead to submissive, pure and pious wives and mothers for colonial men of equally prestigious families.

Ironically, women who were deemed less than ideal candidates for marriage and motherhood had a better chance of education and, if they were inclined, a life of learning. When families were rich, their pious or plain daughters lived in elegant and comfortable convents, where they were waited on by enslaved Africans or servants and enjoyed ample libraries and spaces for entertainment.

Protestantism and Old World and New privileged literacy for women as well as men, which meant that many colonial English, German and Dutch women could at least read. They received their education either from one of their parents or, for the English, at a dame school, which taught simple literacy skills. Literacy in French Canada and Louisiana was far less common for females, but that did not mean that the colonies did not have some very fine schools for the daughters of the elite. As described by Roger Magnuson, French girls in the New World often received their education from convent schools, which were founded by various orders of nuns that came to the colonies' major settlements. They also learned the 'decorative' arts of needlework and music.

Although many women spent their lives deprived of even the basics of literacy, others had parents who nurtured their daughters' intellectual abilities. Anne Dudley Bradstreet, a poet who lived in Massachusetts, was educated by her zealously Puritan father, who granted his daughter access to his extensive holdings of books. Abigail Adams and Sarah Livingston Jay, both of whom married important American revolutionaries (John Adams and John Jay, respectively), had access to large libraries and were encouraged to explore their contents. Sarah Jay also received a more structured, intellectually rigorous education that rivalled those of her brothers. Eliza Lucas Pinkney, who became the mother of two other members of the founding generation (Charles Coatsworth and Thomas Pinkney), received a classical education from her father, who delighted in his daughter's intellect. Supremely confident in his daughter's erudition and sound judgement, he left her in exclusive charge of his South Carolina plantation when he was detained in Antigua. A young Mexican woman with a thirst to learn, Juana Inés de la Cruz de Asbaje y Ramirez found the only legitimate way to satiate her interests was to enter a convent.

Clothing

The Atlantic world was visually encoded with status, and people could recognize the status of almost anyone they encountered. Many regions of the Atlantic world had sumptuary laws – codes governing who was entitled to wear what, and under what conditions – that limited the colours and clothing styles of the poor, middling and up-and-coming. Clothing still varied according to climate, status and availability of fibres for processing and, as the seventeenth century gave way to the eighteenth and beyond, finished cloth. At the highest end of the social scale, elites wore rich fabrics that often had to be imported.

Shoes were a telling dimension of any dress. Often expensive and easily worn out, shoes were an expense that not everyone could afford for each stage of life. Families in warmer regions conserved the shoes of their children by having them go barefoot for significant portions of the year. Shoes and their relationship to class are evident in Latin American *casta* paintings. The elite men and women at the top of the social hierarchy wear boots for hunting, and slippers – shoes clearly for leisure and fashion, not for work. Even their children wear specialty footwear, a special luxury given that such shoes would quickly become obsolete with the rapid growth of small feet. Moving down the social scale, the labouring classes wore more practical, gender-neutral shoes meant more for protection and less for fashion. At the bottom of the social spectrum were the poor, who, if shod at all, wore sandals at best. Children in these scenes are almost always barefoot, not only a testament to poverty, but evidence that the poor in the Atlantic world were placed at a greater disadvantage for contracting diseases or dying of simple wounds. Parasites such as ringworm gained easy entry through the foot, and even the smallest wounds could become infected, leading in some cases to sepsis and early death. Europeans also adapted Native American forms of footwear. Moccasins not only protected feet, they provided excellent cover for quiet stalking during hunting and warfare.

Clothing, however, still served to distinguish Europeans from colonial elites. Observers assumed colonists were behind the times in terms of fashion and did not even know it. But the colonists generally did know; one colonial, George Washington, complained to James Lawrence, a London clothier, about a shipment of goods that Washington considered 'could only have been worn by our forefathers in days of yore'. The assumption among many Europeans that colonists were provincials who did not realize they were behind the times bred resentment and anger.

As late as the first decade of the nineteenth century, the Atlantic world's Europeans and their descendants dressed all children in skirts until the age of six or so, when boys and girls transitioned into dedicated gender-appropriate dress. Historically, scholars have interpreted this phenomenon as a sign that parents held themselves aloof from their young ones. A more practical interpretation takes into account the expense of textiles and the time it took to convert them into wearable clothing, as well as the 'easy access' skirts provided for changing a young child's soiled undergarments and training a child to relieve itself in an appropriate place. As the eighteenth century gave way to the nineteenth, however, cheaper imported textiles and changing concepts of childhood led to an earlier differentiation of clothing, one in which little boys, who a generation before would still have worn skirts, now wore 'skeleton suits', which consisted of a tight jacket and trousers.

Slaves were the most oppressed people of the Atlantic world, and their clothing often reflected this reality. Throughout the colonies, enslaved people who worked in the fields wore osnaburg (a coarse linen) or cotton, which protected their bodies but provided minimal considerations for modesty. Women in some cultures, including the Caribbean sugar colonies, often worked bare-breasted, which served to further demean them in the eyes of white observers. Whether their masters provided them with the means to dress in ways that made them comfortable and covered them in ways they deemed appropriate for themselves is less certain. Regardless, pictorial period evidence suggests that enslaved people, especially those who ventured out in public by themselves or in the company of slaveholders, might have had the means to personalize their garb. In South America and the Caribbean in particular, enslaved women often sported brightly coloured head wraps. In North America, it was common for slaves in Virginia to dress in clothes similar to those that English labouring men and women wore.

Native American dress also varied according to climate. Before contact with Europeans and Africans, the Indians of the western hemisphere's warmer regions wore animal hides to protect their genital regions. Women usually wore much the same, keeping their breasts bare to feed their children. Hairstyles, jewellery, tattooing and other adornment was often gendered and served to separate social classes within Native American society. Among pre-contact Mexicans, the dress and adornment of the royal and priestly classes set these individuals apart from the common folk. In contrast, Christopher Columbus described the Taino Indians of the island he named San Salvador as all 'naked as their mothers bore them', though with hair carefully cut and uniformly styled. To Columbus, the lack of distinctive dress according to gender and class made these Indians 'a very poor people'. Yet his own imported experiences from Europe could not accommodate the possibility of a world where dress and hierarchy were not one and the same.

After contact, Europeans, Africans and Native Americans all wore assortments of coverings that came from three sources: plant fibres, animal fibres and animal skins (including fur). Each had their advantages and drawbacks. While plant fibres such as flax (cotton would come later) were renewable and could often be made into light-weight, climate- and season-sensitive clothing, extraction and preparation of the fibres, as well as the actual spinning, dying, weaving and finishing, were enormously time consuming. Animal fibres presented many of the same limitations. Animal hides were also versatile, but they often required hunting and killing the animal, as well as an extensive tanning process that turned a perishable animal part into something supple and permanent. Many North American Indians wore animal hides. The pelts of fur-bearing animals such as beaver, moose and bear could be turned into extremely warm and durable pieces of clothing, but those from hides had serious limitations for warmth and comfort. Eastern Algonquians became increasingly biased towards European textiles, which became a lively trade component between the two cultures. Leather was less warm, but it allowed for greater personal mobility. To combat suede's propensity to roll and shrivel when wet, Native clothiers cut the edges of hide garments into fringe. Numerous images of Native Americans from seventeenth- and eighteenth-century sources show their subjects wearing articles of clothing of both Indian and European origin. Clothing of blended origins appears clearly in the paintings of Iroquois chiefs that Dutch painter Jan Verelst created for his patron, Britain's Queen Anne, in 1710.

The clothing, and even the bodies, of Atlantic world people often carried badges of religious identification. Despite popular belief to the contrary, Puritans wore many colours, and the style of their clothes reflected personal taste. Nevertheless, they strove for greater simplicity than the average seventeenth-century English man or woman. Quakers took this several steps further, dressing in the religiously circumscribed simplicity that became a badge of their beliefs. Nevertheless, as Quakerism grew in acceptance and Quakers themselves prospered, their dress evolved to encompass better fabrics and styles that, though specific in shape, changed with the times. In Latin America, elite Catholic men and women, and even those of lesser means, frequently wore jewellery that was religious in nature and was intended to suggest to others the piety of the wearer. In frontier regions where Christianities converged, Protestant women and men could encounter Catholic Indians, whose bodies might be covered in overt religious symbols such as crosses, beads and medals. Catholic Indians who had access to rosaries often wore them around their necks, not only to proclaim their faith but also to act as 'a defence from temptation'. Their fingers and necks might boast 'Jesuit rings', inexpensive trade goods made of a copper alloy that were commonly given to Indians by French priests. Though small, their escutcheons could be decorated with crucifixion groupings, crosses or short Latin phrases, all things that would have identified them as vaguely Euro-Christian in origin. Other Indians had similar Christian symbols permanently incised into their bodies through tattooing. Called *piquage* by the French, tattooing was common among most Native American groups, including the Wabanakis and their indigenous neighbours. Some Native groups incorporated Christian symbols into a broader iconographic repertoire. Europeans found this phenomenon worthy of note: in 1708, a French surgeon named Dièreville wrote that Indians he encountered were lavishly tattooed with 'all kinds of Devices' including 'Crosses, Names of Jesus, Flowers; anything in fact that may be desired'.

Food

Historically as today, food was a centrepiece of human life and culture. The origins of human organization coalesced around the need to cultivate and protect food sources. Life's many passages and communal celebrations more often than not consist of feasting or fasting. Some foods are considered sacred in origin, or their consumption gives one an immediate connection to the divine. Conflict and war often revolved around its control.

In crossing the Atlantic, Europeans and Africans encountered new foods (as described above in Chapter 2). These included tomatoes and potatoes, maize, cassava, manioc, peppers and squashes. Europeans in particular brought with them domesticated animals that could give edible products or be eaten themselves. Their relentless quest for trade also imported foods from one part of the western hemisphere to another, adding another way of augmenting local diets.

Agricultural production obviously varied according to region and climate. Therefore, so did the food that the Atlantic world's people consumed. But availability was not the only thing that affected food choice and preparation. Issues ranging from tradition to religious observance determined Atlantic world diets. Eating was one of the few acts that adults, rich and poor, and of varying levels of freedom, were able to determine for themselves. Children, of course, had little control over their diets.

The Puritans embraced local foods as a display of God's will. According to David Hackett Fischer, plain cooking and unadorned ingredients from the earth were reflections of one's piety. Multiple meals relied on peas, from which 'pottage', a thick porridge considered suitable for any meal, was made. It could be eaten either cold or hot and, unlike many other foods, could be prepared in advance – an important attribute for Puritan women, who had multiple claims on their time. The landscape made other contributions to Puritan diets, with fresh fruit and shellfish in abundance in season. The Puritans, however, did not always embrace their new environment's edibles. Eating food prepared along the lines of English cuisine was a way of connecting with home, and served to remind its consumers that they were, fundamentally, English men and women. They had to be pushed to eat foods such as wild duck and oysters, preferring instead plain, unseasoned boiled meat and vegetables. Meals were supplemented by baked goods – varied breads, cakes and pies – that added a bit of texture and flavour to otherwise bland meals. Puritans also included liquor in the forms of beer and ciders from various fruits. Fermented beverages were consumed by New Englanders of all ages, including young children. Though it was acceptable to consume alcohol from an early age, getting drunk on it was not. For that reason, New Englanders were careful to regulate licences for the creation and sale of alcohol. The popular perception of New Englanders as teetotallers, however, is patently false: like others in the Atlantic world, they knew that water could be unhealthy, and milk (by definition unpasteurized) was often put to uses other than drinking. Liquor could also be used as medicine and anaesthetic.

Non-English immigrants also imported their foodways with them. The Dutch in New Amsterdam left permanent marks on American diets with culinary delights such as cookies, waffles and doughnuts. The German immigrants to Pennsylvania persisted in their foodways as well, with various sausage- and cabbage-based preparations becoming American staples.

Wealthy Virginians enjoyed rich diets patterned on those of the well-off back in England. Roast beef was a favourite meal, as were game, fowl and fish. Asparagus and strawberries were also indulgent local delights. One famous popular southern dish – fried chicken – was not a poor person's food, but derived from 'fricassee', a method of cooking food in one pan with herbs and vegetables. As Fischer describes in his book, the tables of the rich contrasted sharply with those of the middling and poor – but that does not mean that those of lesser means simply dealt with cheap and unappealing food. Instead, they dressed their 'mess' of greens and salted meat, hominy or mush, with herbs and other seasonings.

In all Atlantic world cultures, a bountiful table was an important way to honour esteemed guests. When a visit by French Jesuit priest Gabriel Druillettes, on diplomatic mission from French Canada to New England in 1649, resulted in impromptu entertaining at the home of Plymouth Puritan John Bradford, the priest was flattered when the Puritan hosts arranged for a fish dinner for him, a respectful nod, as the priest saw it, to his Catholic dietary practices.

The diets of Catholic New World people were determined as much by the seasons as by religious devotion. The Catholics who crossed the Atlantic from Iberia and France lived in a world punctuated by their liturgical calendar. Chief among these devotions were feast days, which numbered almost half the calendar. On such days, Catholics refrained from eating meat. On others, for the so-called 'black fast', they avoided animal products altogether. In this religious dietary climate, the availability of fish carried heavy significance. Occasionally, fish was not available. Concerned that Catholics would either go hungry or, more likely, ignore the fast, church officials gave a dispensation for colonists to eat the flesh of beavers whose hides supplied the French fur trade. They reasoned that, as a swimming creature, it met the standard! As with other Atlantic peoples, the French in Canada innovated with what they found in their environment that looked interesting and, ideally, tasty. They adapted to both agricultural and religious calendars and enjoyed diets richly flavoured with native onions, maple sugar and syrup, and berries.

Like their counterparts from other parts of Europe, the Spanish diet adapted Old World foodways to New World foodstuffs. Fish was already a staple for many of the island and coastal Indian cultures of Central and South America and the Caribbean. This was something they had in common with the invading Iberians. Corn, beans and peppers became staples of New World diets, which still conformed to the meatless days of the Catholic calendar. For non-meatless days, however, settlers had an array of domesticated animals. Beef, pork and chicken, among many others, were infused with New World flavourings to make distinctly American creole dishes. The settlers also experimented with eating animals that had hitherto been unknown. Christopher Columbus ate alligator (in his *Diario* he claimed it tasted like chicken), and South American Spaniards seemed to enjoy eating such new and unusual delicacies as guinea pig and avocado.

Heat, and lack of refrigeration, led to easy spoilage. Europeans transplanted old techniques of food preparation to make their food last longer. One group was the 'buccaneers' of the Hispaniola, who cured meat on coastal drying racks called buccans. Though the name 'buccaneer' developed a later connection with piracy, the persistence of the word speaks to the importance of the original buccaneers' skill. Fish were likewise cured in open racks, called flakes. The resulting preserved fish was rock-hard and saltier than the Atlantic's waters, which kept well for transport in all climates and sold well in parts of Europe where diets were dictated by the Catholic cycle of feasts and fasts.

Contrary to popular belief, enslaved Africans enjoyed a more varied diet than just the rations that slaveholders gave them. This was due largely to their own labouring in small garden plots provided by slaveholders. Such arrangements were considered a win-win situation for slaves and slaveholders alike. In making at least a few choices a day for themselves, slaves used food to take back some of the self-determination that slavery robbed them of. In their preference for cultivating African foodstuffs such as okra, yams and beans, which grew well in diverse climates, they preserved elements of Africa that somehow survived the trauma of the Middle Passage. Finally, the sale of the surplus produce in nearby markets allowed slaves to accumulate either money or goods such as textiles, jewellery and domestic goods. Most slaveholders approved of the arrangement because they could take a substantial cut of whatever their slaves owned. Slaves producing their own food also meant, for the slaveholders, a reduction in the cost of owning slaves.

There is a popular perception that people of the sixteenth to nineteenth centuries were well below the average height and dimensions of twenty-first-century people. Though essentially correct, a distorted version of early American and Atlantic height suggests that this is somehow linked to human evolution, rather than genetics and diet. In truth, a diverse diet that included protein, dairy, vitamins C and D and roughage were, as they are now, keys to good health. The Atlantic world peoples who enjoyed complex and varied diets were capable of attaining similar height, weight and body dimensions of contemporary Americans.

But even those who had the means to indulge in a rich variety of foods were not always equipped to enjoy them. Tooth decay and loss haunted rich and poor alike, even the young. Since this made chewing difficult, it contributed to the popularity of pottages, gruels and corn puddings that were both digestible to the toothless and nourishing. Nicholas Creswell, an English visitor to North America between 1774 and 1777, assumed that early tooth decay was attributable to the hot bread that Americans ate at every meal. The more likely culprit, however, was the absence of dental hygiene.

With almost all arable land turned over to the production of plantation crops, the Caribbean colonies produced only limited foodstuffs. To supplement the diets of their free workers, who oversaw slaves and the processing of their crops, and in an effort to improve the chance of keeping reliable employees, absentee planters kept 'provisioning plantations' on the mainland to supply them with a varied diet. The Philipse family, whose holdings consisted of 54,000 acres along the lower Hudson River, trade buildings and warehouses in Manhattan, and sugar plantations, with hundreds of slaves, on Barbados, fed their staff with food produced at their farm and mill on the Pocantico River, near Tarrytown, New York. The hands of the property's enslaved Africans created butter and cheese, and cultivated and packed produce and grain for export to the Philipses' far more lucrative Caribbean sugar plantations.

For the transplanted peoples of the Atlantic world, food was one of the most powerful links to their former land. Native peoples, however, saw their world transformed by Atlantic travellers, and this affected their diets too. It started with corn. On the eve of encounter, many of the Indian groups of North and South America had some connection to corn. The kernels of so-called 'Indian corn', or maize, were hard, and the meal created from them made for a long-lasting starchy staple that stored easily and travelled well. Corn was the basis for a variety of cakes, breads and porridges, to be enjoyed with fresh game and fowl, locally grown wild edibles, other cultivated foods such as beans and pumpkins and, where available, fish and shellfish. Corn was the most reliably available food in this line-up, provided it was cultivated. This, however, came with its own problems, requiring some groups to remain sedentary in order to tend their fields. This sometimes led to conflict between Indian bands, as some nomadic groups found it easier to steal or fight for their neighbours' food supply than change their own ways. For their part, the agricultural groups bore their own share in these tensions as their expansion of growing fields led them to fiercely protect their territories – or claim others in a quest for more space to plant. Indians, Europeans and Africans shared new foods, as well as food-related technology, that often transformed more than just diet. Native Americans who came into contact with Europeans tended to appreciate the tools and food-related weapons they brought with them. But a greater reliance on these trade items added encumbrances to Indian groups and hindered their ability to travel lightly, or even at all.

● **UP FOR DEBATE**   New cultures or adapted ones?

Did crossing the Atlantic result in the creation of new cultures, or the simple transplantation and adaptation of old ones? Take a position on this issue and support your ideas with the chapter's content.

Pastimes

All the peoples who converged along the Atlantic littoral enjoyed private and public entertainments. Then as now, small-scale pastimes relieved stress, provided pleasure, bonded families and neighbours, and added a sense of fun to lives often consumed with work. Public events reinforced a sense of community and common purpose, added public spectacle to religious life, and even made hard seasonal work more enjoyable.

Wealth and status often determined access to entertainment. Even before the encounter with Europeans, Mexica and Taino elites enjoyed privileged spots at ball tournaments and seasonal ceremonies. Such events often carried extremely high stakes: upon loss of a game, the victors enslaved or executed the losers.

Elites in the English colonies enjoyed travel to relatives and friends on a seasonal basis. These allowed elites to reinforce their status in society. Prolonged social visits also allowed elite colonial parents to show off unmarried children to eligible partners. Talents in music, dancing, manners and conversation, as well as physical beauty enhanced by elegant dress, were put on display during elite parties, and helped spread the word that the daughter of any given person was a good catch on many levels.

Some entertainments were shockingly cruel by modern standards. Public executions were a particularly popular form of public entertainment, complete with dramatic final statements that were sometimes published as pamphlets or inspired sermons. And as much as they cherished certain animals, such as pet dogs and horses, others were bred for sport alone and deemed expendable. Virginians, for example, revelled in games like 'pinning the bull', a sport in which specially bred dogs were released to attack the larger animal and set their teeth into its snout. Bullfighting migrated across the Atlantic to the Spanish New World, where it took particular hold in Mexico. Cockfights and dogfights were blood sports that required less investment than a horse or bull, as the animals needed for the fights were readily available in most New World communities.

Despite contemporary attitudes about the utility and human mastery of animals, elite families in particular often included pets, that is, animals kept as companions and status accessories. Dog breeds ranging from hunting to companionship canines appear frequently in early American paintings. Their inclusion told observers something of the tastes, interests and status of the sitter. Other animals were also kept as companions to men, women and children. Songbirds were common pets, as were, at least in North America, squirrels. These animals in particular served double duty: they not only amused little boys, but also served as visual metaphors of the process of 'taming' childish impulses. Other pets were even more exotic and ranged from deer to peacocks. Other pets were so beloved that they travelled with their masters. Such was the case with Charles Lee, a Revolutionary War general who rarely went anywhere without his pack of adored dogs. People relied heavily on animals, but such reliance was not only based on the textiles, meat, leather, feathers and eggs that could be got from them. Domesticated animals enhanced status, provided children with opportunities to develop responsibility, and gave affection and companionship to their masters. Priests and ministers from Mexico to Quebec complained bitterly of congregants who went so far as to bring cherished dogs into church with them!

Horseracing likewise migrated from Europe, and many colonists, particularly in the American South, were enthusiastic supporters of the sport. As the most common means of transportation, horses were widely available. Many, however, could not afford to own a horse, making ownership of even the most decrepit specimen a display of status. For the Atlantic world's often self-styled gentry, horseracing became a singular indulgence, one which demonstrated social status, wealth and masculinity all at once. Indeed, people of more modest means were forbidden from competing anyway; as David Hackett Fischer notes, a Virginia tailor named James Bullock was fined one hundred pounds of tobacco for competing with his mare against a gentleman. Though permitted to watch, non-elites were also barred from placing bets on potential winners. Gentlemen, however, challenged one another to thousands of pounds of tobacco, making the capacity to participate in horseracing and bet on its outcomes a public reinforcement of one's place in society. Gambling and games of chance of various kinds, however, were popular pastimes for people with at least some property. Excessive gambling was frowned upon in societies with deep religious underpinnings and at times even outlawed, but other cultures either turned a blind eye or saw no cultural inconsistencies with allowing it to exist openly. Sometimes the stakes were very large: in the seventeenth-century Chesapeake or Caribbean, it was not uncommon for wealthy planters to gamble away slaves or indentured servants.

Dancing was a pastime that knew no class boundaries. The wealthy throughout the Atlantic world enjoyed assemblies, balls and religious festivals, which in turn allowed them to introduce their daughters (or 'doncellas', as they were called in Iberian culture) to the eligible sons of their fellow elites. The same principle put strict boundaries around who was invited to such events. For the poor and middling folk, festivities involving dancing likewise provided a socially acceptable way for young women and men to get to know one another. It also provided a venue for men who lacked material prosperity to display other assets, including their grace and physical prowess.

Social drinking also allowed for relaxation and entertainment. For most people throughout the Atlantic world, alcoholic beverages were often the drink of choice. The reasons for preferring alcohol ranged from the unhealthy alternatives of contaminated water and unpasteurized milk to the desire to escape hard, tedious and sometimes brutal lives. No colonial society banned alcohol outright, though a few tried to curb its distribution and abuses. Yet many societies regulated liquor sale and production. Permits and licences were common, and public drunkenness became a pretext for legal public punishment. In many cultures, making a distilled or fermented beverage out of locally cultivated grains or fruits was a way of turning valuable foodstuffs into something that was both durable and useful. Beer and whiskey preserved grain; cider and perry were produced from apples and pears that might otherwise have been unusable. Women, for the most part, were brewers of beer, a domestic skill they managed until immigrants from Germany brought their own large-scale, and masculine, brewing traditions in the nineteenth century.

In Latin America, women were also the primary brewers of *chicha* and *pulque*, fermented beverages of corn and agave leaves, respectively, which were valued forms of preserving both foodstuffs. Spanish priests who attempted to ban the ceremonial aspects of drinking *pulque* did so at their own peril. Native North Americans had virtually no previous experience of intoxicating beverage at the time they encountered Europeans. They quickly adapted its use to ritual practices. As alcohol became cheap and common, however, its capacity to support irrational and violent behaviour became evident. At the urging of Jesuit missionaries, the French crown moved to limit the sale of alcohol to Native peoples. The trade was valuable to French colonists, however, and they sought to subvert the regulation whenever possible.

Pastimes specifically for the young were few among the poor and middling. Atlantic world children had few personal objects that modern observers would consider toys. Yet is does not follow that they did not play. Most children had little choice but to respond creatively to the world around them, incorporating nature, animals and other children into their play. In contrast, wealthy children often had specific playthings, some of which were imported from Europe. Elite girls had dolls, though not for the obvious reason of teaching motherhood skills. Such dolls were modelled on adults, and taught important lessons of elegance, grace and fashion. For elite girls, these were important skills indeed. Boys had sports equipment and toy versions of tools of future trades, including models of ships and toy horses. Noah's Arks as popular toys were, as one might guess, attuned to waves of evangelical enthusiasm and were widely found throughout the early nineteenth century.

The poorer the child, the more his or her life was likely to be absorbed by work. Nevertheless, children of all backgrounds adapted adult work into the pleasures of childhood. Native American boys, for instance, played at hunting skills until they were old enough to actually join their fathers in the hunt. Boys and girls alike stretched their talents for outdoor activities, in which many excelled. The skills of one particular Maliseet girl in the borderlands between New England and French Canada mortified English captive John Gyles: she saved his life after he fell into a river and could not swim well enough to save himself. Poor children of European extraction likely enjoyed more personal contact with their parents than the rich did, simply because they were more fully integrated into the adult world of work. As fellow contributors to family resources, they worked in kitchens, fields, shops and other workspaces, often from an early age. Though these are highly idealized images in some ways, Iberian *casta* paintings of the eighteenth century depict the mixed-race children of colonial parents helping prepare food, weave, and even manufacture cigarettes.

As we already know, forms of servitude and slavery impacted on children from every cultural background. For some children, the households that held them bound also had the capacity to introduce them to the skills needed for successful entertainments and diversions. Some slave children were exposed to traditional European-style instruments, such as the violin, and learned to play them with great skill. Others retooled African musical traditions to suit contemporary situations. As with any master musician, the greater the skill, the more esteemed the person. Some enslaved 'musicianers' even earned enough to purchase for themselves and their families some significant material comforts.

Travel and Community

Many of the Atlantic world's Euroamericans never travelled more than 30 miles from the place where they were born. Even those born on the other side of the Atlantic Ocean tended to migrate and then stay put. Still, travel within that limited sphere was frequently necessary and often arduous.

Most common people relied on their own feet for travel, even for long distances. The need to move goods, however, required animals such as horses, donkeys, mules and oxen. Despite assumptions to the contrary, not all people owned these animals. In areas where people were many and these helpful animals were few, the latter were in great demand. Even those who possessed the means of easy movement – good horses, the skills to manage them, and even carriages and skilled coachmen – likely faced the proposition of long distances on rough, unpredictably maintained roads with trepidation. It is little wonder, then, that the sense of community that developed in places like North America was focused almost exclusively on local issues, including civil order and defence.

Class could also determine the exposure one had to the world outside the family. In Latin America, many elite young women left their homes only for church or for social visits to one another. In contrast, young women in British colonial society might travel significant distances to visit relatives and gain exposure to a new pool of eligible marriage partners. That being said, young women were prone to the same geographical limitations as other colonials.

Despite the increase in safe passages, the Atlantic Ocean remained a formidable challenge for most transatlantic travellers. Passengers suffered from seasickness, small rations of unappetizing food and water already of dubious quality, and communicable diseases that spread easily in tight, poorly ventilated sleeping quarters. Adding to the journey's discomforts was the sheer tediousness of an Atlantic crossing. Tight quarters and lack of privacy allowed for few personal activities, including reading, private contemplations or intimacy with others. When the weather was fair, travellers could choose to spend time on deck, though that too might be disrupted by the work of the sailors and expose genteel and devout ears and eyes to the profane world of the average European mariner.

Living Together

Urban life in the Atlantic world was experienced by multiple senses. Buildings fine and humble greeted the eyes. Sounds spilled forth from the doors and windows of houses of worship as well as the mouths of street hawkers and peddlers. Noses detected the unpleasantness of freshly dropped animal dung on streets and the more pleasing aromas of wood smoke and cooking food. As the cityscape changed, so did its sensorial elements. Closer to the wharves was the 'forest' of masts of the busier ports, which smelled of tar, pitch and hemp; of wood saturated with salt water; and of commodities packaged and waiting to be loaded onto ships.

By the middle of the eighteenth century, the well-off, the poor and the 'middling sort' in between lived in cities such as Montreal, Boston, New York, Philadelphia, Charlestown, Bahia, New Orleans, Mexico City and Bridgetown. Small by modern standards (none of the cities in what is now the United States had more than 10,000 people on the eve of the American Revolution), cities of the Atlantic world were centres of trade and colonial administration. But they were also home to many colonists, who owned warehouses, lent money, built furniture and musical instruments, sold imported manufactures out of storefronts, cooked and peddled prepared food, and offered their bodies for sex.

In addition, cities came to provide for their residents some of the same privileges that cities in Europe did: they became a form of public theatre in and of themselves, a stage for showing taste, mingling with social equals, and introducing children to suitable friends and marriage partners. Many wealthier families had multiple homes that linked city and country society. Urban homes allowed elites to keep an eye on their business interests and, where relevant, participate in political activity, which like everything else was seasonal in nature. Country homes were refuges from urban hazards, which ranged from the unpleasant (already-aromatic city streets baking in the hot summer sun) to the potentially deadly (outbreaks of highly contagious diseases such as smallpox and yellow fever). Cities were preferred in the winter, when disease was usually at ebb and the short, cold days yielded to indoor entertainments. Country residences, however, were places to entertain family and friends, often for extended periods of time. They also provided opportunities for enjoying outdoor pursuits, especially hunting. When Atlantic world elites engaged in these pastimes, they self-consciously patterned their behaviours on European nobles and gentry.

A rising self-consciousness about their physical surroundings among colonial elites of the British Atlantic world coincided with what historians have called the 'Consumer Revolution', defined in Chapter 4 as a transition in the safety and speed of moving raw materials, goods and people. The revolution brought new products into elite households, such as china, silver and textiles. Through the dissemination of pattern-books, colonials also became aware of the latest styles in British architecture, furniture design and dress. Though eager to emulate the upper classes on the other side of the Atlantic, colonial consumers were often at the mercy of European purchasing agents thousands of miles away. Some of these agents made the fatal mistake of believing they were dealing with poorly informed provincials and sent over unfashionable goods. But colonists often knew they were being duped, and resented it.

A World Imprinted with Religion

Religious environments and public expressions of religion were found among every Atlantic world belief system. A visitor to an overwhelmingly Catholic region of the Atlantic world would have experienced sounds, sights and perhaps even aromas that were distinctly Catholic in nature. Churches and cathedrals (churches that served as the seat of a bishop) were often the largest and most prominently placed structures in a town. Their cruciform shape, bell towers, steeples and distinctively shaped windows made them easy to identify, as did the activity that often buzzed in or around them. Wealthier and more established parishes might boast churches that resembled those in Europe, complete with exterior decorative statuary. Inside, and particularly in Latin America, art forms mingled, with statues and paintings often created using indigenous techniques.

Unlike many colonial buildings, church structures were built to provide as much natural light as possible. With candles expensive, dirty and dangerous, colonial clergy and religious adapted building techniques that minimized their use as lighting elements. Still, candles played a key part in Catholic liturgy throughout the New World and were therefore an absolute necessity. As far afield as frontier Maine, a Jesuit missionary, Sebastien Rale, bragged to his family back in France about the bayberry candles he had for his mission church.

Anglican churches also claimed a commanding position in Atlantic world society – albeit one that was somewhat more diffuse. Anglicanism was just about universal in early Virginia, and quickly became the dominant religion in Maryland as well. Anglican ceremonies conformed neatly to a society that already relied heavily on displays of status and hierarchy. Its rich liturgies and rituals reinforced a common sense of Englishness among the settlers. After Virginia's disorienting early decades, the dominant Anglican church stood as a unifying force that stabilized colonial society. Weddings, funerals, births and weekly sacraments were celebrated within its churches or at home by its clergy. Churches were common landscape features as well. Unlike those in New England, Anglican churches announced themselves as houses of worship. Steeples, distinctive windows and cruciform shapes to the buildings spoke of their function.

Religious institutions were also important landmarks. Frequently, these communal homes of nuns and priests also served as schools, hospitals, hostels for the poor, and seats of missionary enterprise. Any given day would see the comings and goings of children, the poor and the sick who sought the services offered within. Often these buildings were distinguished by the image of a divine patron – Jesus, the Virgin Mary or a patron saint – who protected the institution's work and identified the caregivers.

Religious communities made their own daily contributions to the cityscape, usually in the form of music. During the clement time of year in places like Quebec, the chanting of the divine office and the liturgies of holy days would have escaped cloister walls and bled onto the street, helping people with few or no clocks to mark the time of day.

Streets were likewise filled with Catholic people whose appearance spoke of their religious affiliations. And while strict religious enclosure often limited or forbade nuns from walking the streets, lay women demonstrated their piety by wearing large decorative crosses, carrying rosaries and pious books, and covering their heads in public. Portraiture of Spanish Latin American subjects underscores the ubiquitous presence of religious symbols on clothing. Protestant communities carried their own hallmarks. Chief among them for Puritans was the simplicity of the churches, which were barely distinguishable as houses of worship. As David Hackett Fischer notes, these buildings were built along the same lines as market buildings and town halls. The lone surviving Puritan religious structure in colonial Massachusetts, Hingham's Old Ship Meeting House, helps illustrate how these structures created a specifically 'Puritan' religious landscape, which rejected the architectural religious exuberance of Catholicism and Anglicanism. In this case, the term 'meeting house' is highly suggestive and connotes multiple functions. Reserved for religious services during the Sabbath and on days of thanksgiving, Puritan meeting houses were also places where the community gathered to hear news, address communal problems and, when the circuit court was in session, house trials and other legal proceedings. While Puritans defined virtually all church icons and decorations as idolatrous, they were known to adorn their pulpits with an image of the all-seeing eye of God.

In times of tension between competing Euroamericans, religious structures were frequent targets. New World Protestants of many backgrounds practised iconoclasm against Catholic buildings, an act that was common in England particularly in the period of the English Civil War. English sailors who attacked Catholic settlements in the Spanish Caribbean turned to the usual techniques of burning chapels, smashing statues and hosts, shredding the vestments that priests used for Mass, and pulling apart pious books. But they also looted for both items of value and other objects that would appeal to curious Protestants. When forces under William Phips attacked the French Acadian settlement of Port Royal in 1692, they brought consecrated hosts back with them to Boston, which they displayed as relics of their successful mission. And despite their association with the taint of Catholicism, some items were just too valuable to destroy or cast away and were recycled into Protestant worship spaces. Catholics and Protestants took church bells, which were heavy and expensive, from each other when they could and hauled them back home to be used in their own communities. And in one case truly reflective of the Atlantic world, English raiders counted among their booty from a French merchant ship a baptismal font purchased in Senegal. The font was then given to Saint John's Anglican Church in Portsmouth, New Hampshire, where it resides to this day.

Conclusion

Life in the Atlantic world forced early modern people to adapt to new circumstances. When opportunity arose, many replicated what they could from the Old World. These efforts, however, were hampered by the capacity to move goods throughout the Atlantic world and for the New World societies themselves to survive and thrive. But Old World migrants were resourceful and adaptable, eager to explore new goods and recast them to fit new purposes. Similarly, the New World's Native peoples proved even more inventive, perhaps, in borrowing, adding and adapting the tools and techniques of the invaders, remaking their worlds in their own ways.

CHAPTER CHRONOLOGY

1519   Horses and 'dogs of war' brought with Cortés and his forces in the conquest of Mexico. Other domesticated animals from across the Atlantic will soon follow.

1549   The Portuguese establish the city of Salvator on the coast of Bahia, Brazil.

1621   Wampanoag Indians teach English immigrants to cultivate native crops.

1728   *The Book of Architecture*, by James Gibbs, is published.

1789   British whaling vessel *Amelia* pursues its prey into the Pacific Ocean, reorienting that trade away from the Atlantic; whale oil lamps and candles create cleaner, brighter, longer-burning light sources that enhance domestic life in the Americas and Europe.

1830   The founding of the Baltimore and Ohio Railroad hastens the movement of North America's people away from the Atlantic and towards the western interior.

■ **PRIMARY SOURCES AND STUDY IMAGE**

'Novum Belgium' by the Jesuit Isaac Jogues (1643)

New Holland which the Dutch call in Latin *Novum Belgium*, in their own language Nieuw Nederland, that is to say, New Low Countries, is situated between Virginia and New England. The mouth of the river called by some Nassau river or the great North river (to distinguish it from another which they call the South river) and which in some maps that I have recently seen is also called, I think, River Maurice, is at 4030'. Its channel is deep, fit for the largest ships that ascend to Manhattes Island, which is seven leagues in circuit, and on which there is a fort to serve as the commencement of a town to be built there and to be called New Amsterdam.

    This fort which is at the point of the island about five or six leagues from the mouth, is called Fort Amsterdam; it has four regular bastions mounted with several pieces or artillery. All these bastions and the curtains were in 1643 but ramparts of earth, most of which had crumbled away, so that the fort could be entered on all sides. There were no ditches. There were sixty soldiers to garrison the said fort and another which they had built still further up against the incursions of the savages their enemies. They were beginning to face the gates and bastions with stone. Within this fort stood a pretty large church built of stone; the house of the Governor, whom they called Director General, quite neatly built of brick, the storehouses and barracks.

On this island of Manhate and in its environs there may well be four or five hundred men of different sects and nations; the Director General told me that there were persons there of eighteen different languages; they are scattered here and there on the river, above and below as the beauty and convenience of the spot invited each to settle, some mechanics however who ply their trades are ranged under the fort; all the others were exposed to the incursions of the natives, who in the year 1643, while I was there actually killed some two score Hollanders and burnt many houses and barns full of wheat.

A Voyage to South America, Jorge Juan and Antonio de Ulloa (1748)

The inhabitants of Lima are composed of whites, or Spaniards, Negroes, Indians, Mestizos, and other casts, proceeding from the mixture of all three.

The Spanish families are very numerous; Lima according to the lowest computation, containing sixteen or eighteen thousand whites, Among these are reckoned a third or fourth part of the most distinguished nobility of Peru; and many of these dignified with the stile of ancient or modern Castilians, among which are no less than 45 counts and marquises. The number of knights belonging to the several military orders is also very considerable. Besides these are many families no less respectable and living in equal splendour; particularly 24 gentlemen of large estates, but without titles, tho' most of them have ancient seats, a proof of the antiquity of their families. One of these traces, with undeniable certainty, his descent from the Incas. The name of this family is Ampuero, so called from one of the Spanish commanders at the conquest of this country, who married a Coya, or daughter of the Inca. To this family the kings of Spain have been pleased to grant several distinguishing honours and privileges, as marks of its great quality: and many of the most eminent families in the city have desired intermarriages with it.

All those families live in a manner becoming their rank, having estates equal to their generous dispositions, keeping a great number of slaves and other domestics, and those who affect making the greatest figure, have coaches, while others content themselves with calashes or chaises, which are here so common, that no family of any substance is without one. It must be owned that these carriages are more necessary here than in other cities, on account of the numberless droves of mules which continually pass thro' Lima, and cover the streets with their dung, which being soon dried by the sun and the wind, turns to a nauseous dust, scarce supportable to those who walk on foot. These chaises, which are drawn by a mule, and guided by a driver, have only two wheels, with two seats opposite to each other, so that on occasion they will hold four persons. They are very slight and airy; but on account of the gildings and other decorations, sometimes cost eight hundred or a thousand crowns. The number

Study image 6 *Die Stadt Havana, from Alain Manesson Mallet, Description de l'Univers …, 1685.*

of them is said to amount to 5 or 6000; and that of coaches is also very considerable, tho' not equal to the former.

'American Cookery, or the Art of Dressing Viands, Fish, Poultry and Vegetables, and the Best Modes of Making Pastes, Puffs, Pies, Tarts, Puddings, Custards and Preserves, and all Kinds of Cakes, from the Imperial Plumb to the Plain Cake. Adapted to this Country and All Grades of Life.' By Amelia Simmons, an American Orphan (1796)

Minced Pies, A Foot Pie

Scald neets feet, and clean well, (grass fed are best) put them into a large vessel of cold water, which change daily during a week, then boil the feet till tender, and take away the bones, when cold, chop fine, to every four pound minced meat, add one pound of beef suet, and four pound apple raw, and a little salt, chop all together very fine, add one quart of wine, two pound of stoned raisins, one ounce of cinnamon, one ounce mace, and sweeten to your taste; make use of paste No. 3 – bake three quarters of an hour.

Weeks after, when you have occasion to use them, carefully raise the top crust, and with a round edg'd spoon, collect the meat into a bason, which warm with additional wine and spices to the taste of your circle, while the crust is also warm'd like a hoe cake, put carefully together and serve up, by this means you can have hot pies through the winter, and enrich'd singly to your company.

A Nice Indian Pudding

No. 1. 3 pints scalded milk, 7 spoons fine Indian meal, stir well together while hot, let stand till cooled; add 7 eggs, half pound raisins, 4 ounces butter, spice and sugar, bake one and half hour.

No. 2. 3 pints scalded milk to one pint meal salted; cool, add 2 eggs, 4 ounces butter, sugar or molasses and spice q. f. it will require two and half hours baking.

No. 3. Salt a pint meal, wet with one quart milk, sweeten and put into a strong cloth, brass or bell metal vessel, stone or earthern pot, secure from wet and boil 12 hours.

Recommended Reading

Virginia DeJohn Anderson, *Creatures of Empire: How Domestic Animals Transformed Early America* (Oxford, 2004). Examines how keeping livestock changed American environments, habits and economies.

William Cronon, *Changes in the Land: Indians, Colonists and the Ecology of New England* (New York, 1983). An environmental history of New England's historical residents (Native American and European alike), and the ways they shaped and altered the natural world.

Alfred Crosby, *The Columbian Exchange: Biological and Cultural Consequences of 1492* (Westport, CT, 1973). A classic study of the consequences of converging living organisms passing between the Old World and the New.

Brian Fagan, *Fish on Friday: Feasting, Fasting and the Discovery of the New World* (New York, 2007). Examines how diet, preservation, religion and politics pushed Europeans across the Atlantic in search of codfish.

David Hackett Fischer, *Albion's Seed: Four British Folkways in North America* (Oxford, 1989). Analysis of four regional migrations from England to America, and how these specific regional variations influenced the growth of North American colonial culture.

Peter Moogk, *La Nouvelle France: The Making of New France – A Cultural History* (East Lansing, MI, 2000). A social history of French Canada.

Edmund Morgan, *The Puritan Family: Religion and Domestic Relations in Seventeenth-Century New England* (Cambridge, MA, 1966). Landmark study that separates Puritan rhetoric on family relationships from real practices.

Frederick Douglass Opie, *Hog and Hominy: Soul Food from Africa to America* (New York, 2008). Probes the origins and influence of African American food culture on Atlantic diets.

Jan Rogoziński, *A Brief History of the Caribbean: From the Arawak and Caribe to the Present* (New York, 2000). Narrative of the exploration, invasion and colonial development of the Caribbean islands.

Susan Migden Socolow, *The Women of Colonial Latin America* (Cambridge, 2000). Focuses on the diverse interactions, experiences and relationships of colonial women in Central and South America.

TEST YOUR KNOWLEDGE

1 What basic human needs and traits linked the peoples of the Atlantic world? What were some of the cultural variations of these traits?

2 How did families use these early structures? How did living spaces of elites and the commercial classes evolve during the eighteenth century?

3 How did marriage practices among Atlantic peoples vary from our understanding of marriage?

4 How was family structure affected by the Atlantic movement and encounter?

5 How did the significance of clothing differ according to class? Why were these distinctions important?

6 Why was food, and the quest for predictable food, such a dominant theme in Atlantic history? What does it tell us about this period of study?

7 What pastimes were enjoyed by Atlantic people? How did class and gender affect the ability to participate?

8 What was the interplay between social class and neighbourhood in Atlantic port cities?

9 How did religious identity affect the visual nature of Atlantic communities?

7 Dependence and Independence: the Parameters of Identity and Freedom

For nearly three hundred years, the Europeans who branched out into the greater Atlantic attempted to make the new places they encountered dependent in some way. Trade and security were their chief areas of focus. When challenged, however, Europeans were not above demanding submission, a situation that obviously created dislike of the would-be overlords and, eventually, resistance movements. Enlightenment philosophies of human rights and personal liberty crossed the Atlantic like any other commodity, and gave voice and shape to popular discontent. Eventually, revolts and popular pressures gave way to calls for independence from European powers. By the middle of the nineteenth century, these movements had profound consequences, including the destruction of chattel slavery and the smashing of mercantilism, the Atlantic world's major reason for being, as far as its European invaders were concerned.

This chapter focuses on the movements and activities that ended up contributing to the end of various Atlantic systems. This in turn created new relationships, where colonists who were once expected to submit to the requirements of their mother countries now demanded sovereignty and respect. The conditions that led to these movements, as well as the movements themselves, will be explored.

The Atlantic: Forged in Dependence, Opportunities for Independence

By the middle of the sixteenth century, Europe, the Americas and Africa were a collection of interdependent land masses, spanning out along a common body of water and linked together by increasingly fast, predictable, powerful and often well-armed seafaring vessels. In protecting their interests, Europeans frequently engaged one another in wars of trade and geographical expansion. Some of these conflicts were European or African in origin and spilled over into the New World. Others began in the Americas and crossed the Atlantic in the other direction.

Turbulence in the Atlantic world was not limited to the ocean. As various European powers fought to establish themselves as the pre-eminent Continental power, their Atlantic world land claims became targets for attack by enemies, more forceful assertions of authority, and, specifically in North America, a compromise position in which laws on the books were enforced lightly to the colonists' advantage, presumably to secure their allegiance. Sometimes these hostilities resulted in the destruction of entire families or communities; sometimes they actually benefited the local European populations and the 'haves' among Africans and Native Americans. The 'have nots' – Africans targeted for kidnapping and slavery, poor frontier farmers, and Native American groups who lacked powerful European allies and did not control goods of value – were the ones who stood to suffer the most. But throughout the Atlantic world, the shifting of allegiances, movements among Native Americans, and intellectual and spiritual developments gave both rich and poor powerful motives for rising up against real or perceived oppressors. While one tends to think of the American and Haitian revolutions as the most important uprisings to challenge the Atlantic system, it is important to note that warfare was a near-chronic state of affairs along the littoral on both sides of the ocean.

Colonies on the western rim of the English Atlantic world were often managed by crown officials, or friends and supporters of various European monarchs who were invested with the authority to create or carry out matters of colonial policy. Though these administrators suffered the same diseases, shortages and violence as their fellow colonists, they were often better positioned to benefit from the New World's resources. Some particularly powerful administrators, however, became thorns in the side of their mother countries. Corruption was common, and its frequent occurrence robbed the mother country of revenue and subverted its rule of law. What cannot be discounted is that administrators lived far from the leaders who had appointed them. With an ocean between themselves and those they reported to, they often juggled the demands of duty to the crown, the local conditions with which they had real experience, and the call of self-preservation and promotion. One such administrator, Virginia's colonial governor William Berkeley, managed to straddle these demands with skill for more than 30 years. In New Spain, colonial administrators who could not implement – or resisted implementing – official colonial policy, used the phrase, 'I obey but do not comply', to illustrate their knowledge of laws that, given local circumstances, they were unable to enforce.

As they matured, Atlantic colonies throughout the European sphere of influence were expected to become microcosms of the mother country, which implemented the rule of the monarch's law precisely and strictly. Yet vast distances, time lags in communication, and laws that were unenforceable in the face of local realities contributed to the creation of new cultures, and new cultural outlooks. Though they shared many folkways and civic systems, new beliefs about self-determination and individual rights shaped the western Atlantic peoples' views of themselves. Furthermore, the distance across the Atlantic made it possible for people from many backgrounds to reinvent themselves. Now far distant from rigidly enforced, ancient codes that tied economic success to family, lineage, blood and honour, they were free to use what they had to recreate both themselves and their position in society. Distance always made a difference.

People of more modest means, or those who were oppressed and held captive by their self-described masters, realized the implications of new concepts of freedom and seized the opportunity to free themselves. The Haitian Revolution was one such event. As Haiti's free people of colour grasped the ideas that underpinned France's own radical revolution, its slaves took advantage of the fragmentation of free society and threw off their masters. In revolutionary America, colonists who had long been forced to live in the shadow of cultural inferiority imposed on them by elites appropriated ideas of personal liberty and human rights to assert their own dignity. This group came to include merchants and tradesmen, enslaved Africans, and women.

Competition: Patriotism, Privateering and Piracy

The widening influence of Europeans and their desire for dependence and submission grew and expanded over the course of centuries. Growth sparked envy, upset global balances of power, and contributed to pre-existing Old World conflicts. At various times, Europeans formed predictable and unlikely alliances to combat their enemy of the moment. Religious affinities linked royal houses and cultural ties, and pre-existing conflicts often paled in comparison to immediate needs to defend territory and maintain cultural influence.

A common strategy was to strike at the colonies of an enemy whose colonial management appeared lax or haphazard. This is what the Dutch did in the 1580s. They rebelled against their Iberian overlords by attacking the trading communities of the Spanish-allied Portuguese on the west coast of Africa. Eventually, real penetration into these new markets by the Dutch was achieved though trade rather than violent coercion. By the first decade of the seventeenth century, the United Provinces of the Netherlands had more or less replaced the Portuguese throughout their eastern trade empire. These trade relationships were managed by the Dutch East India Company, whose sister firm, the Dutch West India Company, settled New Amsterdam. The consequences for Africa were significant, as the Dutch took temporary control of the highly lucrative slave trade that linked Angola and Brazil. Though they ultimately lost these possessions, the Dutch did also take control of Surinam, which became one of the most brutal and lucrative plantation societies in the Americas.

Though they were once allies in Protestantism, the Dutch and the English competed for New World primacy during the seventeenth century, engaging in a series of conflicts known as the Anglo-Dutch Wars. Concerned over the Netherlands' spreading influence over trade in the Atlantic world, the English enacted in 1651 a series of trade regulations meant to break Dutch control. The Dutch went to war, hoping to force England to reverse its policies. But that did not happen, and the First Anglo-Dutch War (followed by two others) ended up contributing to the decline in the Netherlands' influence in the Atlantic world. Perhaps most significantly, it spurred England to greatly increase its navy – an innovation that would create the concept of English primacy on the seas and carry global implications into the twentieth century. It was during the second Anglo-Dutch War that the English took control of New Amsterdam, the major Dutch settlement in North America. The settlement was rechristened New York.

The French too competed with the Dutch, and launched their own *guerre de commerce* ('war on commerce') against them, chiefly in Africa. And though the Dutch managed to maintain a strong presence in slave trading in Guinea, they now had to struggle with the aggressive English Royal Africa Company, which by 1671 was a major competitor. Already no friend of the Portuguese or Spanish, and with new, increasingly powerful enemies, Dutch primacy in Atlantic world commerce came to an end.

Conflicts with religious dimensions continued to shift the Atlantic world and often involved the French, English and Spanish. The English Civil War (1642–51) witnessed the beheading of King Charles and the replacement of the monarchy with the Puritan-leaning Protectorate of Oliver Cromwell. English Puritans took this popular victory to the seas. One of their strategies was to seize Spain's sugar islands in the Caribbean in the name of the English Commonwealth, and thus secure revenue for the newly established government. The once Spanish-claimed sugar colony of Jamaica fell into English hands in 1651.

Privateering and piracy was another strategy for breaking an enemy's hold on a given region on commodity. Privateering, a form of piracy in which civilian seamen are authorized by a state or crown to attack an enemy, was frequently practised by nations that did not (yet) have, or could not afford to maintain, a strong colonial presence in either Africa or the New World. By the late sixteenth and early seventeenth centuries, French and Dutch raiders were busy plundering the various Caribbean islands of Spain and Portugal, and coastal Brazil and Venezuela. They engaged in this work largely for patriotic reasons: by attacking the settlements and sources of revenue of their enemies, they dented their potential war chests and added more to the coffers of their own nations. Later pirates would not have the same sense of patriotism or duty to monarch as these early privateers.

More than anyone else, the English relied heavily on privateering during times of war. This move was practical on England's part; as a relatively poor nation in the late sixteenth century, with neither a navy nor the means to support an ambitious colonizing programme to rival Spain's, England had few alternatives for striking out against its increasingly threatening enemy. Its best means of doing so was by attacking their shipping, claiming significant hauls of New World treasure that the Spanish themselves had looted. As England developed as a colonizing and seafaring power, however, authorizing privateers became increasingly unnecessary. Without official sanction, many privateers became fully fledged pirates (seaborne bandits), ceased limiting themselves to Spanish shipping, and took any vessel they could subdue and plunder. With this transition from privateering to piracy came a growing reputation for lawlessness, especially among the islands of the British Caribbean. Fearing for their own ships and commerce, the British took steps to rid themselves of one-time allies who had become seaborne pests.

There was more than a kernel of truth to the 'pirates of the Caribbean' of popular lore. Their connection with the Caribbean's dense network of islands, coves, caves and beaches was obvious: such an arrangement provided ideal cover for quick strikes and retreats. Yet pirates could also be found in bays and inlets from Maine to Florida.

They found particular welcome in New York, where the notorious William Kidd, who shifted from piracy to privateering and back again, lived well in plain sight. But when his reputation as a hero was eclipsed by a far more negative one, Kidd was hanged from a gibbet, his body left dangling on London's Execution Dock for a full three years. His comrade in banditry, Henry Morgan, had better luck with the law: after years of raiding Spanish ships and ports (and looting many others), Morgan retired to Jamaica and lived out his days as a gentleman.

Pirate vessels became cultural units unto themselves, with their own laws, customs, traditions and social structure. To reinforce a sense of common purpose and brotherhood, each pirate received an equal share of the pilferage, with the captain receiving slightly more. Unlike merchant or naval vessels, however, the captain's word was not law: a respected pirate captain considered the input of his crew before he acted. Pirate ships contained multinational crews, with Europeans from various backgrounds, free men of colour and ex-slaves, Indians, and even women. Captain Charles Johnson, a contemporary chronicler of the so-called 'golden age of piracy', recounted the stories of Anne Bonney and Mary Reed, two of Captain 'Calico Jack' Rackham's fiercest crew members. The stories of Johnson and others helped create the colourful, picaresque legend of piracy.

The colourful anecdotes and complex social character of many pirate ships have inspired scholars to pay more attention to these features. Joining a pirate crew made one a person without a country. Nevertheless, pirates seem to have developed their own egalitarian principles and practised a limited form of democracy – a radical step for what were hitherto considered 'lawless' women and men. But these democratic innovations seem to have done little for the average pirate. In fact, most pirates lived short, miserable lives with only limited chances of spending the booty they amassed. They often died violent deaths. And while equality of voice and distribution of resources might have been a pirate ideal, it only lasted as long as it suited the most powerful among the pirate crew. Pirates, in short, were people of neither high nor proto-democratic ideals. Ultimately, they prized the thrill of the chase and the sacking of their victims over anything else.

Power and Resistance: the Revolt of Roldán

Politics in the Atlantic world often revolved around the competition of larger political entities fighting for control of resources. But these revolts unfolded on a local level as well, often involving small numbers of people bonded together in common interest. At a time when many men bore arms, these revolts could be particularly challenging to put down, or even deadly. Christopher Columbus learned this lesson when he first encountered hostile Indian leaders on Hispaniola. Called *caciques*, these local rulers were initially intrigued by the Spanish. But they soon came to resent the Spaniards' presumptuous incursions. Columbus and his men, whose official directions from the Spanish crown called for conciliation with local tribes, were quick to turn to violent coercion, and one of Hispaniola's most powerful *caciques*, Caonabó, was captured and sent to Spain on a vessel that was lost at sea. Some chiefs who witnessed these events allied themselves with the Spanish, to whom they soon lost their ability to lead. Obvious displays of Spanish power disturbed the *caciques* – and raised concerns about abuse of the powerful among some of the Spanish colonists as well. These concerns were highlighted when Columbus returned to Spain, leaving his brother Bartolomé in charge as an *adalantado* (governor of a Spanish colonial province). In a display of his connection to the powerful admiral, Bartolomé Columbus proceeded to move the seat of government from the town of Isabela to a new location. This angered Isabela's mayor, Francisco Roldán, who sought to curb the *adalantado*'s power by allying himself with the few *caciques* who still retained power. Roldán and his followers, accounting for about half of the Spanish on Hispaniola, drifted to the western end of the island. It was there that the promises they made to Native peoples fell apart, as did the idea of setting up a separate regime. Upon his return, Columbus cannily disarmed the rebellion, giving landholdings to Roldán's supporters and, in effect, forcing a geographical separation among the one-time allies. The *caciques* lost the connection to Spanish sympathizers, and abuse of Native people on Hispaniola only worsened.

The Revolt of Roldán demonstrates that, from the earliest days of settlement, some settlers recognized that the colonial situation differed from that of the mother country. Different circumstances called for different rules. Both Francisco Roldán and the Columbus brothers used the fact of separation by the Atlantic to take matters into their own hands, to exceed authority, and to create new political realities that conformed to the visions of people 'on the ground', so to speak, in the colonial environment. Formed by the realities of the age of sail, these behaviours became common practice throughout the Atlantic world.

European Events, Atlantic Repercussions: the Glorious Revolution

A smoothly running mercantilist system required the American colonies to acquiesce to English power – specifically the English monarch. The key people to implement the king's demands were crown officials – men of stature in England who were appointed to New World posts. These often led to great personal gain and were, of course, highly prized. But crown officials faced particular challenges in the New World. Those who carried out unpopular dictates from Europe stood well with the monarch but were despised by the colonists among whom they had to live and work. Those who led with a lighter touch and hedged their bets according to local feelings often had an easier time with their fellow colonists, yet might find themselves accounting for their failure in duty to their monarch at a later time.

When that monarch was a member of a reviled religion, as was the case with the Catholic Stuart king James II, Massachusetts was determined to resist. By 1684, the crown had succeeded in asserting authority over the colony and dissolving its charter, the document that outlined its responsibilities and freedoms. In its place, James rolled Massachusetts and the rest of New England into a larger colonial unit that included

New York and both halves of present-day New Jersey. Known as the Dominion of New England, this 'supercolony', as Alan Taylor terms it, came with a host of administrators from Europe who received their positions because they were favourites of the king. One of these, Edmund Andros, was a devout Anglican from the French-speaking island of Guernsey, and his religion and cultural attributes rendered him from the start an object of suspicion among New Englanders. Andros cemented this immediate dislike by replacing Puritan magistrates (the most important people administering local laws) with Anglican ones, and converting a Puritan meeting house into an Anglican church so that he and his associates could worship. Neither move was popular, nor was his insistence that landowners now had to pay a perpetual fee to the English monarch. But dislike, suspicion and anger also gave way to fear, as Andros travelled up the Maine coast to harass the belligerent French who competed with the English to claim the province.

When the birth of a son to his second wife promised Catholic continuity to the English throne, James II was deposed by his daughter from his first marriage, Mary, and her husband, William, of the Dutch House of Orange. The king was forced to flee with his young wife and newborn son to Continental Europe. As a result, England once again had a Protestant king. Colonists in Massachusetts were eager to demonstrate their loyalty to the new king, and likely just as eager to rid themselves of the much-despised Edmund Andros and his faction. In 1689, Massachusetts magistrates ordered the gaoling of 25 of Andros's appointees. The governor's soldiers and sailors fled or surrendered. With the administrators in gaol and the military might disabled, the New England colonies proclaimed these patriotic acts in support of the new monarchs, William and Mary. Massachusetts in particular hoped to re-establish its old charter, which James II had repealed, and to reconstitute its pre-Dominion system of government.

Massachusetts colonists believed the new king would be delighted with their actions, which they thought to be a show of loyalty to the new rulers and to Protestantism. But even though they did some of William's work for him, they also aroused the king's concern that the New Englanders were used to too much power, and that these powers needed curbing. When Massachusetts sent the Maine-born Sir William Phips to London to appeal for a new charter, it was granted, but the colony's rights were curtailed. In these events, one can see two consequences: the crown's concern that colonies, unmonitored and unregulated, could get out of hand; and Massachusetts' drive to preserve what it considered to be the rights of Englishmen who just happened to live on the other side of the Atlantic.

Old World Rivalries, New World Conflicts: the Early Wars of Empire

Between 1688 and 1748, the English and the French engaged in a series of conflicts that spilled out into the Atlantic world. Known collectively to historians as the 'wars of empire', these conflicts each had serious repercussions for the shape and survival of the Atlantic system. For the people who lived through them, however, these wars were terrifying ordeals that unfolded on the local level.

The first of these conflicts was known locally by American colonists as King William's War. Supported by events in Europe (the outbreak of the War of the League of Augsburg, which pitted England against France), its North American dimension began when allied French and Indian forces launched numerous attacks on frontier settlements in Maine, New Hampshire and New York. In these terrifying events, in which many English colonists were taken captive and some put to grisly, public deaths, historian Mary Beth Norton and others see the horrific origins of the Essex County witchcraft crisis. To stem the French threat, a group of English and New Englanders, headed by the aforementioned Sir William Phips, attempted to take Quebec. The effort failed, boosting French determination to resist the English on any border. Peace was declared after a decade of border flare-ups, but there was no clearly defined victor. The situation between Indians and English colonists in particular remained tense.

Inspired by concerns over who would ascend to the throne of Spain, Queen Anne's War (the War of Spanish Secession) saw conflicts of equal brutality, with clashes from French Acadia to Florida. The French, the Wabanaki Indians of today's eastern Canada, Maine and New Hampshire, and affiliated groups of Iroquois people pursued strategic frontier targets; the English attacked by water. Though assaults on Saint Augustine and Quebec ended in failure, the English succeeded in taking French Acadia. With this victory, the English (or British, after 1707) bargained with the French to redraw colonial boundaries. Though the resulting Treaty of Utrecht alluded to such changes, the border itself was left, as James Axtell has described it, 'dangerously undefined', which sowed the seeds for even more tension and bloodshed.

The 1720s saw the outbreak of even more fighting, but with more elusive origins and results. The English and French accused each other of instigating a conflict on the Maine frontier. Known variously as Lovewell's, Dummer's or Rale's war, one of its major objectives was to remove a Jesuit priest, the powerful and assertive Sebastien Rale, from his post at Norridgewock, a Jesuit mission that was located on the Kennebec River, which both France and England claimed under the Treaty of Utrecht. Several attempts to detain the elusive Rale failed, but the English ultimately succeeded in taking their prize – Rale's scalp – and burning his mission and dispersing his followers. Thus ended a key threat to the English interpretation of Utrecht's boundaries.

By 1744, Britain was again at war with Spain and France. The French once again struck at exposed frontier settlements, and the New Englanders once again attacked their enemies by sea. What followed was an unanticipated and much-celebrated victory over the French fortified stronghold of Louisbourg on Canada's Cape Breton Island. Though eventually bargained back to the French, the attack's success showed New Englanders that they were capable of scoring major strategic victories. British and colonial engagements against the Spanish were mixed. An attempt to take Cartagena, one of the Spanish empire's most valued cities, ended in disaster, but the new colony of Georgia was successfully defended in 1742.

The 1740s also raised concerns about England's local challenges expanding into Atlantic ones. In 1745, Charles Edward Stuart, a grandson of James II and claimant to the English throne, landed in Scotland with a group of Continental supporters. Some Scots – Protestants and Catholics alike – were quick to rally to his cause and achieved a significant triumph at Prestonpans in 1745. The rebellion lasted until 1746, with a decisive English victory under the Duke of Cumberland (George II's younger son), at Culloden Moor. Fallout from 'the '45', as the rebellion came to be known, reverberated throughout the Atlantic world. In the English colonies, colonial newspapers carried terrifying predictions that the Pretender (yet another name for Charles Edward Stuart) had French agents inciting Indians against the English on the frontiers, especially among the already discontented Shawnees and Delawares. Fears mounted that these groups would make common cause with French and Spanish agents. For the Scottish Highlanders, however, the repercussions were very real. The English broke up the local power of the clan system, which had long prevailed as the form of local government and protection. Many of the Highlanders were forcibly deported to North America. Others left of their own accord, and settled in North Carolina, Georgia and New York.

The early wars of empire demonstrated to many colonists that the Atlantic was perhaps smaller than they had thought. Europe's wars became colonial wars wherever two hostile empires met. Their battles took place in a variety of settings, and frontier regions were common places for these hostilities to burst out into violence. During King William's and Queen Anne's wars, the frontier dwellers of New England bore a particularly heavy burden to protect themselves and their interests. They frequently failed and paid with their lives, their property and their freedom. But these conflicts taught important lessons about leadership, the importance of knowing the landscape, and the need to rely on oneself and one's neighbours. These would serve Americans well in their own rebellion against the British.

Pombaline Reforms

The Iberian New World territories languished under lax, corrupt and archaic administration until the eighteenth century. For centuries, poor management had undercut Spain's and Portugal's attempts to make their empires profitable. Starting with Philip V, Spain's kings moved to assert monarchical and cultural control over their territories. These reforms asserted Spanish colonial pride in the country's arts and letters, which flourished in the eighteenth century. In addition, the Bourbon kings (descendants of France's dynamic Louis XIV), sponsored new learned societies, scientific explorations and schools. They also tightened the economic hold of empires on their colonies – the ultimate goal of mercantilism, provided all involved remained happy and committed to the arrangement.

Similar reforms took place in Brazil under the direction of Portugal's prime minister, Sebastião de Cavalho, Marquis de Pombal. Pombal instated a programme of tax changes, trade regulations and standardization, and innovations that spurred new industries. As was the case with Spain, these changes were all aimed at increasing the Portuguese crown's wealth, power and global reach. Reflecting tensions between monarchs and established churches that were also common features of eighteenth-century Europe, Pombal's reforms were also aimed at curbing the power of the Catholic Church in Brazil. He met with little resistance, especially from the Brazilian colonists themselves, who had long envied the landholdings and wealth of the church's major religious orders, especially the Jesuits. The Jesuits also had large numbers of slaves and great herds of cattle. By expelling the Order in 1759, Pombal opened this property for exploitation by the king's administrators and supporters, thus freeing this valuable asset from what could be considered the 'foreign hands' of colonists whose first loyalty was to Rome.

In terms of human rights within the Portuguese Atlantic sphere of influence, the reforms instituted under Pombal were a mixed bag. While they moved to prohibit persecution of New Christians (Jewish converts to Catholicism) and sought to curb the power of colonial clergy, Pombal was eager to solidify Portugal's share of the Atlantic slave trade, which under his influence moved tens of thousands of Africans to Brazil.

The desire to raise revenue for the ever-increasing expense of running a transatlantic empire was a common impulse among European monarchs. Pombal's contemporary, George III of England, aimed to do the same with the various revenue acts that became law in England's colonies during the 1760s. Many colonists in North America, however, found such reforms objectionable, as their system of taxation differed markedly from the structures imposed in Spanish and Portuguese territories. Taxation had been considered a gift of the colonists to the crown, who taxed themselves. The imposition of an external tax, one set by Parliament in which the colonies themselves had no direct representation, was considered an abridgement of English liberties.

Throughout the mid-eighteenth century, colonists of means, intellect and education increasingly equated personal liberties with economic self-determination. While the impulse of Europe's monarchs and ruling bodies was to tighten their economic grip on their colonies, the colonists themselves increasingly sought methods of – and authoritative justifications for – resistance.

The British Economic System on the Eve of Revolution

On the eve of the American Revolution, many American merchants and producers were required to conform to trade regulations imposed by Britain. Known as the Navigation Acts, these restrictions had been on the books since they were first issued in 1651. What followed was years of refinements and adaptations to both suit Britain's imperial needs and maintain a relationship with its colonies that benefited them both.

Mercantilist theory posits that a strong nation is one that keeps raw goods and cash within its borders, while building dependencies on those raw goods and its manufactures elsewhere. State intervention in economic affairs was key to making this philosophy a working reality. It had given the colonies a guaranteed market. For the most part, the economic system of mercantilism had suited Britain's North American colonies perhaps better than the mother country itself. The American colonies had ready markets for their enumerated goods – those items that had to be shipped through English ports, on English vessels and with mostly English mariners – and received plentiful finished goods in return. And they still had an array of goods that they could sell on the open market to the best international customers. Increasingly throughout the eighteenth century, however, England bore the brunt of managing and protecting the overseas colonies (including its valuable sugar colonies of Jamaica, Barbados and the Leeward Islands). By 1763, England's old enemy, France, had been driven from the continent. This was an event of epic proportions in regard to the colonies' collective futures. No longer fearful of French influence among the Indians to the west, the Americans considered themselves free to look westward for their economic and personal futures. Spreading west towards the Mississippi logically meant a possible reorientation *away* from the Atlantic – England's only connection to its colonies. With a possible dispersing population, Britain's mercantilist principles were threatened – just at the very time England required their enforcement to raise badly needed revenue.

Smuggling and Salutary Neglect

Smuggling, or the illegal movement or sale of commodities, was a staple part of Atlantic world life that peaked during the seventeenth and eighteenth centuries. It was undertaken initially by European residents and later by American colonists. At first, smuggling was linked to piracy, and the Protestant nations of England and the Netherlands were the most successful in their attacks on Catholic Spain. But pirates were also able to claim territory for their mother country, as the French showed during the mid-seventeenth century when their contraband traders colonized Saint Domingue, Martinique and Guadeloupe. While the imperial governments turned a blind eye to smuggling and piracy for strategic reasons, local authorities in the Americas took advantage of it for financial gain. Because the authorities knew that the populations of America had no desire to see smuggling prosecuted, smugglers were often pardoned or let go. Customs officials and members of the colonial government often took bribes to 'look the other way'. As Trevor Burnard has said, in the British Atlantic, 'the imperial touch was light'. Despite occasional governmental attempts to control trade, such as through the Navigation Acts, these were unpopular and were not properly enforced. In reality, these laws did not work. In contrast to the 'salutary neglect' of the British, the French maintained a tight, centralized control over their colonies. The French imperial structure allowed the king and his court at Versailles to have a 'direct influence over policy, and he held fast to mercantilist principles', especially concerning the lucrative sugar trade from Saint Domingue (later Haiti).

Towards the middle of the eighteenth century free trade was suggested for the first time as a solution to the problem of smuggling, such as the 1766 British Free Ports Act, but this did not reduce the levels of contraband trade. Efforts such as the

Molasses Act of 1733 (to enforce the payment of duty) failed because it cost more to collect the tax than would be raised in revenue itself. The Sugar Act of 1764 succeeded by cutting duty but encouraging local enforcement. But the cost of this success was the fermentation of widespread colonial disquiet.

Philosophies of Liberty and Freedom: The Enlightenment in the Americas

The Enlightenment was an intellectual movement that reflected a struggle between two conflicting desires: for order and for freedom. The French Enlightenment, a predominantly middle-class movement, developed thinking that had three facets: contractual government, following the work of Locke and Montesquieu; natural rights, propounded by Voltaire; and social justice, as defined by Rousseau. These authors did not advocate revolution, but rather proposed the idea that all classes of men should not be merely used by those in authority. These notions were based on the understanding that 'reason' should be used to improve human society. Reason showed that authority no longer rested within religion, as it had done since the days of Saint Augustine, but with science; and for the first time, that man was truly in control of his own destiny. The concepts of divine revelation and miracles were attacked but Enlightenment figures were not atheists. Many Enlightenment thinkers were deists who wanted to subordinate religion to human need and denied the necessity of organized religion.

These ideas spread quickly in North America because of high literacy rates and an admiration for European culture among the elites. The movement of ideas is just as important as the movement of goods and people in causing change in the Atlantic world. The world of print transmitted many of these ideas as newspapers, gazettes and journals spread around the region. Word of mouth was also important, though, because many people's knowledge of the Atlantic world was defined by personal experience or experience of a family member or friend. Revolution in the Atlantic world was not about a peasant class claiming power but rather a new commercial class emerging out of the forum of Atlantic exchange.

Developments in scientific thinking in the eighteenth century were not only driven from Europe. Spanish America was also a fertile ground for intellectual development. In the mid-eighteenth century European commentators such as La Condamine and de Pauw began to write attacks on the natural world of the Americas, implicitly suggesting that the Americans themselves were inferior to Europeans. Their ideas emerged from those of the French traveller Comte de Buffon, who argued that the humid New World climate had degenerated nature there. New World authors responded by emphasizing their own objectivity and claiming their part in the Enlightenment trajectory. Unlike Europeans, they said, they were not corrupted by patronage and fashions. They emphasized that America did have its own history and that Native sources were reliable in helping to define that history. Many Enlightenment thinkers such as Rousseau believed that primitive peoples had only blank slates for minds, but Spanish American historians rejected this. These humanist traditions led to the development of a 'creole patriotism', arguing that the heirs of the creole elites were the pre-Columbian aristocracy of Central and Southern America. This gave the new elites a sense of racial continuity and defined them as different from Iberian Spanish. The Spanish crown did try to take control of the Enlightenment by creating a storehouse of historical documents, but it was unable to stop the ideas of cultural difference from manifesting themselves in the colonies.

Indians and Africans also took part in the scientific exchange in the Atlantic world. Knowledge of local plants for medicinal purposes was the most important way of doing this. Africans had had centuries of experience in curing tropical diseases and sometimes were willing to pass this knowledge on to Europeans (for a price). An example was the effort to cure yaws, a disfiguring disease for which a white carrier would be ostracized. Slaves treated this illness by banishing the sick person to a 'yaws hut' in a far corner of the plantation and using sweating and poultices (medicated wrappings) as cures.

The most significant revolutions in terms of the Atlantic story are those in North America, France and Haiti. But they were not the only regions in which 'the crowd' of ordinary people was showing discontent. This disorder has a global context too, as simultaneously in Russia the Pugachev Rebellion challenged the empire of Catherine the Great. Also, some historians have chosen to look at the *longue durée* of revolution and see a revolutionary Atlantic, beginning with the English Civil War in the mid-seventeenth century. The 'Glorious Revolution' was also important and much of the British government's activity was designed to enforce the ideas of that revolution onto its colonies. Thus, control was enforced over Navigation Acts, but at the same time, the government began offering naturalization to colonial residents of non-British origin, and religious toleration.

The Seven Years' War

France and Britain had been at war for much of the eighteenth century when a fragile peace was declared in 1748. It was the emerging colonial interests of both powers that then triggered the Seven Years' War. The two nations faced each other not only in Europe but also in four other theatres of war: North America, the West Indies, Africa and India. Commercial rivalry defined the relationship of the two nations in a colonial context but the presence of privateers and smugglers on both sides complicated this relationship. The British resented the French hold on the lucrative sugar production of Saint Domingue because the profits from this single colony outstripped the output from all of Britain's Caribbean holdings. In West Africa along the Gold Coast, the British tried to remove competition from the French, despite themselves having little real control over the region. The Africans maintained their sovereignty throughout the eighteenth century because of their dominance of the lucrative slave trade, and so the British could not yet be said to be a colonial power in the region. But they still resented French intrusion in their commercial world, and their struggles to remove the French traders became part of the Seven Years' War. Outside the Atlantic world, in India, where the trade in cotton and other textiles was financed by American bullion, the increasing imperial pretensions of the French pushed the British into aggression.

The contrasting styles of imperial control, revealed in the different mercantile policies of the two nations, were most obvious in North America. The French ran their colony as an organized military enterprise, whereas the British colonies were disorganized and disunited. They could not even agree on forming a united colonial army at the Albany Congress in 1754 because they were loath to spend the money. They were also reluctant to get involved in European power squabbles because they often saw their prizes returned under subsequent peace treaties, as had happened in the Treaty of Aix-la-Chapelle in 1745 when Louisbourg, the French fortress town off Cape Breton Island, was swapped for Madras, in India. But while the French were Europe's acknowledged land power, the strength of the British navy helped to achieve balance. Also, Canada and Louisiana had few settlers and made the French government little money. The North American colonies were of little concern to either nation at this period. It was really only the imperial rivalry that kept news from them in the minds of those in the mother countries.

War was officially declared in May 1756, but a phony war had been waged between France and Britain for two years prior to that, so the name 'Seven Years' War' is a misnomer: it lasted nine years from 1754 to 1763. In Europe, the war transformed the traditional alliances as Britain took a new ally, Prussia, and France allied herself with Austria. This explains why German mercenaries were used in the British North American army, to the annoyance of the colonists. The British experienced a series of embarrassing failures in the war until William Pitt the Elder (later known as the Earl of Chatham) entered a coalition with the Duke of Newcastle in 1757 and took charge of the prosecution of the campaigns, uniting the whole nation behind him. Pitt was closely associated with the concerns of Atlantic colonists and merchants. He was great friends with William Beckford, the most powerful of the Jamaican sugar planters.

In North America, Britain's aim was to defeat the French in Canada so that they could acquire the Ohio Valley, seen as the passageway to the far west and continental superiority. The Virginians disputed the French claims to the Ohio Valley, and their militia (a small force of 600 men) was led by a young soldier named George Washington. The British initially sent two weak regiments to support the Virginians in February 1755, but the British commander, Edward Braddock, had little respect for his American counterparts and their superior knowledge of the terrain, and their initial attempts to hurt the French were costly failures. The British regular forces, unhappy to be in North America, supported by colonial militia, then successfully attacked Louisbourg, Montreal in Canada from the south and French forts such as Fort Duquesne in the Ohio Valley via the Allegheny Mountains. The final showdown in North America came in 1759 at Quebec where the generals on both sides (James Wolfe for the British and the Marquis de Montcalm for the French), gave their lives.

The peace treaty represented a victory for the French who had a true understanding of global power politics. The concerns of the weaker British politicians were provincial in comparison. One debate was over whether the British should give back Canada or Guadeloupe, one of France's most lucrative sugar possessions. The achievement of dominance in Canada had been a war aim, but keeping Guadeloupe would make more sense financially. However, the British retained Canada and in doing so gave the British North American colonists peace of mind. In fact, it gave them the security to believe, only 13 years later, that they did not need the protection of the British at all. France's ally Spain was forced to cede Florida to the British, but apart from providing security to the southern colonies and allowing the ignominious failure to establish a colony at New Smyrna (Florida) in 1768, little was done with the territory and the United States gave it back to the Spanish at the end of the American Revolution. The United States regained Florida by treaty in 1821 but despite the mid-nineteenth-century pacification of its Indian residents in the Seminole Wars, the region was not properly settled until the early twentieth century, when the advent of electrical air conditioning meant that the Florida climate could be made hospitable to settlement.

By the Seven Years' War (its European name – in America, the conflict actually lasted nine years), both the French and the English were handing the conflict over to the leadership of professional fighting forces who were brought over from Europe. This innovation had mixed results, especially for the Native peoples who fought alongside European allies. Of particular note is the failure of French general Montcalm to understand the reciprocal relationships between the French and their Indian allies during times of war. Montcalm deplored Native American customs of fighting, seeking retribution and distributing tribute. The general's arrogant dismissal of the cultural ways of France's allies contributed to France's ultimate loss of its North American colonies by undermining this successful, decades-old frontier partnership.

The impact of the Seven Years' War could be felt as far away as India, and decisions made in Europe had geographically far-reaching implications. When Spain entered the conflict on the side of France in 1762, it jeopardized its Caribbean sugar-producing colonies, which soon became targets of the British. France itself lost Guadeloupe and Martinique; Spain temporarily lost control of Cuba and Puerto Rico. The Treaty of Paris returned these valuable possessions to France and Spain, but in return, Britani claimed Canada and Florida. Spain emerged as a victor as well and gained control of the huge French territory of Louisiana. This redrawing of the map would have huge geopolitical implications in the late eighteenth and early nineteenth centuries. In the short term, Britain's seizure of Cuba stimulated the island's foundering sugar industry and, with it, slavery on Cuba.

Revolution in America: Breaking the Bonds of an Atlantic Empire

The American Revolution began as a dispute over tax. The British government believed that colonists should pay for their own protection. The financial expense of the Seven Years' War was heavy, so the British began to tighten their control of colonial trade in order to raise revenue. To that end, the Sugar Act was passed successfully in 1764, which emboldened the government to devise more revenue-raising legislation. In order to fund a permanent colonial militia, the British government passed the Stamp Act in 1765, which brought the tax paid by the colonists in line with that paid by residents of England, Scotland and Wales.

But Britain's revolutionary ideology gave the colonists the language they needed to protest: 'no taxation without representation'. Colonial mobs formed and mobilized resistance to the tax, meaning that it lasted only one year before being repealed. In 1770 the worst act of anti-British violence yet resulted in five Bostonians being shot. However, the most symbolic act of the pre-revolutionary build-up was the so-called Boston Tea Party, in which groups of rebels dumped 90,000 pounds of tea into the harbour while dressed as Native Americans. This costume is very significant because they, like the Spanish creoles admiring the Aztec and Inca past, were claiming to be Americans, not Europeans. But it was not until 1776 that the rebels threw off the shackles of imperial government and declared independence. The Declaration of Independence, as written by Thomas Jefferson and the members of the Continental Congress, defined the United States as a republic in which it was the duty of each citizen to uphold the values of republican virtues. However, the fledgling nation could not succeed alone. In their fight against their British masters the North American colonists sought support from the French. The financial and political support that they won helped to swing the war in their favour. The British cause was not helped by strategic problems in the prosecution of the war itself, as well as the heavy toll that disease took on the British army. Malaria and smallpox were rife and this, along with indecisive generals, meant that the British retaliation was weakened considerably. The struggle between the French and the British also spilled over to the African coast as tribes trading with each of the European powers were caught up in the partisan feeling of the 1770s. This led to the outbreak of war with the Dutch in 1780–4.

The British had their supporters in North America. In many areas the War of Independence was a civil war with American colonists fighting their neighbours. But white loyalists left when the tide of the war turned, moving into Canada or back to Europe. Blacks who had run away to join the British following Lord Dunmore's proclamation of 1775 were shipped first to Nova Scotia, where they fared very poorly, and then, because so many of them arrived destitute on the shores of England, they were sent to Sierra Leone, where the diseases and hostile locals also made life difficult for the migrants. Many Native Americans remained loyal to the British following the Proclamation line of 1763, which had protected Native territories in the West from French and Anglo-American encroachment. American Indians had little choice but to side with the British to try to protect their land, but they soon found that their allies abandoned them to their fate as the tide of the war turned.

Whether the American Revolution was a revolution at all is debatable. Although the ruling colonial power was removed and an independent nation was established, very little social change took place at grass-roots level. However, as Gordon Wood has said, in terms of political change, the establishment of the Constitution and Bill of Rights was indeed a radical act. And although the Constitution ended up in a compromise that pleased no one, especially over slavery, it – along with the European Enlightenment – formed the basis of democratic documents of government throughout the world and strongly influenced the thinking of nineteenth-century leaders such as Simón Bolívar and Francisco Miranda (who was a close friend of Benjamin Franklin). In America, post-revolutionary leaders engaged in fierce debates over whether the new nation should protect and value merchants or farmers.

UP FOR DEBATE   Was the American Revolution a radical event?

Some historians suggest that the American Revolution was a radical event; others see it as a limited act with a rather conservative outcome. Take a stand, and support your answer.

Popular Discontent in South America

The Spanish imperial government tried to regain control by expelling the powerful Jesuit order in 1767, creating a climate of anger and fear among the priests and their supporters in America and Europe. Hostility developed between the local-born creoles and the Spanish-born *peninsulares*, who looked to Spain itself for guidance and did not see America as their *patria* or fatherland. As in North America, protests often started over taxes, such as those in Quito in 1765, which were triggered by Bourbon attempts at financial reform. In 1780 a Peruvian Indian rebellion shook Spanish America. It was led by Tupac Amaru III (named after the last Inca leader who had attempted to resist the Spanish onslaught and was executed by them in the sixteenth century) and was used by creoles to indicate an American rejection of Bourbon absolutism. Tupac Amaru III was descended from Indian royalty, but lived like a wealthy Spanish aristocrat. Initially the rebellion appealed to creoles for support, but when this was refused, it became more radical and attacked all people of Spanish descent. The rebellion was eventually defeated because some of the Indian *caciques* remained loyal to the Spanish. However, the creole discontent grew. In 1799 a pamphlet appeared in Spanish, published in London and written by the exiled Peruvian Jesuit Viscardo y Guzman, exhorting creoles to overthrow the Spanish imperial regime and asking for British backing to liberate South America. In 1781 the Comunero revolt in Columbia, led by creoles but with Indian support, also started over economic discontent but failed due to their plans being betrayed to the authorities. Another rebellion in Peru in 1814 also failed and in fact the region was the last to be liberated from Spanish rule. Ministers in Madrid and London were taken aback by the strength of colonial feeling against the imposition of order and control from the mother countries. But the Spanish managed to contain the discontent in the late eighteenth century, whereas the British could not.

The French Revolution and Its Atlantic Repercussions

The French Revolution began in 1787–9 as an aristocratic revolution, but this was not sustained and soon the bourgeoisie and later the peasantry took over. Thomas Jefferson, the ambassador for the new United States to France, was present when the revolution started and he discussed reforming measures with leaders of the cause such as the Marquis de Lafayette, a French nobleman who had helped the Americans win their independence from Britain. In 1789 rebels seized Paris and made sure that across the country the revolution stuck to its radical roots. The Jacobins began to support the unrest that was sweeping the Caribbean French holding of Saint Domingue, including the first leader of the rebels there, Vincent Ogé, who was also supported by the *Amis des Noirs*, the French abolitionist society.

The French Revolution is significant because it fanned the flames of revolution elsewhere. Under Napoleon, revolution was exported to the French empire and even into the Spanish New World after he forced the abdication of the Bourbon monarchy in 1808. Creoles such as Bolívar welcomed the revolution but they were determined to avoid the excesses of mob rule. Anywhere where Frenchmen were present in numbers began to have a debate about the revolution, such as the port towns of Smyrna and Aleppo. But the North American revolution was also important too. It showed the world that overthrow of a powerful master was possible and influenced the French Revolution and unrest in Ireland. The United Irishmen fought for equality and rights for Catholics in Ireland and were inspired by the American revolutionaries with whom they had close contact. Thomas Paine's pamphlet *Common Sense*, published in January 1776, was one of the most popular printed works of its day, and it influenced not only North Americans in their struggle for independence but also Spanish American creoles in theirs.

The reaction to the French Revolution in Britain was divided. Initially clubs were set up in support of the revolutionaries and unrest brewed in the new industrial towns of the Midlands and North, but as the French Revolution became more violent and chaotic after 1792, Edmund Burke was central in formulating British ideas of counter-revolution. He felt that the French Revolution had gone bad because it did not tap into the lessons of history and instead was trying to do something completely new. The British government was good at maintaining the support of residents in England, Scotland and Wales both during the American Revolution and during the Napoleonic Wars. Once war broke out between the two nations, this determined how the new United States would react. Initially many in America were keen supporters of the French Revolution, but once it began to turn violent, and not wishing to make enemies of the British, some Americans retracted their support. Francophile Thomas Jefferson remained an impassioned supporter of the revolution, but many of his compatriots wanted to avoid an alliance and the decision was made to remain neutral. John Adams, who came to the presidency in 1796, tried to maintain a balance between the two European superpowers. Adams also negotiated a trade agreement with Haitian leader Toussaint L'Ouverture and regarded him with respect and admiration as a black Edmund Burke. By 1797, the United States was so concerned about revolutionary ideas infiltrating its own nation that the Alien Act was passed to permit the expulsion of French radicals. When Napoleon Bonaparte took over France and declared himself emperor, the French Revolution as a movement giving power to ordinary people was over. Gradually, despite the war of 1812, the United States and Britain came to a financial understanding that allowed Britain to maintain her imperial power elsewhere and the United States to develop as a regional and then global power herself.

Revolution in Haiti

After the Seven Years' War, the French turned their attention away from North America and towards their lucrative holdings in the Caribbean. Haiti (or Saint Domingue, as it was known before the Revolution) was its most important because of its hugely successful industrialized sugar industry. During the eighteenth century, its exports were worth more than that of the whole of Spanish America. The Haitian Revolution was the most radical of the three Atlantic revolutions and, like that in North America, caused the birth of a new nation. Resistance from the slave population to his plan to reinstate slavery forced Napoleon to sell his holdings in North America. Refugees from Haiti also influenced the future of Cuba as they fled there and took their sugar production with them. Haiti had a very small creole white population (as did most of the French Atlantic world) but it did have a large slave population.

Toussaint L'Ouverture led the Haitian Revolution. He was a former slave, respected among the island's black community, who led the rebels, sometimes supporting the French against the British and other times vice versa. He began as a monarchist fighting for the French king and then the British but later favoured Haiti becoming a republic. One of his key goals was to change the way that black residents of Haiti were treated. In 1794, when the French revolutionary government freed all slaves, L'Ouverture declared his support for the French government and abandoned an alliance with the British. Following the withdrawal of United States support for L'Ouverture when Jefferson came to power, Napoleon took L'Ouverture captive in 1800 and shipped him to France, where he died three years later, and tried to reintroduce slavery on the island. However, he was unable to hold on to power and black revolutionaries under Jean-Jacques Dessalines began a massacre of white Haitians in 1804. By this time, the sympathy of the world had been lost and the spectre of slave revolution haunted whites across the Atlantic world. Nearly two-thirds of the 1789 population of Saint Domingue had been killed by 1804. Haitians had won their freedom but the French reinstated slavery in the rest of their Atlantic holdings.

The Haitian Revolution is one of the reasons why slave unrest was put down so aggressively in places like Jamaica and the Deep South. The unrest and political instability in Haiti's early years, and the interference from other regional powers such as the United States, has left Haiti today in a very precarious political and economic position. However, the language of liberty and freedom from tyranny used by revolutionaries during this period did have some impact on improving the lives of the region's slave population by influencing the abolition movement and making it easier for abolitionists to discuss the issues of social justice and equality.

The Louisiana Purchase and Western Reorientation

Napoleon's costly wars in Europe meant that he had to raise money to keep France afloat financially. The resistance to Haiti's rebellious black population also drained his resources by depriving the French of sugar revenue and encouraging costly military actions. Without revenue, Napoleon's plan for a resurgent French New World empire foundered, and he came up instead with the idea of selling French holdings in North America to the United States. And so the Louisiana Purchase was negotiated under the presidency of Thomas Jefferson; arguably it was his greatest achievement after the Declaration of Independence. He bought a huge swathe of territory for a mere $15 million.

With the Louisiana Purchase in 1803 the United States changed its focus and began to look westwards rather than eastwards in order to define itself. Jefferson immediately commissioned two men to explore the new territory to the Pacific Ocean. Meriwether Lewis, one of Jefferson's aides, and William Clark, a retired soldier, spent two years, from 1804 to 1806, mapping the region, creating alliances with the Natives they encountered and recording potential sources of wealth. The eighteenth century had been defined by world wars between the British and the French in which the United States and Caribbean had become embroiled. By the early nineteenth century the Atlantic world and its old world of empires was no longer the sole economic and political relationship in which the United States found itself. Instead, it had a huge new territory to the west to explore, map and settle. But she also defined herself as a hemispheric power, as shown by the Monroe Doctrine of 1823, which declared that European interference in American affairs would be viewed as an act of aggression. United States confidence grew as the nation took increasing control over the economic destiny of the Latin American region too.

Historians such as J. R. McNeill see this period as the 'unraveling' of the Atlantic world. The British and the French also turned their attention away from the Atlantic, and moved towards an interest in the Pacific region after the Seven Years' War. The revolutionary period had turned the Atlantic from being a colonial space to a national one. However, the focus would turn to Africa, which was to become a colonial space in its turn.

The War of 1812 and Its Consequences for the North American Continent

The use of the term 'Atlantic world' emphasizes the importance the Atlantic Ocean – its navigation, technological conquest and harvest of resources – played out in the years between 1450 and 1888. The first decade of the nineteenth century witnessed a vital reorientation towards the sea and a refined focus on westward movement, especially for the new United States. Before that happened, however, there was one more great showdown between Britain, France and what had been Europe's colonies to secure the capacity to look westward. The War of 1812 provided just such a moment. For years, historians have puzzled over the significance of this conflict. Few would disagree, however, that America's negotiated victory over the British freed the new nation to reorient west.

It all began, however, with the sea. Britain's mastery of it was unparalleled and unchallenged among western nations of the late eighteenth and early nineteenth centuries. In addition, it was a time of near-chronic conflict with France. The British turned to impressment – the forcible conscription of young, able men into its Navy – to sate its seemingly unending appetite for human power. In addition, Britain was furious with America's attempts to retain its right to trade with partners of its choice. What the Americans termed neutrality was to the British the potentially fatal capacity for the Americans to help fortify the French war machine. With a more powerful military presence on the Atlantic Ocean, the Navy turned to attacking American ships, seizing cargoes and forcing sailors who sounded or seemed British into the Navy. What ensued was a 'second American Revolution' of sorts, in which the Americans demonstrated their ability to maintain the authority of their new government.

The Americans also won key victories on water against a seemingly invincible naval enemy. The end of the conflict drained almost all British influence from the Great Lakes region, the existence of which had concerned would-be American settlers and hindered westward expansion. Indeed, the British made the most of Indian antipathy towards American settlement when it supported Native American uprisings on the United States's frontier fringes. The end of this threat provided yet another reason for Americans to look westward, away from the Atlantic, to secure their future.

Independence in Latin America

In the early nineteenth century, the spirit of independence raged throughout the Spanish Atlantic world. By the time its embers had cooled, Mexico, Bolivia, Venezuela, Mexico, and eventually Brazil, among others, had claimed their freedom from the Spanish crown. These events caused the networks and structures we call the Atlantic world to crumble even further.

Two of these leaders, Simón Bolívar and Francisco de Miranda, led the way for vast areas of northern South America to claim their independence. Like many of South America's revolutionary leaders, Bolivar and Miranda were schooled in Europe. They travelled widely to places as diverse as Haiti, the United States, London and revolutionary France. They studied the Constitution and political structures of the new United States, from which they borrowed some ideas, but, feeling they were unsuitable to their own local realities and heritage as Spaniards, rejected others. Many were determined to crush the Catholic hierarchy in South America, long a powerful institution and a premier influence on local politics.

Simón Bolívar went on to urge Venezuela's Congress to declare independence, making it Latin American's first independent republic. In a move that echoed America's own drive for independence, the Spanish sent a military force to squash the independence movement, offering freedom for Venezuela's slaves in exchange for help. Other issues, including a disastrous earthquake in 1812, ended the short-lived republic, but Bolívar continued to seek new opportunities to reify radical reforms. Some of Bolívar's ideas, such as the need for a balance between hereditary and lifetime appointments to office, strike modern thinkers as retrograde.

Simón Bolívar was an enormously influential and effective leader, inspiring legions of British, American, French and Irish volunteers to join forces to throw off the Spanish empire. The empire itself, having long been in a period of decline, was ready to fall in many corners of South America. The end product was the liberation of Bolivia, Peru, Venezuela, Argentina and Chile from Spanish control. The new republics faced many challenges, including the incursions of power-grabbing elites and attempts by local Catholicism to reassert its authority. The internal strife these created hampered the growth of political systems and institutions.

The movement of New Spain, or Mexico, towards independence had decidedly different origins. Its primary leader was Miguel Hidalgo y Castillo, a priest born to wealthy Spanish parents. He too, however, was inspired by Enlightenment ideas, including humane treatment of and economic development for New Spain's Indians. Hidalgo's message to indigenous people was a then-unusual mix of revolutionary, anti-colonial ideas and Catholic piety. He eventually assembled tens of thousands of followers, who became an army intent on driving the Spanish out. They inflicted a good deal of damage before they were overcome by Spanish Imperia troops. Hundreds, including Hidalgo, were executed. Another priest, José María Morelos y Pavón, followed in Hidalgo's footsteps until he too was executed.

The wearing down of the Mexican army was key to the nation's quest for independence. Independence was brokered by Vincente Guerrero, a part-African rebel, and Agustín Iturbide, an army general changed with breaking the rebellion. The resulting independence, however, was more of a break from Spain's viceroyal structure than its Spanish imperial past. It allowed for a constitutional monarchy and the Catholic Church as the official state religion. The new government came into being in 1821 with Iturbide, an admirer of Napoleon, as its first monarch. It would not be long, however, before Mexico was repeatedly challenged by internal and external strife, including military coups and war with the United States.

The 1810s also saw an anti-monarchical revolt in Brazil. This quickly segued into rampant anti-colonialism, which called for throwing off a monarch shared with Portugal. In a limited act of rebellion, Brazil declared independence from Portugal and set up the Portuguese prince Pedro as emperor. The primary advocates of independence were wealthy mine owners, landowners and planters. These creole elites did not advocate change in the system of slavery, as others in South America had in the wake of their independence movement. As a result, Brazil's quest for independence was a highly conservative one, and slavery would linger for more than 60 additional years.

The Jamaica Slave Rebellion of 1831 and Its Consequences

The increased consciousness of human rights led to a new breed of abolitionist, who advocated freedom for freedom's sake and pointed out the contradictions of a free society supporting the institution of slavery. This concept of uniform human rights was not exclusive to the reformers. Many of the enslaved were well aware of the hypocrisy of chattel slavery and were determined to end the institution, at least for them and their families, by any means necessary. The end of the British slave trade in 1808 was supposed to trigger a new era of race relations in the Caribbean. It was hoped that slavery would become so inconvenient and morally repugnant that planters would accept a system of gradual emancipation. But that did not happen, and in Jamaica, Barbados and the other English sugar colonies, enslaved Africans rose up against their masters, but with mixed results: while Haiti's revolt evolved into a full-scale revolution, Barbados's 1816 rebellion had only fleeting success, and was soon brutally suppressed.

In the early nineteenth century, white evangelicals could be found throughout the Caribbean, preaching the message of slavery's incompatibility with Christian society. Most nineteenth-century slave revolts had a religious dimension. The Jamaican Slave Rebellion of 1831 was no exception. Some planters called the event 'The Baptist War' because of the number of church members involved. The leader was widely reputed to be Samuel Sharpe, a Baptist deacon who was closely associated with white evangelicals. What set the rebellion apart was the way it started: Sharpe called not for a full-scale overthrow of white overlords, but for a strike among enslaved workers to pressure whites into granting them wages and better working conditions – many of the same things that white working people in places like New York and Boston agitated for. During the ten days of conflict, however, one-fifth of the island's 300,000 slaves participated in the action, some violently.

As was common in the Atlantic world, far more people of colour than whites ultimately suffered in these conflicts. For every white who lost his or her life, 35 blacks lost their lives either in attempts to suppress the rebellion or in retribution. Ultimately, over 300 of Jamaica's blacks were executed for their connection to the rebellion. The response to the uprising also targeted black evangelical Christian establishments: in total, 15 Baptist and Methodist churches were burned by vindictive white Jamaicans.

The brutality of the crackdown shocked Britain's Parliament, which came to realize that slave societies would always remain dangerously antithetical to egalitarian principles of any kind. Within two years, the movement to abolish slavery in Jamaica and elsewhere in the British commonwealth was underway, with final emancipation occurring in 1834. Still, the 'emancipated' slaves faced a mandatory, sequenced apprenticeship for up to six additional years. And the stigma of slavery and persistence of racism continued to haunt relationships between races in the Atlantic world for almost two centuries.

Conclusion

The end of the Atlantic world's colonial system meant, by necessity, the end of mercantilism. Parent counties in Europe could no longer compel colonies across the Atlantic to deal in their wares according to restrictions the countries themselves had set. The blossoming of free trade opened up colonial merchants from Buenos Aires to Nantucket to trade with any connections that would prove profitable. These conditions allowed more of the Atlantic world's people to create and explore new markets, encourage investment, and compete economically with each other. For many, this became the truest exercise of personal liberty and the pursuit of happiness.

CHAPTER CHRONOLOGY

1688   England's 'Glorious Revolution', which removes Catholic James II from the English throne.

1750   A spate of economic and cultural reforms under the Marquis de Pombal begin; these will eventually spread to include Portugal's Atlantic world sphere of influence.

1776   The British North American colonies officially declare separation from the British empire, the first step in becoming the United States of America.

1791   Haitian slaves and *gens to couleur* lead fight for independence.

1815   The Treaty of Ghent is ratified, ending the War of 1812.

1821   Mexico declares its independence from the Spanish and uses the Constitution of the United States as a model.

1847   Liberia declares independence from the United States.

■ **PRIMARY SOURCES AND STUDY IMAGE**

'Captain Preston's account of the Boston Massacre' (5 March 1770)

On Monday night about 8 o'clock two soldiers were attacked and beat. But the party of the townspeople in order to carry matters to the utmost length, broke into two meeting houses and rang the alarm bells, which I supposed was for fire as usual, but was soon undeceived. About 9 some of the guard came to and informed me the town inhabitants were assembling to attack the troops, and that the bells were ringing as the signal for that purpose and not for fire, and the beacon intended to be fired to bring in the distant people of the country. This, as I was captain of the day, occasioned my repairing immediately to the main guard. In my way there I saw the people in great commotion, and heard them use the most cruel and horrid threats against the troops.

In a few minutes after I reached the guard, about 100 people passed it and went towards the custom house where the king's money is lodged. They immediately surrounded the sentry posted there, and with clubs and other weapons threatened to execute their vengeance on him. I was soon informed by a townsman their intention was to carry off the soldier from his post and probably murder him. On which I desired him to return for further intelligence, and he soon came back and assured me he heard the mobb declare they would murder him. This I feared might be a prelude to their plundering the king's chest …

The mob still increased and were more outrageous, striking their clubs or bludgeons one against another, and calling out, come on you rascals, you bloody backs, you lobster scoundrels, fire if you dare, G-d damn you, fire and be damned, we know you dare not, and much more such language was used. At this time I was between the soldiers and the mob, parleying with, and endeavouring all in my power to persuade them to retire peaceably, but to no purpose. They advanced to the points of the bayonets, struck some of them and even the muzzles of the pieces, and seemed to be endeavouring to close with the soldiers. On which some well behaved persons asked me if the guns were charged. I replied yes. They then asked me if I intended to order the men to fire. I answered no, by no means, observing to them that I was advanced before the muzzles of the men's pieces, and must fall a sacrifice if they fired; that the soldiers were upon the half cock and charged bayonets, and my giving the word fire under those circumstances would prove me to be no officer. While I was thus speaking, one of the soldiers having received a severe blow with a stick, stepped a little on one side and instantly fired, on which turning to and asking him why he fired without orders, I was struck with a club on my arm, which for some time deprived me of the use of it, which blow had it been placed on my head, most probably would have destroyed me.

On this a general attack was made on the men by a great number of heavy clubs and snowballs being thrown at them, by which all our lives were in imminent danger, some persons at the same time from behind calling out, damn your bloods –why don't you fire. Instantly three or four of the soldiers fired, one after another, and directly after three more in the same confusion and hurry. The mob then ran away, except three unhappy men who instantly expired, in which number was Mr. Gray at whose rope-walk the prior quarrels took place; one more is since dead, three others are dangerously, and four slightly wounded. The whole of this melancholy affair was transacted in almost 20 minutes. On my asking the soldiers why they fired without orders, they said they heard the word fire and supposed it came from me. This might be the case as many of the mob called out fire, fire, but I assured the men that I gave no such order; that my words were, don't fire, stop your firing. In short, it was scarcely possible for the soldiers to know who said fire, or don't fire, or stop your firing. On the people's assembling again to take away the dead bodies, the soldiers supposing them coming to attack them, were making ready to fire again, which I prevented by striking up their firelocks with my hand. Immediately after a townsman came and told me that 4 or 5000 people were assembled in the next street, and had sworn to take my life with every man's with me.

Letter from Toussaint L'Ouverture to Napoléon Bonaparte on the 1801 Constitution

27 Messidor, Year IX [16 July 1801]

Citizen Consul:

The minister of the Marine, in the account he gave you of the political situation of this colony, which I devoted myself to making known to him, should have submitted to you my proclamation of last 16 Pluviose [5 February 1801] on the convocation of a Central Assembly, which would be able to set the destiny of Saint-Domingue through wise laws modeled on the mores of its inhabitants. I today have the satisfaction of announcing to you that the final touch has just been put to this work. I hasten to send it to you in order to have your approval and the sanction of my government.

Given the absence of laws, and the Central Assembly having requested to have this constitution provisionally executed, which will more quickly lead it to its future prosperity, I have surrendered to its wishes. This constitution was received by all classes of citizens with transports of joy that will not fail to be reproduced when it will be sent back bearing the sanction of the government.

Greetings and profound respect.

[signed: Toussaint Louverture]

'Message to the Congress of Angostura', by Simón de Bolívar (1819)

We are not Europeans; we are not Indians; we are but a mixed species of aborigines and Spaniards. Americans by birth and Europeans by law, we find ourselves engaged in a dual conflict: we are disputing with the natives for titles of ownership, and at the same time we are struggling to maintain ourselves in the country that gave us birth against the opposition of the invaders. Thus our position is most extraordinary and complicated. But there is more. As our role has always been strictly passive and political existence nil, we find that our quest for liberty is now even more difficult of accomplishment; for we, having been placed in a state lower than slavery, had been robbed not only of our freedom but also of the right to exercise an active domestic tyranny ... We have been ruled more by deceit than by force, and we have been degraded more by vice than by superstition. Slavery is the daughter of darkness: an ignorant people is a blind instrument of its own destruction. Ambition and intrigue abuses the credulity and experience of men lacking all political, economic, and civic knowledge; they adopt pure illusion as reality; they take license for liberty, treachery for patriotism, and vengeance for justice. If a people, perverted by their training, succeed in achieving their liberty, they will soon lose it, for it would be of no avail to endeavor to explain to them that happiness consists in the practice of virtue; that the rule of law is more powerful than the rule of tyrants, because, as the laws are more inflexible, every one should submit to their beneficent austerity; that proper morals, and not force, are the bases of law; and that to practice justice is to practice liberty.

Although those people [North Americans], so lacking in many respects, are unique in the history of mankind, it is a marvel, I repeat, that so weak and complicated a government as the federal system has managed to govern them in the difficult and trying circumstances of their past. But, regardless of the effectiveness of this form of government with respect to North America, I must say that it has never for a moment entered my mind to compare the position and character of two states as dissimilar as

Study image 7 *Haiti: Slave Revolt, 1791.*

the English-American and the Spanish-American. Would it not be most difficult to apply to Spain the English system of political, civil, and religious liberty: Hence, it would be even more difficult to adapt to Venezuela the laws of North America.

Recommended Reading

Colin Calloway, *The American Revolution in Indian Country* (Cambridge, 1995). Explores the motives, actions and outcomes of Native American populations involved in the American colonists' conflict with Britain.

Laurent DuBois, *Avengers of the New World: The Story of the Haitian Revolution* (Cambridge, 2005). Comprehensive narrative of the fight of Haiti's enslaved to free themselves from bondage.

J. H. Elliott, *Empires of the Atlantic World: Britain and Spain in America 1492–1830* (New Haven, CT, 2007). A comparative study of the colonization methods of Spain and England.

Wim Klooster, *Revolutions of the Atlantic World: A Comparative History* (New York, 2009). Compares key features of various Atlantic world revolutions, including the roles played by various peoples in colonial society and the mechanisms that helped mobilize them.

Andrew Jackson O'Shaunessey, *An Empire Divided: The American Revolution and the British Caribbean* (Philadelphia, 2000). Examines the reasons why Britain's sugar colonies failed to support the North American colonies' bid for independence.

Carla Gardina Pestana, *Protestant Empire: Religion and the Making of the British Atlantic World* (Philadelphia, 2010). Examines the differences and commonalities among the various peoples of the British Atlantic world.

Ray Raphael, *A People's History of the American Revolution: How Common People Shaped the Fight for Independence* (New York, 2008). A detailed examination of the lives of the men and boys, women, Native Americans and Africans who were caught up in America's conflict with Britain.

Marcus Rediker, *Villains of All Nations: Atlantic Pirates in the Golden Age* (New York, 1995). Explores the trajectories that transformed mariners into pirates and created their unique cultural organizations.

John Thornton, *Africa and Africans and the Making of the Atlantic World, 1400–1800* (Cambridge, 1998). Discusses the historical economies, civil and social structures, and beliefs and practices throughout the continent of Africa.

Gordon Wood, *The Radicalism of the American Revolution* (New York, 1993). Reveals the complex dimensions of America's war for independence and its outcomes.

TEST YOUR KNOWLEDGE

1 What is mercantilism?
2 Why did the advocates of mercantilism strive to make Atlantic colonies dependent on their European 'mother countries'?
3 What are two key differences between pirates and privateers?
4 What were two of the major ideas about human freedom to emerge from the writings of the great Enlightenment theorists?
5 What was the major imperial consequence of the Seven Years' War, and why did it matter so much?
6 How did the American Revolution influence future Atlantic freedom movements?
7 How did the French Revolution do the same?
8 What role did class play in the American and Haitian revolutions, and the formation of the Mexican Republic? What does this suggest about the importance of class and status in the Atlantic world?
9 What role did religion play in freedom movements in places such as Jamaica, Brazil and Mexico?

8 The Quest for Abolition

Why Abolition?

The abolition of the slave trade and the emancipation of slaves was a truly Atlantic quest. Activists consciously worked with like-minded individuals to bring an end to slavery in all parts of the Atlantic world, and the letters, pamphlets and poetry they produced spread their ideas further. Abolition of the slave trade was part of the late eighteenth-century Enlightenment tradition, encompassing many other aspects such as the reform of prisons in Britain. A civil society – a public sphere in which men and women came together to campaign on moral issues – developed. As a rational and commercial modern world emerged, slavery seemed out of place. J. R. McNeill believes that the abolition of the slave trade accompanied a decline in the Atlantic system and, along with the revolutions, brought an end to the Atlantic world by 1888.

In the early nineteenth century the Atlantic world was trying to move away from a mercantilist system and towards open, free trade. Ports were opened to all ships and colonies were allowed to trade with other European nations. However, the British economic system was in difficulties because of the competition from French sugar and the growing costs of American goods. Soil erosion and bad weather had also threatened the profits of planters. Eric Williams argues that these factors weakened the slave system so that no abolition movement was really necessary. The changes were not forced on the New World by idealists in Europe. Campaigners in both the Old and the New World worked together to bring about change. The role played by Africans in the diaspora and in Africa itself should also not be forgotten. Free and enslaved Africans were not passive receivers of abolition; many played a key part in the abolition movement while others fought to preserve the slave system for their own economic gain.

Slaves made a very important contribution to the early abolition effort. Every attempt at resistance, from the localized go-slows or spoiling of crops to runaways, revolts and rebellions, undermined the slave system, both by costing the planters money and by showing the world that Africans did not passively accept slavery, as some planters argued. From the outset slaves sought their freedom by rebelling against their masters. In 1521 on Hispaniola, slaves revolted on the plantation owned by the son of Christopher Columbus, and in Virginia in 1676 the rebellious force led by Nathaniel Bacon included 80 black men. Slaves also used more peaceful ways of gaining their freedom, seeking to be manumitted or suing for their freedom in court, especially in New England where slaves had legal rights.

Maroon communities in the West Indies and South America sometimes existed unmolested for years. They resulted from coordinated runaway attempts, and could also be created when the masters were distracted by an external threat. For example, when their masters fled a French invasion in 1712, groups of slaves in Surinam established their own communities in the forests. They were structured along the lines of West and Central African societies and their existence reminded Europeans that it was possible for Africans to flourish independently without white support. Maroon communities, often home to former slaves, free people of colour and Native Americans, were also active in raiding plantations and freeing more slaves. The best example is the Quilombo dos Palmares in Brazil, a fugitive slave community that survived for nearly a century between 1605 and 1694.

But it must be recognized that these acts were attempts at individual freedom, not an attempt to bring down the slave system as a whole. Nevertheless, they undermined it and gave ammunition to the abolitionists campaigning for an end to the system in its entirety. But in many cases, slave unrest triggered a tightening of slave codes, the laws by which slaves were controlled. For example, the slave revolt of 1712 in New York City caused the colony to add more restrictions on the movement of slaves, and forbade slave owners from freeing their slaves because it was thought free blacks were instrumental in fomenting unrest.

Why did abolitionists want to end both the slave trade and the system of slavery? Slavery was an obvious moral evil and it was natural that good people such as William Lloyd Garrison, who was active in the United States between the 1820s and 1860s, should want to end that system. However, in the Atlantic world of the eighteenth and nineteenth centuries the decision for everyone was more complex. Many pro-slavery campaigners argued that slavery was good for Africans, and that to end it suddenly would leave those whom abolition was designed to help in a state of chaos and distress. The most extreme argument was that Africans were unable to survive in the world without the guidance of the white man and so to end the system of slavery was the equivalent of throwing your children out of the family home and forcing them to fend for themselves. Some moderate abolitionists argued that ending slavery gradually would be much kinder, so that slaves and slave owners could get used to the new way of life. Their ideas caused others who were sympathetic to the plight of the slaves but not true abolitionists to want to ameliorate (i.e., improve) the lives of slaves.

Historians have asserted that while a few people held genuine moral beliefs that slavery was evil, many of those who called themselves abolitionists were much more pragmatic. Sometimes, economic motives trumped humanitarian impulses. If the slave system was dying anyway, modern thinking claimed that free labour and industrial capitalism meant that the abandonment of the old-fashioned system of forced labour was inevitable. Scottish Enlightenment thinkers Adam Smith and David Hume held this view, which was reinforced by the fear of slave revolt. The spectre of slaves taking political control had been raised with the Haitian Revolution in 1791 and many Europeans were worried that this might also happen in their colonies.

This 'decline' thesis has been put forward by historian David Brion Davis. He believes that at the turn of the nineteenth century slave economies were becoming less important to the mother country. Abolitionists were promoting their cause for economic gain for themselves, not for moral reasons. This has led some historians to label the entire abolition movement 'a sham'. However, this thesis is controversial. Other scholars such as Seymour Drescher have argued that the slave system was in good health at the end of the eighteenth century and, although soil erosion was damaging the output of some plantation regions, slavery was moving into new areas such as Demerara, Essequibo and Berbice in Guiana, and the islands of St. Vincent and Trinidad.

Early Opposition to Slavery

The abolition movement came to fruition in the late eighteenth and nineteenth centuries. The holding of one human being in bondage by another was hotly debated from the first days of the plantation system. Objections to the use of slaves were based either on economic or on religious grounds. Initially some colonists in seventeenth-century Virginia were resistant to the idea of using slaves, because of their belief that black people were inferior and because they did not want to live alongside them. The cost of buying and keeping an African slave also led some to argue that white inden-tured labour was a preferable system. These were objections to slavery that still denied the essential humanity of slaves. The abolition movement constantly struggled with the issue of racial difference and whether opposition to the institution of slavery meant acknowledging the humanity and equal rights of slaves.

There is a strong connection between personal religious belief and the abolition movement. While there is a long tradition of Christian objections to slavery, the record of various churches on abolition has been chequered. The Church of England through the Society for the Propagation of the Gospel owned slaves on the Codrington estate in Barbados (although it was also involved in the education of slaves), and there was ambivalence in the behaviour of Catholic missionaries towards slaves and their owners in the Caribbean and South America. The earliest objectors to the holding of slaves on religious grounds were the Quakers. They came to North America in large numbers at the founding of the colony of Pennsylvania in 1677. A few Quakers were present in the colonies prior to that, some in the Caribbean, some in Massachusetts. They were victims of persecution in England under the Puritan government of Oliver Cromwell. Their unusual brand of Protestantism aroused such fear and hatred that suggestions were made by the early adventurer Ferdinando Gorges that Quakers be shipped from Britain to the Caribbean for use as forced labour on sugar plantations. But they did not receive a friendly reception in the New World either, with Massachusetts in particular threatening Quakers with exile and death if they refused to conform.

Quakers are known for their pacifism. This is just one example of how their behav-iour in the world reflects a strongly moral outlook. Not all Quakers were abolitionist. Many 'friends' held slaves and defended their right to do so. For them, slavery was not an evil in itself, provided slaves were treated with decency. But from other

Quakers came the first voices for the abolition of slavery. In 1693 George Keith published *An Exhortation and Caution to Friends Concerning Buying and Keeping of Negroes*. This was the earliest use of the medium of print to persuade others of the moral peril endangering those who kept slaves. Within the next 50 years, anti-slavery Quakers such as Keith and later John Woolman, Ralph Sandiford and Anthony Benezet managed to convince their 'friends' to end their connection with slavery. Many of these men had visited the southern colonies and the West Indies and had witnessed plantation slavery at first hand. These early campaigners did not desire racial equality but rather sought to free the white man from the sin associated with the holding of slaves. Between 1773 and 1777 Quakers in the northern colonies of North America freed their slaves. Not until 1796 did Quakers acknowledge the equality of African Americans by admitting that there was no reason why they should not be full members of their church.

Others followed the Quaker lead. In 1700 Samuel Sewell, a Puritan of Massachusetts, published *The Selling of Joseph*, which argued that slavery was incompatible with Christianity. Also, nonconformist ministers who were involved in the eighteenth-century religious movement known as the Great Awakening were not prejudiced in their treatment of the people of the Atlantic world. When preachers such as George Whitefield and Jonathan Edwards came from Britain to North America to spread the revival message, they preached to outdoor gatherings that included African Americans and Native Americans as well as whites. The Revivalists believed that all people were equal in God's eyes and that everyone was capable of a personal relationship with God. They encouraged the provision of a Christian education for poor whites and for racial minorities. This religious movement, combined with the developing revolutionary doctrine in North America that emphasized liberty and equality, encouraged many North Americans to think about slavery for the first time.

Early abolitionists were reacting to the pseudo-scientific racial doctrines of the eighteenth century, which argued either that the races had always been separate or that there was originally one human race and that other races 'degenerated' from the main European ancestor. The Jamaican planter and judge Edward Long argued that three species existed separately: 'human', 'negro' and 'orangutan'. Long thought it was possible for 'negroes' and 'orangutans' to mate, and Thomas Jefferson, founding father and third president of the United States, shared this view. The connection between racism and the arguments over slavery are complex. Some pro-slavery planters such as William Beckford Jr had no strong feelings about race, and subscribing to the scientific racist doctrines did not always lead to pro-slavery views.

Not all arguments against slaveholding emphasized the cruelty and sinfulness of the institution; instead they focused on the effect on the slaveholder. Some commentators such as James Oglethorpe, founder of the colony of Georgia, believed that slaveholding was bad for the whites that participated in it. The redeeming power of hard work was the main tenet of his new colony, and he fought hard to prevent Georgia from following Carolina, its neighbour to the north, into becoming a slave state. Oglethorpe's view mirrored the attitudes of abolitionists in early nineteenth-century Britain who thought that the planters of Jamaica and Barbados were corrupt and lazy because of their over-privileged lifestyle. Oglethorpe faced a great challenge; the settlers who moved to Georgia from Britain and Carolina did not share his idealistic vision. They wanted slavery to be permitted in the colony for two reasons. First, they believed that African slaves were better suited to the difficult labour and challenging climate. And second, they envied the wealthy lifestyle of the planters in Carolina and the Caribbean and wished to emulate it. They had no ambition to become self-sufficient yeoman farmers. Oglethorpe was unable to enforce his slaveless colony and Georgia rapidly developed into a plantation society.

Abolishing the Slave Trade

The campaign against the slave trade was led by men such as William Wilberforce, Thomas Clarkson and Granville Sharp, but in recent years historians have acknowledged the importance of public opinion in ending the slave trade. Revisionist historians have deflated the reputations of men like Wilberforce, challenging their importance and the purity of their motives. It is now understood that the campaign was not solely driven from metropolitan London, but that abolitionists around Britain, including Scotland, played a key part. The slave trade came to public attention with a series of high-profile legal cases. In 1772 Granville Sharp, a member of the Society for the Propagation of the Gospel who also supported the colonization programme designed to resettle former slaves in Sierra Leone, was involved in the Mansfield case, which ruled that slaves could not be sent out of Britain. In effect this was seen as emancipating all slaves in Britain. Soon afterwards, a popular movement began to mobilize against slavery and, in response, the pro-slavery supporters found their voice. In 1781 the Zong case, again with Sharp and Lord Mansfield involved, horrified the British public. A ship's captain was accused of throwing 122 ill slaves overboard to their deaths because in that way he would get insurance compensation for them, whereas if they died on board he would not. Sharp tried to prosecute the captain for murder, but failed, and no charges were brought; however, the case captured the public imagination and became part of the abolitionists' armoury of examples of the cruelties of the slave trade. Sixty years later, the painter J. M. W. Turner used the Zong case, among others, as a reference point for his painting *Slavers Throwing Overboard the Dead and the Dying* (1840).

At the end of the eighteenth century there were three groups of abolitionists who formed a coalition: the evangelicals led by Wilberforce and the Reverend John Newton (former slave trader and composer of the hymn *Amazing Grace*), the Quakers and the Whigs. These groups had different reasons for opposing the slave trade. Evangelicals and Quakers saw the slave trade as a sin and wanted to save Britain from a national moral crisis. The radical Whigs were influenced by secular Enlightenment ideas and saw slavery as the oppression of human beings.

The political and religious leadership were motivated in their struggle partly by their beliefs but also in the knowledge that the British public were increasingly opposed to the cruelties of the slave trade and that there was grass-roots support among middle-class professionals and their wives for the abolitionist cause. Abolitionist prints became popular, especially the graphic plan of an overcrowded slave ship. Abstention from the purchase and use of West Indian products became common, encouraged by the distribution of abolitionist pamphlets, newspapers and periodicals. The boycott of sugar was orchestrated for the most part by middle-class women, who became politically organized for the first time in 'ladies' societies'. The decision concerning which products to serve at the dinner table rested with the lady of the house, and if she chose to boycott West Indian sugar this was a powerful political move. Consumption of sugar had become a symbol of wealth in Britain; parishes used the 'sugar test' to determine whether or not an individual was poor enough to be offered relief. In 1791–2, the abstention campaign affected as many as 300,000 people. Female authors published poetry on the subject, although it was not thought fitting for them to enter the formal world of political debate. Petitioning was also an important way for local abolitionist societies to make their feelings known, by putting pressure on their Members of Parliament.

Another minority group, of former slaves and free blacks, took a central role in the abolition movement and became a figurehead for the campaign, publishing abolitionist pamphlets and participating in lecture tours. Of these, the most influential was Olaudah Equiano, also known as Gustavus Vassa, a former slave who had bought his own freedom and who became a Methodist after hearing George Whitefield preaching. His 1789 work *The Interesting Narrative of the Life of Olaudah Equiano* was significant because it informed readers of the horrors of the capture, the Middle Passage and being sold as a slave in the New World. Equiano became a hero of the abolition movement by giving public lectures, and he also exposed the Zong case to the public. The letters of Ignatius Sancho, a free African man and wealthy property owner living in Britain, were also significant in helping to ignite the question of black people's humanity, showing that they were capable of rational thought and of creating works of literature. Literature written by black women was also used by abolitionists to convince others to join the cause. *The History of Mary Prince* was a very popular book, although the words of Mary Prince herself are hidden behind the messages of the book's white amanuensis, editors and critics.

In 1807, after the British Parliament abolished the slave trade, the British Navy and Foreign Office worked together to ensure that other countries joined the movement for abolition. Negotiations and military force were used equally as other nations were suspicious of British motives for policing the slave trade. For example, in Brazil and Cuba, due to the high mortality rate importation of slaves from Africa was still needed, and these nations strongly resisted the end of the trade. When the slave trade to Brazil was finally abolished in 1851, the numbers of slaves in the country dropped dramatically. Because of the decrease in supply the prices of slaves rose and this prevented poorer members of Brazil's slaveholding class from entering the market. The end of the trade had only been achieved by the Royal Navy's presence in Brazilian waters and its policy of stopping and searching slave ships.

But it was not only planters in the Americas who resisted the abolition of the slave trade; African leaders, too, recognized that their financial security depended on it.

Slowly, the British used their influence in the region to discourage the trade, but this changed the relationship between the British empire and her African allies. Missionaries and Royal Navy vessels were a growing presence on the West African coast. The abolition movement was part of an increasing drive towards the spread of Christianity through a missionary education. Outside the Atlantic world, there were similar developments, for example the anti-sati movement in India that registered the British dislike of the custom of the burning of widows. Pressure from government and missionaries led to some success – for example, King Pepple of Bonny agreed to give up the trade in 1841, signing a treaty with the British that gave him £500 worth of goods in return – but many African leaders resisted strongly. The British and Americans were very keen to pursue the idea of a free labour colony being established on the West African coast, an idea initially mooted by Henry Smeathman, a natural historian who had lived for four years on the Banana Islands in the 1780s. The Sierra Leone Company, part mission and part colonization society, was founded in 1787 and a voyage departed from Britain taking former slaves to the west coast of Africa, while Granville Sharp led the campaign at home for a 'province of freedom'. Once the slave trade was abolished in 1807, the Royal Navy took seized slaves to Sierra Leone, where they were freed.

Influenced by this British example, mixed-race black and Wampanoag Native Quaker mariner Paul Cuffee, from Massachusetts, planned voyages from the United States to carry supplies in support of Sierra Leone, and took 38 families to the colony. Just before his death, Cuffee hesitantly joined the American Colonization Society (ACS), which was established in 1816 with the intention of giving freed slaves the opportunity to move back to Africa. Despite many of its members being abolitionists, the society's motives were not purely altruistic. In the early nineteenth century fears of slave uprisings and the detrimental consequences of racial mixing dominated American discourse and some supporters saw the activities of the ACS as a way of removing black Americans. This is partly why, from the 1830s onwards, radicals such as William Lloyd Garrison were opposed to colonization. It had also made Paul Cuffee nervous about joining the fledgling society. Garrison saw colonization as a delaying tactic by slave owners: he wanted immediate emancipation for all the slaves in the United States.

The American Revolution and Its Effect on Slavery

The institution of slavery in the United States was especially resistant to the campaigns of abolitionists, with southern planters presenting a united front in its defence. The struggle there was as passionate and violent as anywhere in the Atlantic world. Also, unlike elsewhere, the end of the slave trade did not spell the end of the institution in the United States because of the ability of the slave population to reproduce itself. The American Revolution spawned a number of different methods of abolition in the northern half of the country, most of them gradual and legal. Some of the most significant commentators of the generation, such as Thomas Paine, Thomas Jefferson, and

Henry and John Laurens, became involved in the debates over the rights and wrongs of slavery. Paine exposed the hypocrisy of slave owning, saying that Americans struggling to achieve their own freedom from a form of slavery should not then hold others in bondage. He appealed to Americans to bring an end to the institution. Jefferson was extremely vocal in his opposition to the 'slavery' that he and other white Americans were enduring, but he was nevertheless a slave owner, had children with his female slaves and subscribed to the ideas of scientific racism arguing that black people were a distinct species from white, more akin to the orangutan. Henry Laurens and his son John were South Carolinian slave owners. In private letters Henry realized the hypocrisy of proclaiming liberty at the same time as holding slaves and saw that it violated his strongly held Christian principles. However, he did nothing to act on these beliefs, whereas in the face of much hostility his son John publicly campaigned for slaves to be enlisted by South Carolina for the Continental Army. John died in a skirmish before the war was over, so no one knows if he might have joined the abolitionists after Independence.

Three significant factors contributed to the changing attitudes to slavery: firstly, the growth in discussions of liberty and rights, triggered by the perceived tyranny of the British king over his American subjects, led many to consider the position of slaves in society. Secondly, the role played by abolitionists and their societies and petitions, especially in the northern states, was vital. Their intentions were to bring slavery to an end gradually and they certainly did not perceive black people as fully equal to whites. Thirdly, the experience of seeing African Americans fighting in the Revolutionary War changed the minds of many whites who had previously thought black people unable to be citizens of the new country. Running parallel to these ideas was the fear of black insurrection during wartime. In some quarters fears grew that slaves would go over to the British side, following the Dunmore Declaration of 1775 when freedom was offered to any slaves who joined the British army. However, despite these important changes in attitude, the Constitution to define the new nation that emerged out of victory in the war did not rule decisively on slavery, thus enshrining its existence and leading to the showdown of the mid-nineteenth century. And after the radicalism of the Revolutionary War era, the country was subsumed in a new conservatism, particularly after the French Revolution, leading to a decline in anti-slavery feeling. North America initially hailed the hero of the Haitian revolution, Toussaint L'Ouverture, but as his coup descended into violence people became afraid that giving former slaves any sort of power would lead to bloodshed, as it had in Haiti.

Slow Emancipation in the North

In the colonies in the northern part of North America, slaves had been treated differently. They were permitted to sue for their freedom in the courts and they were offered more educational opportunities. From the earliest days of settlement Puritan ministers encouraged masters to educate their slaves so that they could hear the Christian message. Manumission was much more common in the North than in the South, and this tradition increased throughout the revolutionary period. Masters and slaves had a closer relationship in the North compared to those in the southern states and the Caribbean where large plantations and absentee landlords meant that slaves were considered more of a threat. However, they still laboured under slavery in the North and were restricted by a series of slave codes that grew harsher during times of unrest. An abolitionist visitor to New England who had also travelled extensively in the Caribbean, the French Duc de Rochefoucauld-Liancourt, observed that the systems differed only in 'manners', meaning that the style of slavery might be different in the northern states, but in essence it was identical.

During the Revolutionary War, as each colony developed into a state and established its own decision-making convention, the decision to abolish slavery was taken at that level. Vermont was the first to abolish in 1777, followed by Massachusetts in 1780. Although reluctant to acquiesce, there was no significant opposition from slaveholders in these areas. Rhode Island and Connecticut offered slave owners the opportunity to gradually end the institution without a large loss of income. Those states decided that no living slave would be freed but that their children would not be slaves. There were vigorous debates in Pennsylvania in 1779–80 as to whether to free slaves or not. Pro-slavery campaigners defended the institution that they said was justifiable both in law and using biblical evidence. Slavery was a profitable institution for them and they would not give it up without a struggle. However, despite their resistance, gradual abolition was passed and allowed to stand. The most resistance to abolition in the North emerged in New York and New Jersey. Throughout the 1780s pro-slavery campaigners defeated bills to abolish slavery and enacted even harsher slave codes. They justified their arguments by referring to the property rights of an individual. In response, abolitionists, especially Quakers, increased their use of printed propaganda. They emphasized Enlightenment ideas about the rights of the individual rather than religious justifications. Finally, in 1799 the abolition bill was passed in New York declaring that slave children would be made free and that the state would be responsible for their care. New Jersey followed suit in 1804, also allowing slave owners to abandon their slave children to the state. This cost the state a huge amount of money and amounted to compensated abolition for slave owners. In 1807–8, 30 per cent of the state's budget went on supporting former slave children. The struggle by abolitionists in New York and New Jersey did not bode well for the abolition process in Virginia, the Carolinas and Georgia, where slavery was much more entrenched, where property rights were important and where the prospect of a large free black population, a majority in South Carolina, caused much concern.

Abolitionists did not abandon the fight once gradual abolition had been achieved in the North. They knew that the free black population needed support, and also that under gradual abolition some older slaves would languish in the institution for years to come, so the fight for immediate abolition did not end. However, the popularity of the abolition movement declined, partly because of a general swing towards conservatism but also because some people were satisfied that their goals had been achieved. Fewer and fewer black people remained enslaved and many of those were elderly. State legislatures were also vigilant on the issue of slave importations; they were keen to prevent slave owners from elsewhere bringing enslaved people into their territory. Abolition societies played a key role in alerting the legislatures to this problem.

As the free black population increased, and freedom became the normal state of black people in the North, it became clear that emancipation had not brought racism to an end. In fact, racial tension increased as the numbers of free blacks increased. They were treated as second-class citizens. The relationship between abolition societies and the free blacks they helped was often strained. Abolitionists could be overly paternalistic and were embarrassed if free blacks did not behave in a morally upstanding way, blaming them for any public hostility.

Emancipation

After the successful abolition of the slave trade in 1807, the abolitionist coalition in Britain held together to oversee abuses of the law, and then from 1820s onwards to campaign for the abolition of slavery itself. Although William Wilberforce had been a leader in the cause to abolish the slave trade, he feared that emancipating the slaves would cause economic ruin for the British empire, especially the West Indian trade that relied on the slave-grown commodities of rum, sugar and coffee. The government was also sceptical and preferred to pursue a policy of amelioration through negotiation with the West Indian planters. This reflected the economic nervousness of the British and the strength of the plantation lobby. The West Indian planters were not keen to enact the improvements in slave conditions and this resulted in patchy enforcement by local legislatures. They made a comparison between the condition of slaves and that of the free labour workforce in Britain, saying that their slaves were treated better and lived happier lives. Other abolitionists, such as Thomas Clarkson and Granville Sharp, did not share Wilberforce's doubt and intended to pursue the goal of emancipation from the start, seeing the termination of the slave trade as only one part of this process.

The situation of slave women was of especial concern to abolitionists, who were alarmed by the abusive treatment meted out to women and girls. Sexual abuse and inconsiderate behaviour towards new mothers were the focuses of the campaign. Another complaint was over the enforced separation of a slave husband and wife. Abolitionists typified the relationship between a white man and a slave woman as an abusive one. They did not want to acknowledge that the reality was more complex and that consensual relationships sometimes developed, especially in the West Indies and in Louisiana. But the flogging of slave women angered abolitionists, partly because women were physically weaker and could not withstand such treatment, but also because flogging was associated with women's nakedness as they had to expose their bare backs to receive the punishment. Abolitionists accused planters of receiving illicit and immoral enjoyment from having their slaves flogged, but the abolitionist literature also gave graphic details of the nakedness of the women.

However, during the early 1830s the call for emancipation was having an impact on the British government. The slave revolt in Jamaica in 1831, a result of slaves being worked harder when sugar prices fell, caused British public opinion to become mobilized against slavery, especially when news of the harsh punishments inflicted on slaves in the area reached Britain. Missionaries were working to improve slave conditions when planters accused them of stirring up trouble. Many chapels and meeting houses were pulled down as the planters reacted to the perceived threat from missionaries whose effigies were hung in the marketplace, and this mobilized the evangelical wing of the abolition movement across the Atlantic. Slavery was the key factor in the 1830 and 1832 elections in which candidates who declared themselves for abolition won victories over those who did not. The support for abolition in Parliament made the passing of the Act in 1833 a reality. The Act decreed that in return for abolition planters would receive $20 million. This proposal divided the pro-slavery West Indian lobby, and as the Act could not be imposed from London their backing was crucial. In the end, they acquiesced and the Act became a 'parent statute' under which colonial legislatures passed acts to free their own slaves. In Jamaica the system of slave labour was replaced by apprenticeship in which slaves continued to work for the same master but were given wages. For many former slaves the new system brought worse abuses. Workhouses were used to control those workers who could not afford to look after themselves; and although the flogging of women was banned elsewhere, it was rife in the workhouses because their organizing committees were supporters of the plantation system and did nothing to protect the former slaves.

There were many different models for emancipation in the Atlantic world. The French case shows the fragile state of abolition movements and their susceptibility to political change. The earliest French abolition movement in 1788 had modelled itself on the London Society for the Abolition of the Slave Trade, which was founded a year earlier. The two groups frequently corresponded to compare tactics and progress. The French movement was more elitist and made no attempt to engage the people and harness their power, as the British did. Women did not become involved as they had done in Britain and the United States because of the control of the Catholic Church. The movement was also less radical, campaigning only for gradual abolition. The French Revolutionary government was the first colonial power to abolish slavery completely in 1794. But only eight years later the emperor Napoleon, who was married to a creole and favourable to colonial interests, re-established the institution and also the transatlantic slave trade while repressing the abolition movement in France.

The 1833 abolition of British slavery changed the nature of the debate in France. Earlier the French press and popular opinion had mostly remained ignorant of the idea of emancipation. French abolitionists became more vocal, and black and mixed-race people such as the author Alexandre Dumas increasingly participated in the movement. However, they were still cautious about their aims, discussing compensation for slave owners and maintaining an interest in gradual abolition, not moving towards immediatism until 1847. By the 1840s they used petitions as a means to persuade the government, and missionaries also changed their attitudes towards slave ownership. The Pope finally spoke against the mistreatment of slaves, whereas previous popes had appeared tolerant of the institution. However, Catholic clergy in the French Caribbean remained beholden to the planters so were unlikely to speak out. The sugar-growing lobby in France was as powerful as it had been in Britain, so this also hindered progress. The French abolition movement had little effect although it was slowly becoming more radical. Abolition was finally achieved a second and final time through the means of domestic revolution in 1848. In return, French slave owners were offered an indemnity totalling 90 million francs.

Dramatic political change was linked to the abolition movement in other parts of the Atlantic world. In the former Spanish and Portuguese regions of South America the newly independent nations grappled with the issue of slavery and took various lengths of time to emancipate, depending on the power of the conservative elites and how entrenched slavery was in the economy of the nation. During revolutionary struggles slaves fought on both the royalist and rebel sides and others took advantage of the chaos to run away. Some planters lost so much money during the wars that they were unable to maintain their slaves afterwards and simply abandoned them. Whether the independence leaders, such as San Martín and Simón Bolívar, were true abolitionists or merely using the cause for their own political gain is a point for debate. Liberal thinkers focused on the 'liberty' of their nation and not on their slaves, as the founding fathers had done in the North American revolution. Abolition in the South Atlantic was influenced by events elsewhere. The British government supported the rebels' campaigns for independence only when they condemned slavery. The publication of Harriet Beecher Stowe's *Uncle Tom's Cabin* galvanized the abolition movement across the Atlantic world. This serialized novel was one of the most popular of its time and has been compared to *The Pilgrim's Progress* in its religious and cultural significance. It was much admired by Frederick Douglass, Queen Victoria and Abraham Lincoln.

In Peru abolition happened gradually over three decades. In 1821 'the law of the free womb' was passed, proclaiming that all children born after that date would be free. '*Libertos*', or freeborn children, had to be cared for by their master until adulthood, and in return they would work for their masters as servants; but this system was open to exploitation. Slave owners also manumitted their slaves voluntarily and the government held lotteries in which groups of slaves were freed. In the 1850s, some slave owners, such as Alfonso Gonzales Pinillos, experienced dramatic conversions to the cause and freed all their slaves. But most mobilized to defend the existing state of affairs, saying that emancipation would further damage the agriculture of the country. Their position strengthened as liberalism waned after independence. The replacement of slavery with a system of free labour was further complicated by an influx of Chinese labourers known as 'coolies', who were also treated badly because of their race and were restricted by laws similar to slave codes. Slavery was finally abolished after a Civil War in 1854, and slave owners were offered monetary compensation. Unlike in the United States, the war was not about slavery but was a rebellion by a former president against the incumbent president.

In Brazil, slavery was also challenged by the influx of immigrants, this time from Europe. The demographic make-up of the slave system also meant that it was vulnerable to change. In Brazil even the poorest people owned slaves; however, there were far more free blacks in Brazil than in the southern United States. The decline of Brazilian slavery was due to external pressures rather than action by a domestic abolition movement. The end of the slave trade had a dramatic effect on slave numbers, as the slave mortality rate was high and reproduction rate low. Pro-slavery planters found it harder to hold on to their system because of the presence of a large proportion of free blacks. There was no popular movement led by whites or blacks trying to abolish slavery in South America and the Catholic Church did not wish to disturb the status quo. Fundamentally, abolition was achieved gradually and peacefully through parliamentary legislation in line with the desires of the elite. The slave trade itself was abolished in 1851 due to pressure from the British. This was followed in 1871 by the 'free birth law' emancipating the future children of all slaves. The law was put into effect more quickly in the north-east of the country than in the south around Rio de Janeiro and São Paulo, where there was more resistance. Finally, in 1888 the 'golden law' was passed, freeing all slaves immediately. By that stage slavery had collapsed in many places, superseded by free labour areas such as Pernambuco. Slaves fled from their plantations more easily after the coming of the railways. This made the transition to free labour inevitable.

The Abolition Movement Gains Pace in the United States

The abolition of slavery in the southern states of the United States was a particularly protracted and violent business. The power of the pro-slave lobby and its ability to convince the non-slaveholding southerners of the rightness of their cause, the strict control of the slaves and the lack of a free black community in the South, combined with the radicalization of the abolition movement in the North, meant that violence became inevitable. The early nineteenth-century Protestant revival triggered the abolition movement but it also had secular roots in the natural rights tradition of Enlightenment Europe. The way historians view the abolition of slavery has been affected by politics ever since the American Civil War. The South's 'lost cause' mentality encourages a sentimental view of the war, separating the sacrifice from the cause. But it is important to remember that the abolitionists in the North were fighting for a moral cause inspired by religious idealism.

In the United States the free black population in the North was central to the abolition movement. At times it had a tense relationship with white abolitionists and initially many free blacks favoured colonization. These included Paul Cuffee, who was involved in preparations to ship freed slaves to Liberia and Sierra Leone, believing that black people would never be accepted as equals and that the best chance of success for the former slaves was in returning to Africa. The American Colonization Society found unlikely allies among racist whites whose aim was to keep the United States white. Later, the African American abolitionists became more radical, encouraged by abolitionist whites who were making a conscious effort to overcome their own racism and to promote self-help among free blacks.

As well as campaigning for emancipation, they sent missionaries into the South to try to turn slave owners away from the institution; they protected the rights of free blacks, taught black children, tried to bring an end to segregation and petitioned Congress to end slavery. They issued so many petitions that the 'gag rule' was implemented by pro-slavery politicians to prevent the government from considering them. They encouraged southern slaves to run away and offered them protection in the North. Harriet Tubman, a former slave, returned to the South 19 times to help others escape. Abolitionists believed that through education, the black population of the United States would achieve middle-class respectability. Abolitionists led by William Lloyd Garrison were pacifists but radical; they believed that women should play a full part in the campaign and that churches were too slow to respond and only emphasized the privileges of the few. Their policy became known as 'come outerism'. Garrison also denounced the Constitution, believing that an end to slavery would not happen within the Constitution that had permitted it. On these points he split from fellow abolitionists such as Lewis Tappan and Frederick Douglass, who were more conservative over the role of women and the potential of the Constitution to be reformed. Wendell Phillips thought that to worry about the rights of women was distracting and that abolitionists should focus wholeheartedly on freeing slaves. 'One question at a time,' he said, 'this is the negro's hour.'

Garrison is the most famous abolitionist in the history of the United States; his influence has been compared to that of both Thomas Paine and Martin Luther King. He trained as a printer and made his living editing newspapers, his most famous being the longest-running abolitionist paper *The Liberator*, which ran from 1831 until 1865. He also made his name as an inspirational public speaker, and large audiences around the country flocked to hear his oratory. Around the time he founded the newspaper, Garrison realized that the doctrine of gradual abolition was morally unacceptable and he declared his desire for immediatism. He was a member of the New England Anti-Slavery Society, the first abolitionist group to refuse to accept gradual abolition, and then later in 1833 he founded the American Anti-Slave Association, the first national abolition organization. Garrison also criticized colonization projects, saying that they refused to challenge racist stereotypes and allowed white Americans to evade their responsibilities. During the 1830s Garrison began to bring together his radical coalition of abolitionists of both races who shaped the movement until emancipation. They were influenced by abolitionists in Britain, and campaigners such as Frederick Douglass and Harriet Jacobs travelled across the Atlantic to attend meetings and give lectures, where their first-hand experience of the slave system invigorated the movement in Britain as well as the United States.

Garrison was the only man who asserted in print that slavery was an issue of right and wrong, whereas moderates portrayed the differences of opinion as a mild fraternal struggle. A slave rebellion in 1831, led by Nat Turner, aroused the fears of southerners. Abolitionists were inspired by his religious fervour, although some were unsure whether or not to condemn his violence. Turner also demonstrated that slaves were ready to strike out for their own freedom, implying that the time for action had finally come. Northerners were increasingly becoming part of the modern capitalist economy and saw slavery as regressive. Wage labour was seen as an important expression of individual freedom. As in Britain, a court case mobilized public opinion behind the abolitionist cause. The Amistad case of 1839–41 had repercussions that were felt throughout the Atlantic world because the Supreme Court ruled that the Africans accused of murder were illegally held as slaves and should be allowed to return to their homeland. Events in Europe had an effect on the abolition movement: revolution in 1848 initially pleased Garrison, but then, as liberalism collapsed, reformers everywhere were disheartened.

In the 1840s and 1850s, as the debate over slavery became sectional and the positions of North and South hardened, the possibility of using violence became a reality for many abolitionists. The people of the United States always admired the use of violence in struggles such as that for their own independence, and abolitionists realized that they would have to be prepared to fight in their own self-defence. Fugitive slaves and their protectors had to be armed as fights between pro- and anti-slavery groups escalated in Kansas. As the issue of territorial expansion became bound up with slavery, a new, milder type of anti-slavery campaigner emerged, one who did not want to see the spread of slavery but was not willing to call for its abolition in existing states. By the time of the election of 1848, politicians and campaigners were split between those like Garrison advocating disunion, and moderates speaking of free soil (all new states should be free), non-interference (Congress did not have the right to interfere with slavery in any state), an extension of the Missouri compromise line, or leaving the decision to popular sovereignty within each new territory. Free Soilers, who were the first anti-slavery political party, were not devoid of racist feeling despite their ideals. For example, Walt Whitman hoped that white working men everywhere would come together to ensure that they did not descend to the horrible state of black slaves.

The movement was weakened in the 1850s when Garrison disagreed with Frederick Douglass over political strategy. Douglass was more moderate than Garrison and believed that it was possible to reform the Constitution in order to bring an end to slavery. Garrison had long believed that the Union itself would have to fracture before the institution could be ended. Ironically, early on only he and pro-slavery politician John C. Calhoun of South Carolina were talking about disunion. Garrison's slogan became 'no union with slaveholders'. During this period many radical abolitionists came to the conclusion that violence was needed. Even Garrison realized that his pacifism was an unachievable ideal. However, the founding in 1854 of the Republican Party, emerging out of a coalition of Free Soilers and northern Whigs, gave the radical abolitionists cautious optimism that a political solution might be possible. John Brown believed that this would not be the case, and, being more radical even than Garrison, was convinced that violence was justified in the anti-slavery cause. He attacked Harper's Ferry, Virginia in 1859, acting alone but with the support of many other abolitionists including Frederick Douglass. After the attack there was a willingness to go to war to end slavery. In some ways, Brown's mission was a failure; he did not free any slaves and was easily captured. But he became a martyr for the abolitionist cause and he made people realize that war was inevitable: as Garrison said, 'his gunshot merely told us the time of day. It is high noon, thank God'.

Women and Abolition

The role of women in the abolition movement was also important. The fate of women had always been associated with slavery, with Homer and Aristotle linking the lot of women to that of slaves and, from the mid-seventeenth century, Continental philosophers comparing the married state to slavery. When Napoleon took power and reinstituted slavery in the French colonies, he simultaneously protected the rights of husbands, enshrined in law the duty of obedience for the wife and prevented the possibility of divorce. Nineteenth-century white, middle-class American culture idolized its women, emphasizing their domesticity and innocence. This was in stark contrast to the treatment of southern slave women who were physically and sexually abused. The Grimké sisters from South Carolina and the Jewish campaigner Ernestine Rose became involved in the abolition movement and, although they faced resistance from men, used it as a platform to become politically active. Lucretia Mott and Elizabeth Cady Stanton, two early feminists, met in London at the World Anti-Slavery conference of 1840 where they were forbidden from taking the floor because of their gender. The abolition movement, especially in Manchester, had initially been feminized, with female traits and values emphasized over male ones. However, British abolitionist women were less likely than their American counterparts to speak out against the oppression of women because of the class system and the way that it tied women into the 'separate spheres' ideology, and because of the British abolitionists' emphasis on the single issue of slavery. The American female abolitionists developed a 'sisterhood' rhetoric which then fed directly into the new feminist movement. Women debated how far they wanted to take their cause. The question of what freedom meant for a woman was a challenging one. For example, should a slave woman be free to be a wife and mother, or free to be the man's equal? Not all women became abolitionists; many plantation wives in the South thought women should accept the natural order of things. African American women also used abolition to claim a voice. For the first time, they joined together in literary societies and began to use print to combat racist ideas about them. This worried some male abolitionists who saw the struggle for freedom as a way to assert their masculinity.

Free at Last!

Abolitionists did not enthusiastically welcome Abraham Lincoln's presidency but southerners were even more perturbed. Lincoln believed in the natural inferiority of black people and favoured the repatriation of former slaves to Africa. He was worried by the prospect of immediate abolition and when, in 1861, John Fremont, a long-time abolitionist who held Missouri for the Union, tried to declare martial law and free all the slaves in that state, Lincoln over-ruled him because he was afraid the move might push Missouri to favour the southern cause. However, although Lincoln still believed in gradual and voluntary emancipation for slaves in the Union, in his desire to help the war effort he introduced the Emancipation Proclamation that came into effect in January 1863. Abolitionists were disappointed because the Proclamation did not turn their cause into a moral crusade. By itself the Proclamation did not free one slave; it needed further government legislation to enact full emancipation.

By December 1863 the Confederacy was considering freeing slaves for use in the army. President Jefferson Davis initially rejected the proposal because he thought slaves inferior and unable to make good soldiers. He was convinced otherwise by General Robert E. Lee and Judah P. Benjamin despite the fact that most southerners remained opposed to the measure, claiming that it was not necessary and would weaken the South still further. Slaves might also turn traitor and attack the Confederacy. The measure also challenged deeply held racial assumptions. If slaves were freed and allowed to fight then might they also be allowed to determine their own future in the longer term? Planters predicted the downfall of slavery. The decision to use slaves in the army came too late to affect the war; only in Richmond, Virginia were any slave units mustered.

Meanwhile Republicans in the Union had decided that an amendment to the Constitution was needed to bring full emancipation, thus changing the way that Americans viewed the Constitution. It was now a document that could be amended without being undermined. On 5 January 1865 the amendment was voted through by 119 votes to 56. The decision then had to be ratified by each state in the Union. Southern states that were on the verge of being accepted back into the Union after the war rushed to ratify the amendment, although a few diehard Confederates refused.

Conclusion

The abolition movement across the Atlantic world was influenced by many factors: evangelical religious revival, the development of a discourse on human rights emerging out of the natural philosophy of the Enlightenment period, the public reaction to court cases revealing the horrors of the slave trade or of slavery itself, the development of a popular print culture and increased literacy, the emergence of a public sphere in which the middle classes became involved in the political process, liberal revolutions implementing new ideas about personhood and race, a waning of the mercantilist system and increased emphasis on the value of free labour.

Traditionally the story of abolition has focused on key individuals such as William Wilberforce, William Lloyd Garrison and Simón Bolívar, whose religious, philosophical or political beliefs drove the movement forward. Increasingly their role is contested or their motives challenged. Public opinion in Britain and the United States, and to a lesser extent France, encouraged governments to move towards abolition. The movement was not imposed from the metropolis onto the colonies because of the beliefs of a few individuals. Economic forces explain why slavery was abandoned. Sometimes slavery was no longer profitable or free labour seemed a more attractive option, such as in Brazil and Peru.

There are many ways of categorizing abolition movements. These contrasts illustrate the way that the movements differed across the Atlantic world:

1 *Gradual versus immediate.* The abolitions in the north of the United States and in Peru and Brazil were gradual. Children of slaves were freed first and the numbers of slaves decreased as the population died. Immediate abolition occurred in the southern United States and in the British and French Caribbean, although the apprenticeship schemes that replaced slavery in Jamaica were harsher in some ways than slavery itself.

2 *Legal versus economic.* In the case of South American countries many slave owners gave up their slaves because of economic changes that meant other forms of labour were more profitable. However, in most cases abolition was imposed through legal means – a change in the law by the imperial ruler, a newly independent nation or local government.

3 *Voluntary versus imposed.* The ending of slavery everywhere except the southern United States was to some extent voluntary. Even the imposition of abolition by law met with little resistance. In the British Caribbean, for example, local legislatures confirmed the law passed by Parliament in London. The British Royal Navy imposed the ending of the slave trade that was also imposed on Africa and the Atlantic world, and took them nearly half a century to complete. Abolition was imposed on the southern United States by the Union using the Emancipation Proclamation and then the Thirteenth Amendment.

The abolition of the slave trade and of slavery itself coincided with the end of imperial control in many areas of the Atlantic world, apart from the Caribbean and West Africa. Together these developments changed the Atlantic world and even broke it apart.

For the individuals in the Atlantic world, abolition opened the way for political participation for those of the lower classes, women and black people. However, for many former slaves little changed. In the southern United States, after a decade of radical reconstruction, the status quo resumed where former slaves were bound as sharecroppers to their former masters and suffered the institutional racism of the 'Jim Crow' laws. The abolition of slavery in Jamaica led to a short period of apprenticeship, but an uneven transfer of power from the planter elite to the population followed. Despite the efforts of many abolitionists, newly freed slaves initially struggled to overcome centuries of prejudice and legal inequality. They now fought alongside other poor free workers for the few available resources while many elites retained their position and power.

It is also important to remember that slavery has not been entirely removed from the Atlantic world. Some West African nations, although legally abolishing slavery, still tacitly permit the practice. According to the twenty-first-century abolition organization Anti-Slavery International, in Mauritania and Niger nomadic and semi-nomadic tribes have slave castes that, while they permit a slave to buy his or her own freedom, still tie the former slave to the master in the form of tribute payments. Slave women and girls as young as 10 can be taken in forced marriage, sometimes to atone for crimes committed by members of their family. Slave trafficking is prevalent; often West African slaves are moved a long way from their homes, perhaps across national borders. Slavery still exists in Brazil too, with thousands of male workers employed in ranching, deforestation and agriculture. The agri-businesses are very powerful and they resist Brazilian government attempts to legislate and free the slaves. In these troubled parts of the world a new abolition movement still has work to do.

CHAPTER CHRONOLOGY

1521 First slave revolt on Hispaniola.

1605 Escaped slaves found the colony of Palmares in Brazil (lasts till 1697).

1735 Colony of Georgia in North America tries to ban slavery, but allows it after 1749.

1777 Constitution of the state of Vermont abolishes slavery.

1780–4 Massachusetts, Pennsylvania, Rhode Island and Connecticut gradually abolish slavery.

1783 Quakers begin campaign in England against slave trade; the Zong case catches the public's attention.

1789 Slavery is preserved under the new US Constitution.

1791 Toussaint L'Ouverture takes command of slave forces in Saint Domingue.

1807 Britain and the United States prohibit the slave trade.

1834 Slavery abolished throughout British empire, replaced by system of apprenticeship.

1860 South Carolina secedes from the United States triggering the Civil War.

1863 President Lincoln issues the Emancipation Proclamation.

1865 Slavery abolished in United States.

1888 Slavery abolished in Brazil.

1980 Slavery abolished in Mauritania.

▪ **PRIMARY SOURCES AND STUDY IMAGE**

Samuel Sewall, *The Selling of Joseph* (1700)

And all things considered, it would conduce more to the welfare of the province, to have white servants for a term of years, than to have slaves for life. Few can endure to hear of a Negro's being made free; and indeed they can seldom use their freedom well; yet their continual aspiring after their forbidden liberty, renders them unwilling servants.

And there is such a disparity in their conditions, colour & hair, that they can never embody with us, and grow up into orderly families, to the peopling of the land: but still remain in our body politick as a kind of extravasat blood [involuntary resident]. As many Negro men as there are among us, so many empty places there are in our Train Bands, and the places taken up of men that might make husbands for our daughters. And the sons and daughters of *New England* would become more like *Jacob*, and *Rachel*, if this slavery were thrust quite out of doors. Moreover it is too well known what temptations masters are under, to connive at the fornication of their slaves; lest they should be obliged to find them wives, or pay their fines. It seems to be practically pleaded that they might be lawless; 'tis thought much of, that the law should have satisfaction for their thefts, and other immoralities; by which means, *Holiness to the Lord*, is more rarely engraven upon this sort of servitude. It is likewise most lamentable to think, how in taking Negros out of *Africa*, and selling of them here, That which GOD has joined together men do boldly rend asunder. Men from their Country, Husbands from their Wives, Parents from their Children.

How horrible is the uncleanness, mortality, if not murder that the ships are guilty of that bring great crowds of these miserable men, and women. Methinks, when we are bemoaning the barbarous usage of our friends and kinsfolk in *Africa*: it might not be unseasonable to enquire whether we are not culpable in forcing the *Africans* to become slaves amongst our selves. And it may be a question whether all the benefit received by Negro slaves, will balance the accompt of cash laid out upon them; and for the redemption of our own enslaved friends out of *Africa*. Besides all the persons and estates that have perished there.

Translation of the Declaration of Independence from Haiti (1804)

The Commander in Chief to the People of Haiti

Citizens:

It is not enough to have expelled the barbarians who have bloodied our land for two centuries; it is not enough to have restrained those ever-evolving factions that one after another mocked the specter of liberty that France dangled before you. We must, with one last act of national authority, forever assure the empire of liberty in the country of our birth; we must take any hope of re-enslaving us away from the inhuman government that for so long kept us in the most humiliating torpor. In the end we must live independent or die.

Independence or death ... let these sacred words unite us and be the signal of battle and of our reunion.

Citizens, my countrymen, on this solemn day I have brought together those courageous soldiers who, as liberty lay dying, spilled their blood to save it; these generals who have guided your efforts against tyranny have not yet done enough for your happiness; the French name still haunts our land.

Everything revives the memories of the cruelties of this barbarous people: our laws, our habits, our towns, everything still carries the stamp of the French. Indeed! There are still French in our island, and you believe yourself free and independent of that Republic which, it is true, has fought all the nations, but which has never defeated those who wanted to be free.

What! Victims of our [own] credulity and indulgence for 14 years; defeated not by French armies, but by the pathetic eloquence of their agents' proclamations; when will we tire of breathing the air that they breathe? What do we have in common with this nation of executioners? The difference between its cruelty and our patient moderation, its colour and ours the great seas that separate us, our avenging climate, all tell us plainly that they are not our brothers, that they never will be, and that if they find refuge among us, they will plot again to trouble and divide us.

Native citizens, men, women, girls, and children, let your gaze extend on all parts of this island: look there for your spouses, your husbands, your brothers, your sisters.

Indeed! Look there for your children, your suckling infants, what have they become? … I shudder to say it … the prey of these vultures.

Instead of these dear victims, your alarmed gaze will see only their assassins, these tigers still dripping with their blood, whose terrible presence indicts your lack of feeling and your guilty slowness in avenging them. What are you waiting for before appeasing their spirits? Remember that you had wanted your remains to rest next to those of your fathers, after you defeated tyranny; will you descend into their tombs without having avenged them? No! Their bones would reject yours.

And you, precious men, intrepid generals, who, without concern for your own pain, have revived liberty by shedding all your blood, know that you have done nothing if you do not give the nations a terrible, but just example of the vengeance that must be wrought by a people proud to have recovered its liberty and jealous to maintain it let us frighten all those who would dare try to take it from us again; let us begin with the French. Let them tremble when they approach our coast, if not from the memory of those cruelties they perpetrated here, then from the terrible resolution that we will have made to put to death anyone born French whose profane foot soils the land of liberty.

We have dared to be free, let us be thus by ourselves and for ourselves. Let us imitate the grown child: his own weight breaks the boundary that has become an obstacle to him. What people fought for us? What people wanted to gather the fruits of our labour? And what dishonourable absurdity to conquer in order to be enslaved. Enslaved? … Let us leave this description for the French; they have conquered but are no longer free.

Let us walk down another path; let us imitate those people who, extending their concern into the future, and dreading to leave an example of cowardice for posterity, preferred to be exterminated rather than lose their place as one of the world's free peoples.

Let us ensure, however, that a missionary spirit does not destroy our work; let us allow our neighbours to breathe in peace; may they live quietly under the laws that they have made for themselves, and let us not, as revolutionary firebrands, declare ourselves the lawgivers of the Caribbean, nor let our glory consist in troubling the peace of the neighbouring islands. Unlike that which we inhabit, theirs has not been drenched in the innocent blood of its inhabitants; they have no vengeance to claim from the authority that protects them.

Fortunate to have never known the ideals that have destroyed us, they can only have good wishes for our prosperity.

Peace to our neighbours; but let this be our cry: 'Anathama to the French name! Eternal hatred of France!'

Natives of Haiti! My happy fate was to be one day the sentinel who would watch over the idol to which you sacrifice; I have watched, sometimes fighting alone, and if I have been so fortunate as to return to your hands the sacred trust you confided to me, know that it is now your task to preserve it. In fighting for your liberty, I was working for my own happiness. Before consolidating it with laws that will guarantee your free individuality, your leaders, who I have assembled here, and I, owe you the final proof of our devotion.

Generals and you, leaders, collected here close to me for the good of our land, the day has come, the day which must make our glory, our independence, eternal.

If there could exist among us a lukewarm heart, let him distance himself and tremble to take the oath which must unite us. Let us vow to ourselves, to posterity, to the entire universe, to forever renounce France, and to die rather than live under its domination; to fight until our last breath for the independence of our country.

And you, a people so long without good fortune, witness to the oath we take, remember that I counted on your constancy and courage when I threw myself into the career of liberty to fight the despotism and tyranny you had struggled against for 14 years. Remember that I sacrificed everything to rally to your defense; family, children, fortune, and now I am rich only with your liberty; my name has become a horror to all those who want slavery. Despots and tyrants curse the day that I was born. If ever you refused or grumbled while receiving those laws that the spirit guarding your fate dictates to me for your own good, you would deserve the fate of an ungrateful people. But I reject that awful idea; you will sustain the liberty that you cherish and support the leader who commands you. Therefore vow before me to live free and independent, and to prefer death to anything that will try to place you back in chains. Swear, finally, to pursue forever the traitors and enemies of your independence.

Done at the headquarters of Gonaives, the first day of January 1804, the first year of independence.

Letters from American Colonization Society settlers in Liberia

Careysburg, Jan. 28, 1858

My dear Miss.

I now write in answer to your two letters I received this year, I was glad to hear from you and all the freinds [sic] in that part of the Country. I and children are well, and may this find you and all well and enjoying the blessings of kind heaven. I now tells you some thing about Careysburg. This is a fine place and fine country indeed, the custom of the natives is very good they are docile and friendly people, I have not seen one hostile one as yet. Those persons that came out with us, mostall living except those you [have] heard death [sic]. If you pleased to send me 1 Keg of nails, 1 Barrel of Pork, and children shoes and pair for myself, and two axes, pantaloons stuff 1 piece, 1 piece Calico, 1 grumbling hoes and some [of] the cheapest of Cloths which is different kinds of Calico piece of each, 1 Box of soap and two B [unclear] and 1 sett of knives and forks and half dozen of water pails. We have meetings every Sunday and the Baptist Association have appointed a young man from Grand Bassa Country by the name of [unclear] Roberts to teach us all little and big who wished to go to school. My love to sister Jinny tell her I like this country very well and I cannot find no faults.

March 3ᵈ 1857 Carysburgh Mount Faublee
Dr Minor

Dear Sir

I have taken this first opportunity after my arrival in this country, of writing to you I hope that you and family are well, myself & family are quite well, and have been since I been in this country, yet at this time I am not quite well to day. Myself and Maria, Isabella Charles and Richard, have all come to the new Interior Settlement, about 50 or 60 miles from the sea coast. Wm Douglass and his family, Charles Twine and his

Brother Philip, George, Winslow and Hugh Walker 3 Brothers, Washington, Coleman, Allen, Wilson, and Martin 4 Brothers, John and Washington Mickey 2 Brothers, and Thomas and David Scott, 2 Brothers compose the company that came to the new Interior Settlement with us, We have all been quite well, no fever nor any other kind of sickness the place is finely located on top of a very high mountain, we like this place much better than we seen elsewhere, and although things are not like they were at home, yet we are thus far quite satisfied. The rest of our people all settled at Monrovia, and Clay Ashland up the river about 15 miles from the sea coast, And I am very sorry to inform you that the mortality has; been very great by the fever, we have lost by Death the following persons, my father, sister Francis, Uncle Buck Thomson, Billy Douglass, James Scott, Lucy Twines baby, Frank Coleman; Maria Coleman; Lucy Twines Father; Patrick Mickey; Robert Scott is laying very low, indeed all the people down at Clay Ashland are quite sick, Thus far we all have enjoyed good health as when at home. I will now tell you of my wife Maria, and the children, they did not get any of the clothes that was intended for them the box was robbed or something else; as there was no bill of Lading for them, we have never seen any them [sic]. I would like you send me 1 Barrell of Pork 1 Bll of Fish and 1 of flour, and also 2 pair of Black Gaiters No 6 and No 7 also some leather shoes for us all, I would be very glad to receive these by the Mary Caroline Stevens, when she comes in the Spring, so as we may get them by the then our 6 months is up on the Society, I would like to get some Calico, some Bleached and some Unbleached Cotton, and 2 cotton Bed spreads – . some Blue and White womens stockings; and 1 White Swiss muslin dress pattern for Isabella; I wish this to be fine, and a peice of Satin Ribbon, and please to send Maria some Black dresses suitable for mourning. I wish you to send me a few lawn dress patterns, and some cheap calico for country trade, as that is the same as money or better you will please to send me some cloth for myself and the boy, I would like to get a good Bedstead also; I wish you to send me about 20 Dollars in Gold or Silver money, I would wish you to give my respects to Dr Merryweather and ask to send me something. Young Barrett send his love to his Father, [Mother,] Brother and Sisters, Maria and Isabella sends [sic] their love to all, Maria, sends her love to her Brother Wm Terrell we all send our love to Uncle Bob, Aunt Daffiny Jane, Mr Harry Lewis, and Sarah Lewis and all of their family, Tell Aunt Daffiny, Young has seen Dianna and she was well; Isabella sends her love to Sarah Thornton and her family, She is very well and enjoys herself and expects in a short time to be married. You will please to send me some Leaf Tobacco as that is the Money; You will direct your letters to Carysburgh Interior Settlement and in the Care of Mr Saunders A Campion Superinten[dent] of Carysburgh and Agent of Amer Col Society as well as all goods for us by these means I will get them. Please to put my things in a box by themselves and direct as above.

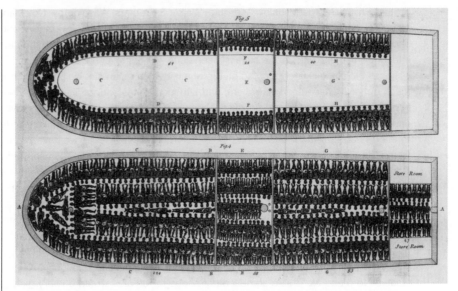

Study image 8 *Hemsley's engraving of a slave ship, nineteenth century.*

Recommended Reading

Robin Blackburn, *The Overthrow of Colonial Slavery 1776–1848* (London, 1988). A wide-ranging survey of the abolition movements during the period of revolution. Examines broad intellectual developments such as the Enlightenment but also focuses on the personal stories of individuals such as Quakers, maroons and pirates.

Brycchan Carey, *British Abolitionism and the Rhetoric of Sensibility: Writing, Sentiment, and Slavery, 1760–1807* (Basingstoke, 2005). Provides a literary survey of the ways that contemporaries talked about abolition, arguing that they developed a sentimental rhetoric.

David B. Davis, *The Problem of Slavery in the Age of Revolution* (New York, 1975). Offers a classic survey of the history of eighteenth-century slavery throughout the Atlantic world, and of attempts to challenge and then end the system.

Seymour Drescher, *Abolition: A History of Slavery and Anti-slavery* (Cambridge, 2009). Provides a global context to the question of why, if slavery was a successful and flourishing system, abolition was embraced so readily in the early nineteenth century.

Eric Foner, *Reconstruction: America's Unfinished Revolution* (New York, 1988). Explores how the United States and black and white individuals came to terms with the end of slavery.

C. L. R. James, *The Black Jacobins: Toussaint L'Ouverture and the San Domingo Revolution* [1938] (3rd edn; London, 1980). Seminal work on the Haitian

Revolution and its Atlantic context, arguing that the class distinctions were as significant as racial ones in causing the upheaval.

Peter Kitson and Debbie Lee (eds), *Slavery, Abolition and Emancipation: Writings in the British Romantic Period*, 8 vols. (London, 1999). A collection of contemporary extracts discussing the case for and against British abolition of the slave trade and slavery in its empire.

Henry Mayer, *All on Fire: William Lloyd Garrison and the Abolition of Slavery* (New York, 1998). Shows that Garrison was crucial to the abolition of slavery in the United States and that he is a true American hero, without whom abolition was far from inevitable.

David Turley, *The Culture of English Antislavery, 1780–1860* (London, 1991). An in-depth look at the British anti-slavery movement and its gradual evolution across a number of alliances using a range of tactics such as propaganda to appeal to the middle-class 'reform mentality'.

Eric Williams, *Capitalism and Slavery* (Chapel Hill, 1944). Classic and very influential account of the relationship between industrial capitalism in Britain and the country's connection to slavery and abolition.

TEST YOUR KNOWLEDGE

1 Did slave resistance trigger the abolition movement?

2 Were all religious denominations against slavery?

3 How did abolitionists convince the British people and Parliament of the justice of their cause?

4 What were the main arguments for and against slavery?

5 When and how did the northern states of the United States free their slaves?

6 Why did abolition happen at different rates in different places?

7 Was colonization ever a viable alternative to the struggle for full freedom?

8 Why was the struggle for emancipation in the southern United States particularly bloody?

9 Did the end of the slave trade mean the end of the Atlantic system?

Conclusion

In the emancipation of slaves in Brazil in 1888, many historians see the end of over four centuries of Atlantic-oriented exploration, encounter, political development and cultural evolution. This period encompassed global events that pre-date Columbus's landmark voyages to the west, and ended after the American Civil War and the completion of a transcontinental railroad that linked the Atlantic coast with the Pacific. The Atlantic world's endpoint as a defined period of study was marked by trends in global history that challenged the Atlantic as the focal point of encounter and human experience.

In the western hemisphere, the focal point of human activity moved distinctly to the west and the interiors of the American continents. In many ways, the development of the United States' transcontinental railroad is a fitting metaphor for the passing of the Atlantic's primacy. During much of the nineteenth century, the peoples on the western edge of the Atlantic littoral looked towards continental interiors for new opportunities and resources. The people of the United States crossed the Mississippi River, and then the Continental Divide, moving into California and displacing Mexican and Native American peoples, before 1850. A similar transition westward happened in Canada. In regions with rich farming potential, such as Argentina, the United States, Mexico and Canada, the open range of the grasslands eventually yielded to a more structured sense of private property and dedicated farming and grazing. Native peoples were displaced and often killed outright; small-time entrepreneurs who depended on the open range of the seemingly unwanted grasslands now faced the challenges of ownership by others, who reinforced their claims with barbed wire. As the nineteenth century gave way to the twentieth, the citizens of various Caribbean islands would likewise turn west. Some migrated in boats, others in airplanes. Still others braved the perils of the open Atlantic to escape political oppression. Seeking opportunity in the West was certainly a characteristic of Atlantic experience documented in this book. But what separates later westward movement is that it pushed farther inland, away from the coasts and the connections to the old worlds they afforded. Technological innovations of the nineteenth century and beyond made the processes involved in transatlantic and interior travel more complete, and more easily achievable, by an ever-widening array of people.

The various independence movements of the late eighteenth and nineteenth centuries also contributed to the erosion of the Atlantic's importance. Atlantic systems owed their existence to control imposed from abroad. In addition, the administration of territories claimed by Europeans brought opportunities for personal advancement and financial enrichment from those 'on the ground'. The ending of these structured connections to Europe resulted at the very least in economic reorientation and often in far-reaching social changes. As a consequence, there was an accompanying break in many of the cultural and economic cords that bound Atlantic people together and shaped 'Atlantic' identities.

Furthermore, the territorial transitions affecting Europe, Africa and the Americas increasingly operated on a *global* scale into the nineteenth and twentieth centuries. Far from drifting into obscurity after the loss of most of its North American mainland colonies, the British empire continued to aggressively extend its influence and power other parts of the globe. Known popularly as the empire 'on which the sun never set', its control spanned from Ireland and the North Atlantic to Tasmania and Hong Kong. Britain's successes in asserting its control over distant places and peoples triggered a land grab among other would-be European colonial powers. French, German, Dutch, Italian and, perhaps most notoriously, Belgian forces 'annexed' territory throughout Africa and South-East Asia. Some displaced legitimate leaders and replaced them with local 'puppet' monarchs who complied with European demands. Other repressive forms of colonial government were more brutal, resulting in the violent deaths of large numbers of Native peoples unwilling to be colonized. Also destroyed were vast reserves of natural resources. The experiences in these parts of the world, which were in many cases decimated and traumatized by these colonial invasions, demonstrate that colonization carries severe, often catastrophic consequences regardless of time and place. Certainly, the land masses that formed what we term the Atlantic world had already learned this tragic lesson.

The discovery of new resources to exploit became global as well, and remained as focused on the seas as it had before: when Atlantic resources dried up, the harvesters of the oceans were forced to turn elsewhere. But such changes in resource exploitation had the added dimension of introducing merchants and mariners to new lands, and consumers to new products to be found away from the Atlantic and its interconnected lands. These changes provided new opportunities for growth for communities that hitherto had had little engagement with the rest of the world. Cases in point are the American and British whaling industries which, having depleted Atlantic whale stocks, were chasing their giant prey around the Cape of Good Hope as early as 1789. Enormous pods of oil-rich sperm whales were located in habitats a thousand miles into the Pacific. On voyages lasting as long as four or five years, whaling vessels were forced to find alternative locations to purchase food and water, repair their vessels, blow off steam in pursuit of physical pleasures, and deposit mail to their loved ones on the western coast of South America, and in the islands of Polynesia and the rest of the Pacific. Places such as Valparaíso, Chile and the Hawaiian islands became well-known destinations for these hunting mariners, not only providing for their immediate needs, but also introducing them to products of the tropics and local crafts. The new economies they spurred were another factor that contributed to a de-emphasizing of the Atlantic and its sphere.

* * *

Still, interest in the Atlantic's role in the history of human contact and encounter remained a vital component of many national histories. But the history of the *study* of Atlantic-based systems is a fairly new idea when contrasted with other well-defined perspectives, such as colonial and imperial history. Yet the concept itself has proved sufficiently innovative to force major rewrites of basic narratives of history from 1450 to 1888, although it only took off as a discipline in its own right within the past four decades or so. This leaves scholars and students alike to wonder what necessitated the development of this alternative model for the study of Old and New Worlds.

First, it is important to acknowledge that, despite more recent popularity, the *concept* of Atlantic history has been part of the historical zeitgeist for much of the twentieth century. As Bernard Bailyn points out in his seminal work on the subject, *Atlantic History: Concepts and Contours*, the idea of framing early modern history Atlantically began to coalesce around the eve of the United States' entry into the Second World War. The timing is highly suggestive, and can be viewed as a reflection of renewed interest in the long-existing ties of culture and society between Britain and its former colonies. The concept lingered in scholarship for decades, but the movement towards social history and its many innovative and exciting historical dimensions propelled the concept forward.

Bailyn asserts that framing history Atlantically addresses the deficiencies of two older historical constructs. In many colleges and universities, Atlantic history has replaced the study of an explicit *colonial* history. Though many of the topics are the same, the perspective of study has been reimagined to encompass the far-flung connections that affected the lives of even the most marginalized colonists. In addition, Atlantic history strikes a blow against the ideology of New World exceptionalism – the idea that colonies in the Americas, in particular the English ones, were founded for lofty political and humanitarian purposes, thus contributing to an American spirit distinct from that of a corrupt, retrograde Europe. Atlantic history had a particular appeal for those who reject this idea because it privileges the study of connections, influences, movements, motives and negotiations. In addition, it also addressed a problem that faced many social historians – the fact that many things in the Americas *did not* change in the wake of the Revolution – by providing them with a framework that de-emphasized that event.

As Bailyn further asserts, Atlantic history is not the same thing as *imperial history*, which privileges the study of the function and administration of empire. Instead, it moves historical stories from the highest, most abstract levels (imperial, administrative) down to the human level. In the process, it stands to provide answers on how policies such as the Navigation Acts *really* affected merchants, colonial administrators and colonists, ranging from the rich to the enslaved. One need only to look at the furnishings of the kitchen of an authentically interpreted house museum to see how integrated these interconnected cultures were, for even the homes of the people of modest means contained objects that were somehow shaped by the Atlantic experience.

So what does Atlantic history provide? As Bailyn points out, imperial history (along with the history of exploration and discovery) privileged the study of discoveries, wars of conquest, laws, political structures and revolutions. They eschewed the study of 'societies and social organizations', as well as exchange and encounter. Atlantic history stood, and still stands, not only to fill in blanks but to inspire new forms of historical enquiry.

Still, as historian Alison Games has pointed out, '[not] all subjects are Atlantic in scope; not all questions require answers that include the entire Atlantic World. An Atlantic perspective should only be invoked if the Atlantic offers a logical unit for analysis.' Some historians even question whether the Atlantic world existed at all, arguing that the chronology is too large and inchoate, and the geography too diverse and far-flung, to be a useful organizing principle. More compellingly, they question whether historical actors *spoke of* or left records that they *thought about* themselves as residents of an Atlantic world. Measured against the demands for this type of evidence, the concept does indeed come up wanting.

But if we use a different yardstick – in this case, the argument that people *behaved* Atlantically – the concept is in a much more defensible position. 'Behaving Atlantically' can be defined as demonstrated acknowledgement of, or dependence upon, the Atlantic Ocean as the main conduit for goods, peoples and ideas. Many who crossed the Atlantic between the late fifteenth and late nineteenth centuries maintained ties with loved ones or business associates in their respective mother countries. People on the western littoral knew that the Atlantic was the 'highway' through which they learned about news from Europe that might affect their lives, that apprised them of new laws and restrictions, which provided notice of the latest in fashion, domestic innovation, technology, philosophy and theology. In Europe, the Atlantic provided the same for raw goods and some finished products, revolutionizing tastes, hastening the transition into manufacturing, and worrying those in power about how these colonies, growing in population and productivity, could best be managed. In Africa, the Atlantic brought desired goods for some but sorrow for the many who awaited the often-lethal voyage into a life of slavery. But slavery's tragic consequences cannot mask the fact that Atlantic connections were an economic boon for some, Africans, Europeans and Euroamericans alike. The Atlantic world's reliance on seaborne travel meant that those who built, prepared and manned the ocean's vessels were engaged in Atlantic commerce of some kind. Those who engaged in even the most marginal of these activities were reliant on Atlantic connections to sustain themselves and their families. They could be found among farmers, planters, slaves and servants, ironworkers, coopers, tanners, small-scale manufacturers, distillers, fishermen and printers, among many others. Those who did not work in some way connected to Atlantic-based production and dissemination of goods would have, at some point of their lives, consumed products that were the result of Atlantic exploration, exchange and innovation.

Atlantic travellers carried the imprint of their origins with them for life. But as discovery and conquest gave way to encounter and exchange, peoples mixed and new cultural identities evolved. Mixed-race and ethnically and culturally mixed peoples could be found among the enslaved and the free in Bahia, Haiti, New Orleans and Baltimore. A man whose lineage was seven-eighths European could rise to the highest levels of Native American leadership. A slave in upstate New York could speak Dutch as her first language. In New France, Jesuit priests communicated more frequently in Indian languages than European ones, and adapted Native American terms to translate theologically complex ideas from Latin.

Recognizing that people 'behaved Atlantically' entails the study of identity and consumption in the service of demonstrating how reliance on the Atlantic shaped human lives. Yet it should not be construed as a new version of American exceptionalism. Instead, the behaviours of the Atlantic world's people demonstrate their very human propensities both to preserve what they had known and to innovate with what seemed useful.

* * *

Echoes of the Atlantic's historical importance are still with us. One can argue that some aspects of it have never changed. Migration from one point on the Atlantic littoral to another was as common a hallmark of the late nineteenth and twentieth centuries as it was of the seventeenth and eighteenth centuries. European immigrants continued to flow into Canada, the United States, Brazil, Mexico and Argentina (to name but a few), with local, national and continental factors still influencing the decision to move. Human migration around the Atlantic continued to be affected by recurring sets of related issues, including innovations in overseas travel, technological and industrial changes affecting the littoral's cities, political movements, and the needs and desires of the migrants themselves. All these modern realities have parallels to the world forged by Atlantic encounters. The Europeans who crossed the Atlantic from as far away as Poland and Russia in the early twentieth century knew that they were leaving their ancestral lands for good. Though winsome ideas of 'making a fresh start' or 'pursuing life in a free land' are generally regarded as hopelessly sentimental and inaccurate, the idea that the Old World pushed as much as the New World pulled is echoed in the odyssey of the Scotch-Irish and German Pietist migrations of the eighteenth century. Atlantic travellers from the Caribbean flocked to new opportunities in New York City, Philadelphia and Miami, but the relatively close proximity of the islands in the age of the jet engine allowed for easy movement between ancestral and adopted homes. In this regard, these migrants and immigrants shared similarities with the seventeenth-century Puritans, who moved about the Atlantic world as opportunity and their own spiritual needs dictated.

Fragments of the Atlantic experience can still be found along the littoral. For generations, the descendants of the original Atlantic travellers and survivors both destroyed and preserved the remainders of the cultures their ancestors had built. Much was lost before historic preservation became a field in its own right, involving government and sometimes international guidelines for protection and care. Preserving cultural legacies has proved even more difficult, as the cultures of pre-literate and non-literate people died with them. Even objects and buildings that were carefully tended and valued are still endangered by the ravages of nature, time and ignorance. A good deal of what does remain from the Atlantic past exists as a curiosity, used for teaching students and attracting tourists. Yet these artefacts, which range from cultural habits to whole buildings and streetscapes, retain their power to illuminate the complexities of Atlantic history. One cannot snorkel in Jamaica over the submerged ruins of Port Royal, take high tea in Bermuda, tour Cape Coast Castle in Ghana or the replica of the *Mayflower* in Massachusetts, celebrate Pinkster in what had been Dutch New York, or walk the streets of Seville without remembering the centuries of human interactions along the Atlantic littoral they represent.

Sources

1 Navigation and Empire

Popol Vuh – Chapter 1: A Mayan Creation Story
Author unknown: Popul Vuh (*c*.1550); first translation by Father Ximinez, *Historias del origen de los Indios de esta Provincia de Guatemala*. Also known as the Manuscript of Chichicastenango (MS copy in Newberry Library).

Traveller Leo Africanus describes Timbuktu (1600)
John Leo, *A Geographical Historie of Africa*. London, 1600.

Richard Hakluyt's *Discourse on Western Planting* (1584) encouraging English involvement in the Americas
D. B. and A. M Quinn, eds., *A particular discourse concerning the greate necessitie and manifolde commodities that are like to growe to this realme of Englande by the westerne discouries lately attempted, written in the yere 1584: known as discourse of western planting. By Richard Hakluyt*. Hakluyt Society, Extra Series, 45 (1993).

Study image 1
Waldseemüller Map of 1507.
http://www.granger.com/results.asp?image=0031683&itemw=4&itemf=0001&item step=1&itemx=2

2 Contact and Encounter

John Smith describes Jamestown (1608)
J. Smith, *A True Relation of such occurrences and accidents of note as hath happened in Virginia ....* London, 1608.

The Mayflower Compact (1620) Agreement Between the Settlers at New Plymouth
Original manuscript lost, printed in William Bradford, *Mourt's Relation*. London, 1622.

Bernal Diaz's account of Cortés and Moctezuma (1632)
Bernal Diaz del Castillo, *The Conquest of New Spain*. Madrid, 1632.

Miantonomo's (Narragansett) plea for unity among the Natives (1630s–40s)
Herbert Milton Sylvester, *Indian Wars of New England*, vol. 1, p. 386. Cleveland, 1910.

Study image 2
Manhattan Purchase, 1626. Painting by William T. Ranney, 1855. http://www.
granger.com/results.asp?image=0259392&itemw=4&itemf=0006&itemstep=1&ite
mx=1.

3 Bondage and Freedom

Early slave codes from Virginia (1660s)
The Statutes at Large; Being a Collection of All Laws of Virginia, from the First
Session of the Legislature in the Year 1619, edited by William W. Hening, II, pp.
26, 170, 260, 266, 270. New York and Philadelphia, 1819–23.

A defence of slavery from antebellum US (1854) by George Fitzhugh
George Fitzhugh, *Sociology for the South.* Richmond, VA, 1854.

Olaudah Equiano on his Middle Passage crossing (1789)
The Interesting Narrative of the Life of Olaudah Equiano. London, 1789.

Capt. J. E. Alexander observes slave life in Guiana (1833)
J. E. Alexander, *Transatlantic Sketches.* Philadelphia, 1833.

Study image 3
Slave trading compounds on the African coast, 1746. http://www.granger.com/
results.asp?image=0130752&itemw=4&itemf=0003&itemstep=1&itemx=28.

4 Exploiting the Atlantic: Trade and Economy

'Diario' of Christopher Columbus (1492–3)
Original manuscript copied by Las Casas in the 1550s, in Biblioteca Nacional in
Madrid.

**'Commercial Orders to Governor Andros, Royal Governor of New England'
(1686–7)**
Published in the *Collections of the Massachusetts Historical Society,* pp. 174–6. Boston,
1838.

The General Advertiser **(New York, 22 October 1767)**

Study image 4
'Tobacco Production, French West Indies', from Jean Baptiste Labat, *Nouveau voyage
aux isles de l'Amerique,* vol. 4. Paris, 1722. http://hitchcock.itc.virginia.edu/
Slavery/detailsKeyword.php?keyword=tobacco&recordCount=25&theRecord=8.

5 Atlantic Religion: Beliefs and Behaviours

Letter from Father Sébastien Rale, S.J., Missionary of the Society of Jesus in New France, to Monsieur his nephew (1722)
Sebastian Rale, *A Maine Tragedy of the Eighteenth Century: EXTRACTS FROM RALE'S LETTER TO HIS NEPHEW*, pp. 117–28, edited by John Francis Sprague. Boston, MA, Heintzemann Press, 1906.

Flushing Remonstrance (27 December 1657)
Series A1809 Dutch Colonial Council Minutes, vol. 8, pp. 626–7. Queen's Library, Flushing, New York.

'You Men', by Sor Juana Inés de la Cruz (1651–95)
First published as *Castillian Inundation*. Madrid, 1688.

Study image 5
'Sinners in Hell'. Woodcut from *The Progress of Sin* (1744). http://www.granger.com/results.asp?inline=true&image=0042095&wwwflag=1&itemx=1.

6 Lived Lives and the Built Environment: Cultural Transfer in the Greater Atlantic

'Novum Belgium' by the Jesuit Isaac Jogues (1643)
Reuben Gold Thwaites, *Jesuit Relations*. Cleveland, 1898.

A Voyage to South America, Jorge Juan and Antonio de Ulloa (1748)
Printed in English by Juan and Ulloa, *A Voyage to South America*. London, 1748.

'American Cookery, or the Art of Dressing Viands, Fish, Poultry and Vegetables, and the Best Modes of Making Pastes, Puffs, Pies, Tarts, Puddings, Custards and Preserves, and all Kinds of Cakes, from the Imperial Plumb to the Plain Cake. Adapted to this Country and All Grades of Life.' By Amelia Simmons, an American Orphan (1796) Hartford, CT, 1796.

Study image 6
Die Stadt Havana, from Alain Manesson Mallet, *Description de l'Univers* .... 1685. http://www.alte-landkarten.de/stock/antique%20map/18085/die%20Stadt%20Havana%20HAVANA/Mallet.shtml.

7 Dependence and Independence: the Parameters of Identity and Freedom

'Captain Preston's account of the Boston Massacre' (5 March 1770)
Publications of the Colonial Society of Massachusetts, vol. 7 (1905), pp. 8–9.

Letter from Toussaint L'Ouverture to Napoléon Bonaparte on the 1801 Constitution
Printed in Victor Schoelcher, *Vie de Toussaint Louverture*. Paris: Paul Ollendorf, 1889.

'Message to the Congress of Angostura', by Simón de Bolívar (1819)
Simón Bolívar, *An Address of Bolivar at the Congress of Angostura (February 15, 1819)*, reprint edition. Washington, DC: Press of B. S. Adams, 1919.

Study image 7
Haiti: Slave Revolt, 1791 (German). http://www.granger.com/results.asp?inline=true&image=0028252&wwwflag=1&itemx=3

8 The Quest for Abolition

Samuel Sewall, *The Selling of Joseph* (1700)
Boston, 1700.

Translation of the Declaration of Independence from Haiti (1804)
From Laurent Dubois and John D. Garrigus, *Slave Revolution in the Caribbean*. Bedford/St. Martin's, 2006.

Letters from American Colonization Society settlers in Liberia
Letters among the American Colonization Society papers held in the Manuscript Division of the Library of Congress, Washington, DC.

Study image 8
Hemsley's engraving of a slave ship, nineteenth century. http://www.granger.com/results.asp?image=0260120&itemw=4&itemf=0005&itemstep=1&itemx=7

References

Armitage, David and Braddick, Michael (eds), *The British Atlantic World 1500–1800*. Basingstoke: Palgrave Macmillan, 2002.

Baker, Emerson Woods. *The Devil of Great Island: Witchcraft and Conflict in Early New England*. New York: Palgrave Macmillan, 2007.

Berlin, Ira. *Many Thousands Gone: The First Two Centuries of Slavery in North America*. Cambridge, MA: Harvard University Press, 2000.

Burnard, Trevor. 'The British Atlantic', in Jack P. Greene and Philip D. Morgan (eds), *Atlantic History: A Critical Appraisal*. New York: Oxford University Press, 2008.

Coclanis, Peter A. 'Beyond Atlantic History', in Jack P. Greene and Philip D. Morgan (eds), *Atlantic History: A Critical Appraisal*. New York: Oxford University Press, 2008.

Davis, Natalie Zemon. *Women on the Margins: Three Seventeenth Century Lives*. Cambridge, MA: Harvard University Press, 2007.

Elliott, John. *Empires of the Atlantic World: Britain and Spain in America, 1492–1830*. New Haven, CT: Yale University Press, 2007.

Engel, Katherine Carté. *Religion and Profit: Moravians in Early America*. Philadelphia: University of Pennsylvania Press, 2011.

Foner, Eric. *Reconstruction: America's Unfinished Revolution, 1863–1877*. New York: HarperCollins, 1988.

Games, Alison. *Migration and the Origins of the English Atlantic World*. Cambridge, MA: Harvard University Press, 2001.

Magnuson, Roger. *Education in New France*. Montreal: McGill-Queen's University Press, 1992.

McNeill, J. R. 'The End of the Old Atlantic World', in Alan L. Karras and J. R. McNeill (eds), *Atlantic American Societies from Columbus through Abolition 1492–1888*. New York: Routledge, 1992.

Pestana, Carla Gardina. *Protestant Empire: Religion and the Making of the British Atlantic World*. Philadelphia, PA: University of Pennsylvania Press, 2010.

Rodney, Walter. *How Europe Underdeveloped Africa*. London: Bogle L'Ouverture, 1972.

Rogoziński, Jan. *A Brief History of the Caribbean: From the Arawak and Carib to the Present*. New York: Penguin, 1999.

Seeman, Erik. 'Jews in the Early Modern Atlantic: Crossing Boundaries, Keeping Faith', in Jorge Canizares-Esguerra and Erik R. Seeman (eds), *The Atlantic in Global History, 1500–2000*. Prentice Hall, 2007.

Sleeper-Smith, Susan. *Indian Women & French Men*. Amherst: University of Massachusetts Press, 2001.

Smith, Mark M. 'Remembering Mary, Shaping Revolt: Reconsidering the Stono Rebellion'. *The Journal of Southern History* 67.3 (August 2001): 513–34.

Taylor, Alan. *American Colonies: The Settling of North America*. New York: Penguin, 2001.

Ulrich, Laurel Thatcher. *Wives: Image and Reality in the Lives of Northern New England Women, 1650–1750*. New York: Vintage, 1980.

Ulrich, Laurel Thatcher. *A Midwife's Tale: The Life of Martha Ballard Based upon Her Diary, 1785–1812*. New York: Vintage, 1991.

Thornton, John. *Africa and Africans in the Making of the Atlantic World, 1400–1800*. New York: Cambridge University Press, 1998.

de Vries, Jan. *The Industrious Revolution: Consumer Behavior and the Household Economy, 1650 to the Present*. New York: Cambridge University Press, 2008.

Wood, Peter H. *Strange New Land: Africans in Colonial America*. New York: Oxford University Press, 2003.

Index

abolition, and abolitionists, 72, 197
  in British Atlantic, 74–5, 191, 199–203,
    206–8
  in French Atlantic, 186, 207
  and 'gag rule', 210
  and gradualism, 198, 204–6
  and immediatism, 198
  in South America, 208–9
  in the United States, 187–8, 198, 202–4,
    208–11
  and women, 212
Acadia, 144, 163, 176
Adams, Abigail, 150
Adams, John, 63, 150, 187
Africa, and Africans, 25, 26, 30, 36, 44
  as Christians, 27, 112
  connection to slave trading, 13, 18–19,
    60–4, 71–2
  connections with Europeans, 13, 28–30, 45,
    105
  encounter Europeans, 1, 13, 17, 20–4, 30,
    39, 45
  in Europe, 35–6, 66–7
  and family, 28, 52, 105
  fear of Europeans, 24, 45
  and misconceptions of origins by
    Europeans, 15, 25, 39–41
  religion in, 29, 99, 114–16, 124–5
  and scientific knowledge, 47
  social organization, 13–14, 39–40
  as 'sons of Ham', 37
  trade goods of, 13, 18–19, 20–1, 46, 83–7,
    89–90, 92
  see also specific kingdoms
alcohol, 90, 99, 127, 154, 159
  and ceremonial significance, 99
  limits enforced on trade of, 159
Alexander VI (pope), 22
Algonquians, 50, 152

American Anti-Slave Association, 210
American Colonization Society, 203, 209
American Revolution, 126, 133, 150, 161, 170,
    178–9, 183–5, 186
  and backlash against consumer goods, 178,
    180
  and issue of slavery, 203–4
  origins of, 171, 180, 183–4
Amish, 131
Andros, Edmund, 175
d'Anghiera, Peter Martyr, 17
Anglicanism, and Anglicans (Church of
    England), 113–14, 118–19, 120–1,
    125–6, 129–30, 132, 162–4, 175, 199
  and attitudes toward marriage, 146
Anglo-Dutch Wars, 87, 172
Angola, and Angolans, 29, 61–2, 64, 72, 171
animals, 37, 47, 67, 104–6, 115, 117, 140, 143,
    155
  domesticated, 49, 153–5, 158
  as part of Columbian Exchange, 4, 48–51
  as pets, 157–8
  as transport, 100
  see also cattle, dogs
animism, 115
Anne I (English/British monarch), 152
Aragon (Spanish kingdom), 16, 21
architecture, 116, 162
  British, 162
  and building materials, 140–4
  Caribbean, 144
  church, 91, 163, 207
  and climate, 3–4, 142–4
  domestic, 101–2, 133, 140–4
  French, 142
  Georgian, 101
  port cities, 92–3
  Spanish, 49
Aristotle, 17, 65, 212